Ruinairski

More bloody cheap flights eastwards with Mick

Ruinairski

More bloody cheap flights eastwards with Mick

Paul Kilduff

Gill & Macmillan

Gill & Macmillan Ltd
Hume Avenue, Park West, Dublin 12
with associated companies throughout the world
www.gillmacmillan.ie

© Paul Kilduff 2009
978 07171 4598 0

Typography design by Make Communication
Print origination by Carole Lynch
Printed by ColourBooks Ltd, Dublin

This book is typeset in Minion 11 on 13.5 pt.

The paper used in this book comes from the wood pulp of
managed forests. For every tree felled, at least one tree is
planted, thereby renewing natural resources.

A CIP catalogue record for this book is available
from the British Library.

5 4 3 2 1

Contents

PROLOGUE   IX

Lithuania   1
Mick's Plane Speaking (1)   18
Latvia   22
Mick's Curriculum Vitae   43
Estonia   46
Tony Ruin   57
The Czech Republic   64
Job Application   79
The Czech Republic (Again)   82
Lidice   95
The Low Fares Airline (1)   99
Poland   104
Annual General Meeting   114
Slovakia   123
The Low Fares Airline (2)   134
Bulgaria   140
Readers' Emails   150
Slovakia (Again)   158
Ruinair Fan Forum   168
Hungary   176
The Ruinair Song   189
Slovenia   191
Advertising Feature   201
Romania   208
Mick's Local   226
Cyprus (and Turkey)   230

The Low Fares Airline (3)   244
Malta   248
Financial Ruination   262
Mick's Plane Speaking (2)   263

EPILOGUE   265

'Take Gdansk. Who wants to go to Gdansk? There ain't a lot there after you've seen the shipyard wall.'

'Twelve months ago I believed it made no sense flying to Poland. I've changed my mind. We're happy to let our higher-cost rivals get in there. We will follow when the time is right. We'll then push the others out to Russia, then Siberia.'

MICK O'LEERY, CHIEF EXECUTIVE,
RUINAIR HOLDINGS PLC

Prologue

Mick O'Leery
Chief Executive
Ruinair
Dublin Airport

Dear Mick,

I am pleased to enclose a signed copy of 'Ruinair', which is about low fares air travel in Europe. Some of my readers told me that they have already sent you a copy but I suspect this is your first signed copy.

I hope that the book, with its attendant free media publicity and the nine weeks spent as Ireland's no. 1 best selling non-fiction title, will in some small way help to increase your traffic this year from 51 million to 58 million passengers. Perhaps you can let me know if you spot any factual inaccuracies, perish the thought.

I am aware that as air fares fall your airline is looking for inno-vative ways to increase ancillary revenues. I can get copies of 'Ruinair' for half price so how about we sell the book onboard your flights and split the profits? We would sell lots of books if we push them as hard as Bullseye Baggies and scratch cards.

I am setting out on my second voyage of discovery to travel to the 12 countries of Central and Eastern Europe which have joined the European Union, and all for another miserly €300 in total air fares (excluding taxes, fees and charges which we both know don't really matter much to passengers).

It remains a daunting prospect to fly to Lithuania, Latvia, Estonia, the Czech Republic, Poland, Slovakia, Bulgaria, Hungary, Slovenia, Romania, Cyprus and Malta, since I was horrified to discover that your fantastically low airline does not yet fly to some of these major European nations.

    I would be grateful for any expert advice you could offer as I set out on my epic journey eastwards.

With best wishes,
Paul Kilduff
(budding author, frequent flyer and loyal shareholder)

PS Keep an eye out for a signed copy of 'The Little Book of Mick' in the post to you shortly.

Two weeks pass by where I am completely ignored by the postman. Then I receive an envelope which contains my original letter with the following handwritten comments scribbled in blue pen:

'Dear Paul, I haven't read it. I heard it should be in the fiction list but keep up the good work. Free publicity won't make any difference to our growth but it all helps. Why don't you travel during our €1 seat sales (including taxes, fees and charges) and do it all for just €30? Fly Ruinair and avoid our vastly inferior competitors. Best wishes, Mick.'

It is just as I thought. Mick is never lost for words.

Lithuania

Flight FR2971 – Friday @ 10.55 a.m. – DUB-KUN-DUB

Fare €0.02 plus taxes, fees and charges €46

I am at the departure gate to take my first flight after several months of abstinence when the girl boarding us looks at my boarding card and my passport and says to me, 'You wrote a book about Ruinair.'

It's the first time that I have been rumbled. 'I did.' I am impressed. I thought they never bothered to read the passenger names on boarding cards and passports. 'I am surprised that you still allow me to fly.'

She laughs at me. Her colleague who heard the conversation is laughing too. They don't hate me. I think they might have got the book, maybe they have even read it, although as yet we have not sold the Lithuanian or Polish translation rights. All I wanted to do was to take the Mick out of Europe's lowest airline.

Our cabin crew supervisor is Irish. 'Yez can't sit in the first three rows. Yez can sit anywhere else.' Someone told me once that because this is an Irish airline, the first three rows of seats are always reserved for leprechauns, in the event that a group of them turn up looking to travel home at short notice.

Another cabin crew girl, Anna Maria Conchita Lopez Suarez, directs passengers to seats, much like a cinema usherette. 'I hava one seat here and I hava one seat there. Eeeeess very full today.' She stands in a row of three seats and tells us, 'I am keeping theeees row for a family.' That's great customer service. They must be an important family, maybe even the Holy Family itself. There'll certainly be three of them. Later she makes an announcement. 'Pleeeease ensure your mobile phones are switch-ed off.'

I approach the cabin crew girl who always stands in the aisle seat of the emergency row, because of the extra room. She is checking incoming text messages on her mobile. I ask her if I can sit here, pray she too doesn't recognise me and she obliges. Because I am sitting in the emergency row, Anna Maria Conchita Lopez Suarez stops by us before we take off and tries to get our attention in vain. 'Can I have your attention. You are seated in an emergency row. In the unlikely event that we have to evacuate the aircraft, you have to open theeees doors. You know what to do? It's on the diagram on the wall. Ok? Is theeees clear?' Er … crystal. *Muchas gracias, señorita.* Despite the importance of my seat today, I know that I am not allowed to have a practice go at opening the door.

One of the last passengers to board is a solo girl who I saw in the terminal building crying her eyes out. She is red-faced, blotchy and still sniffling but she has recovered somewhat. She has either just kissed goodbye to a dearly beloved one at the departure gate, or else she has flown before on this airline.

I relax into my hard non-reclining blue plastic seat. Ruinair once undertook a customer survey where they asked passengers if they would prefer if the seat in front of them could not be reclined into their faces. 75 per cent of respondents said Yes, and this partly justifies these seats. They should have asked the same passengers if they would prefer a seat which reclines. 100 per cent of respondents would have said Yes. Mick explains. *'Five years ago one of our engineers realised that we spent €2.5 million repairing reclining seats. Large people who use reclining seats tend to break the mechanisms. That was when we had 50 aircraft. A few years later if we had 300 aircraft and I thought, shit, we're going to spend €15–20 million repairing these seats. How could we not repair them? We took the revolutionary step of going to Boeing and asking for non-reclining seats so now one of the features of our planes is that they have non-reclining seats.'*

I'd like to place my book and newspaper into a pocket on my seat but there is none. *'One of the key glitches we had was security checks, because of those of you who throw the rest of your crap in the seat-back pockets. One of the things that affects the aircraft turn-around is that individually they have to go and inspect every single one of those seat back pockets. How the hell could we stop them having to do that? Well, the cabin crew came up with the legendary idea that we could get rid of the seat-back pockets.'*

The safety announcement begins but everyone chats away so it is barely audible and no one tells us to shut up. The safety announcements are no longer delivered in *Spanglish*. Now they play a nice tape recording and the cabin crew mime the safety demonstration. Of course the first information they give us immediately we get onto an aircraft is how to get off of it. Anna Maria Conchita Lopez Suarez in a uniform two sizes too big is terrified when standing in our midst. She prefers to hide behind her dangling fringe and she shakes when she shows us what to do if any oxygen masks were to drop down from the cabin roof. Of course this eventuality is very rare and it almost never happens. Except on that Ruinair flight which dropped 26,000 feet over Limoges.

The interior of the cabin is spotlessly clean, apart from the food remnants on the floor, the Ruinair magazines and menu cards strewn about and the blob of white chewing gum stuck to the window in our row. We are late pushing back so the captain apologises and tries to explain why. 'We were down in Italy. Italians like to stand in the aisle and get their luggage down as we taxi towards the airport terminal. So we stopped the aircraft on the runway and we made them all take their seats again.' Just before we take off he comes on air again. 'Cabin crew, take your seats for landing.' I heard what he said and so did a few puzzled others. There's a short pause. Then another bing-bong on the intercom. '… or even for take-off.'

As we hurtle down the runway, we dodge the empty soft-drink cans which rattle and roll back down the cabin interior, destined to go to the rear walls but no further. Our take-off is such a rapid and almost vertical ascent that I am increasingly convinced that most of these enthusiastic Ruinair pilots would much prefer to be flying the Space Shuttle for NASA out of Cape Canaveral, Florida, USA.

Two langers from Co. Cavan sit in the row in front of me in athletic track-suits.

'How long is the flight?' asks one of them.

The less inebriated of the two replies. 'Three hours.'

There's an approving nod. 'Jaysus, 'tis good value for three hours.'

The *Irish Independent* is on sale on the aircraft for €2. A girl walks down the aisle, displaying the newspaper prominently. A passenger a few rows away puts his hand up for a newspaper, he takes one from her and he begins to read the front page with enthusiasm. She stands beside him and soon asks for €2. He looks up amazed; evidently he did not listen fully to the cabin announcement. He grimaces and hands the newspaper back reluctantly. He thought the newspaper was free. Free. On this airline? Ho ho.

I am subjected for the first time to the Ruinair song played on their flights. It is a ghastly, annoying, repetitive, inane tune so on that basis it suits this airline perfectly. Here are the meaningful lyrics:

> 'Let's fly, let's fly, fly, fly Ruinair, We're gonna take you there, fly, fly Ruinair,
> Let's fly, let's fly, fly, fly Ruinair, We're gonna take you there, fly, fly Ruinair,
> Sit down, relax, time to step in, Buy a juice for Little Johnny and get yourself a Gin,
> We got sweets, treats, lots of goodies on the trolley for you,
> Whatever it is that you need, ask the friendly cabin crew,
> Let's fly, let's fly, fly, fly Ruinair, We're gonna take you there, fly, fly Ruinair,
> Let's fly, let's fly, fly, fly Ruinair,
> We're gonna take you there, fly, fly Ruinair…'

The *Daily Mail* described this tune as 'the Vengaboys meets the Crazy Frog'. The tune divides opinion. Ruinair strongly defended the song which it was first introduced across its fleet on April Fool's Day. 'We've had a great response from our passengers and have even heard news of conga lines forming in the aisles.' But the reaction is not shared by all Ruinair passengers to whom the *Daily Mail* spoke. Some complained the music was too loud and intrusive. And if the passengers are not universally welcoming the song, spare a thought for the poor cabin crew. One stewardess on a flight out of Beauvais said, 'Imagine what it's like for us listening to it day in, day out. But at least I get to choose whether I play it or not.'

There are banks of advertisements on the overhead luggage bins in the cabin, all extolling the virtues of Ireland's third mobile telephone company and encouraging me to roam, more than I usually do when writing travel books. Not at their sky-high international roaming rates. Being a dedicated 087 prefix type customer, I'm not switching to the 085 prefix based on in-your-face advertising on this airline. Industry veterans have long acknowledged that half of all advertising is a total waste of money but the same gurus can never agree on which half is wasted. Except in this instance on board a Ruinair flight. On the way back the advertisements are for Ruinair's own gift vouchers so they are clearly running short of genuine paying corporate advertisers. On other flights I have seen them used for Christmas gift vouchers and this was in May. I have seen them used to advertise Ruinair's own city and ski break destinations, encouraging us to 'Book now on www.ruinair.com', which is clearly impossible to do at 36,000 feet, right now. So come on Mick, let's get the internet going whilst up in the air. I will be happy to pay €1 for a 10-minute web surf.

Below these adverts is another strip advising that if we buy a *Bullseye Baggie* (*'Life is Simple, Take What You Want'*) of *Super Premium Select* Gin, Rum, Vodka, Whiskey or Cognac, we will receive another little Baggie for 'free, free, free'. I wonder what determines this alcohol to be *Super Premium Select* and where does this leave other crap drinks like Gordon's, Bacardi, Smirnoff, Jameson or Courvoisier? These alcoholic drinks arrive in square foil packets and they look more like Durex condoms. On offer onboard are fine wines which we learn are a bold merlot and a refreshing chardonnay. It is not widely known but Ruinair employ a full-time team of expert wine sommeliers who travel Europe, California and the New World annually in search of the finest wines for 36,000 feet. Right, Mick? *'Don't say it's cheap: that's nasty. The first question 99 per cent of people ask is, 'What is your cheapest fare to x?' Nobody asks us about the wine list.'*

I fly often on this airline. How often do I see a crew member twice? Rarely, if ever. I read in the *Irish Times* that the average career lifespan of a Ruinair cabin-crew member used to be 18 months but it's now down to nine months. '*I wouldn't believe anything I read in the Irish Times.*' There are some smart personable crew members who work for this airline but none of them are working on our flight today. I believe they primarily work for the airline so as to populate the annual staff charity calendar. '*Loony groups like the various Institutes for Ugly Women are simply jealous of our good-looking girls.*'

The crew remain a largely scruffy bunch. You can always spot food stains, pen marks, ripped hems and split threads on their uniforms. The ladies still wear uniforms in the same shade of bright blue as the Smurfs. Even the sight of these blue uniforms in an airport now has an adverse affect on me. My heartbeat races, my blood pressure soars and I perspire wildly with fear. But this cabin crew seem to be happier than others. It's probably because some of them are going home today. For 25 minutes anyway.

I remain anxious. A friend of mine said that it's likely that Ruinair have fixed my picture on the wall of all forward and rear galleys on their aircraft so that staff will recognise me and then adhere to the instruction to poison me with *Saile and Sabga* gourmet products. So nothing new there then. The pre-recorded sales announcement offers us 'the new range of gourmet hot drinks, which include a dark French roast coffee, an imperial tea, a rich and creamy cappuccino and a very special luxury hot chocolate'. What baloney. Why are drinks 'gourmet' when they consist of dry powder in a paper cup? What is 'imperial' tea? When I last looked, imperial was something that involved the British Raj in India or the Tsar in Russia.

Overall it's the familiar sort of flight from hell. We depart Dublin exactly one hour late, destined to arrive 30 minutes late in Lithuania. The crew don't know what they are selling to us and they cannot add up more than one item nor can they get the change right. There's near hysteria when it becomes clear that the green *Pringles* have run out early. Orders for hot food are forgotten about until passengers complain. Service is so slow and stocks so low that an anxious male passenger gets up out of his seat and walks the length of the aisle to the trolley, hands a €10 note to one of the crew and says, 'Two beers.'

The hard sell continues. They try to sell us 'international telephone cards'. The cabin crew girl begins at row 1 with a serious face, breaks into a smile by row 5 and is cracking up by row 10 as she walks through the cabin holding up such useless cards. We know it and she knows it. Who would want to buy one of these telephone cards? Is there a single person on this flight who does not have a mobile telephone with them today? I saw six-year-olds an hour ago sending texts to their classmates on their mobiles from the departures lounge. Once we land every person here will power up their mobiles. They won't be looking for their Ruinair international telephone cards 'which offer fantastic reductions on international rates'.

They try to sell us Terravision bus tickets. I have only ever been on this bus service to and from Rome Ciampino Airport, where they leave you for 30 minutes stewing in the bus with the air-con off and it's 30 degrees outside, where the tickets are not cheap, there are lots of signs saying that we cannot eat or drink or do anything at all on the bus, the drivers drive like Italians and the buses only depart when the very last seat on the bus is taken. So I prefer to refer to this bus service as Terrorvision. On my one and only round trip I proved to be a hero when I single-handedly rescued three American teenage girls by killing a giant angry bumble bee inside our bus (I mashed it against the window using the very fine velour curtains). They thanked me profusely for killing the 'bug', whilst I explained that it was a bee and that a 'bug' is an error found in computer software code, most usually associated with Microsoft applications, and typically encountered whilst working on large Word documents, e.g. books which are at the time unsaved.

Later they wheel the gifts trolley along the aisle, which encourages the two girls near to me to examine the products on offer in the in-flight magazine.

'Now dat's really cheap,' advises one as she points at a bottle of perfume.

'And dat smells lovely,' confirms the other girl.

The *Irish Times* reported that in this airlines' regulatory filing with the SEC in the USA, they confirmed that 48 per cent of cabin crews' total pay is earned by way of commission from in-flight sales. That's why they push the trolleys so much. Finally the crew try to sell us those infamous scratch cards.

'Anyone like to buy a scratch card? They are for charity,' the cabin crew girl reminds us nicely. 'You can win a million euro with these cards.' Right. Imagine Mick making anyone else into a millionaire.

A narky guy in the row across from me mutters quietly. 'Yeah … for the Mick O'Leery Charity.'

Onboard we have a minor medical emergency. One of the passengers has a serious toothache and is in visible pain a few rows from me. I overhear the conversation as the senior cabin crew girl asks a Lithuanian lady to make an announcement on the PA to ask if anyone has a painkiller. The passenger obliges and about 20 hands go up inside the cabin. Evidently many passengers are in pain on Ruinair.

Later on we hit bad turbulence. The aircraft shudders about. The cabin crew tell us all to sit down and that the toilets are not to be used. The seat belt lights immediately come on and we do all sit down and belt up and tightly grip the non-reclining arm rests for the upcoming white-knuckle ride. I hope that we survive this and we live to tell the tale. But then everything goes calm. The pilot goes to the WC. A coincidence? I am increasingly certain that Ruinair pilots have a red button in their cockpit entitled *'Push for Turbulence'*. I was once on a flight where a very large man was walking down the aisle when we hit bad turbulence at the same time. He turned to his mates in nearby seats and said, 'This happens every time I walk up and down on a plane.'

Lithuanians are the nationality most likely to use their mobile telephones whilst on board aircraft. Many chat to loved ones ('I'm on the plane') as we taxi to our takeoff, which I hear is dangerous. They all feel the need to send that final text in case a disaster befalls us, what I call the last will and textament: *'I, Josef Bloggski, temporarily residing at Dublin, being of sound mind, do hereby declare this text to be my last will and textament, I hereby leave all my worldly possessions (carry-on baggage, maximum 10 kg) to …'* etc. The crew members tell the offenders to power down but they are ignored because the crew have neither the presence nor authority to tell chunky Lithuanian youths to cease and desist until they are damn well good and ready. I sit next to two foreign national blokes who are identical, with leather jackets, jeans, crew cuts, pale complexions and big square foreheads, who play race car games on their telephones mid-flight. Others prefer to text, or attempt to text, their very best friends from 36,000 feet. Later when we begin our descent telephone ring tones sound off all around once we drop within range of Lithuania's BITE GSM. I hear that Ruinair will soon introduce an in-flight mobile telephone service. Lithuanians are ahead of the game and are already mobile.

Vilnius is the capital of Lithuania. Half a million inhabitants live in a diverse, cosmopolitan and vibrant city. Its Europa Tower is the tallest skyscraper in the Baltic States. Vilnius is the 2009 European Capital of Culture. Sadly, Ruinair fly to the second city of Kaunas, 100 km west of Vilnius. In the 1920s and 1930s when Lithuania achieved independence, Poland controlled Vilnius so the capital moved eastwards to Kaunas. The President of Lithuania once lived in Kaunas in the President's Palace, which is now a mere museum. Kaunas has a higher proportion of Lithuanian nationals than Vilnius, so it proclaims itself as the capital of being Lithuanian. The tetchy relationship between the capital and Kaunas is like that of Cork and Dublin. Kaunas is on capital standby on the substitutes' bench should the need arise again. There is so little love lost between the two cities that Ruinair chose not to describe this destination as Vilnius (Kaunas). Sure being only 100 km from the capital is bordering on the convenient, what with Torp being 140 km from Oslo. The *Exploring Kaunas Guide* I later pick up in my hotel lobby has some reassuring words for every visitor on page 10: 'The small airport is in Karmelava, 12 km from Kaunas, and has enough room to land.'

I head off outside immediately because Lithuanian LTV shows the Teletubbies, the Waltons and endless basketball matches. Basketball is huge in Lithuania, the nation came third in the 2000 Olympics, they will host the 2011 European Basketball Championships once they build a new stadium, some of their own players have been voted the best players in Europe and Kaunas sports the best team in the country (named Zalgiris), but I have never had an affinity for the sport of basketball, what with me not being seven foot tall. Lithuanian TV also broadcasts the oddest of reality TV shows. A few years ago they ran a show called *Miss Captivity*, looking for the most beautiful female inmate in the prison system. Participants were excused from work in the prison's sewing factory for the week of the contest. A girl called 'Samanta' won and she said it was the best day of her life but she didn't receive the £750 prize money until the end of her four-year sentence, when she planned to pursue a modelling career. This all followed another equally successful local show called *Miss Disability* in which eight women in wheelchairs, aged 18 to 30, competed for another coveted title. That in turn followed a similar pageant for nice deaf women called *Silent Lithuania*.

My hotel is on the 1.7-km-long Laisves Aleja (Freedom Avenue). It's the longest pedestrian catwalk in Central Europe, and allegedly often enjoyed by the town's 370,000 citizens, although today it is sparsely populated and looks more like an avenue meant for a larger and more ambulatory population. Two rows of linden trees run down the avenue, complemented on both sides by shops, bars, restaurants and casinos. But there's no point coming to Kaunas for shopping since you will only need one thing here and that's an umbrella. When it rains folks stand in the shelter of the Maxima department store entrance at the crossroads of Laisves Aleja and Mickeviciaus. Folks do not enter the department store to pass the time. I made that mistake and stepped back about 50 years in the world of retailing. Inside formidable ladies guard individual displays of horrendous clothes, tacky ornaments and shocking jewellery with the sole objective of not selling anything to anyone without a decent fight. I am not sure that anyone would want to shop here when Benetton, Boss and others are next door. When the rain sometimes stops, folks remain standing in the shelter of the Maxima entrance because they're not sure what to do or where to go next.

In the Miesto Sodas city park is a memorial named 'Field of Victims'. A series of large rusted metal blocks are laid flat on the grass along with an inscribed name and a single rain-soaked wreath. Romas Kalanta stood here on 12 July 1974 and set himself alight in protest at living under Soviet rule. In his farewell letter he wrote, 'Why am I living? This is a system which does not allow me to live. I would rather die by my own hand.' There are 19 blocks on the grass, representing his age upon his self-immolation.

I walk onwards until I spy a 25-metre-high bronze monument in front of the football stadium, at the junction of Sporto and Perkuno. This monument is dedicated to Kaunas's greatest heroes. Steponas and Stasys are so famous around these parts that there are many streets named in their honour, plus the adjacent *S Darius ir S Girenas Soccer Stadium* (capacity of 8,739, all-seater, no roof) and the old Kaunas Airport. The monument is appropriate since it looks like a huge aircraft wing sticking vertically out of the ground.

Flying to Kaunas is easy these days, with Ruinair's industry-leading reliability, punctuality and lost baggage statistics, but it was not always so easy. Steponas Darius and Stasys Girenas were two Lithuanian pilots who emigrated to the USA, and instead of taking an ocean liner back across the Atlantic as most sensible people did at the time, they attempted to make their mark in world aviation by flying non-stop with only a compass for their navigational equipment, and without an in-flight bar service, from New York to Kaunas. They wanted in effect to put Lithuania on the map, which is surprising because it's always been there. In their last letter, the pilots wrote that 'either a successful flight or a complete disaster would be a significant event'. They were right about that and are thus responsible for Lithuanian's obsession with flying.

The aviators collected $3,200 from friends, bought a plane and named it *Lituanica*. They took off from New York in July 1932 without the required permissions and flew over Newfoundland, Ireland and Scotland, covering 4,000 miles in 37 hours of non-stop flight, which at that time was the fourth longest flight ever, even longer than the apparent length of your average Ruinair flight. Their pioneering flight came to a sudden and premature end in a field in Soldin in Germany, 100 miles north of Berlin, only 650 miles away from a sort of homecoming. An old man heard the crash but he didn't go outside because it was too wet. A lady picking mushrooms later found the fatal crash site. Steponas's body was lying beside the wreckage while the body of Stasys was still inside the cockpit. An investigation proved that at the time of the crash, the engine was working and there was sufficient fuel. Some suspect the aircraft was shot down by the Germans who thought it was a spy plane. Lithuanians like that theory but no bullet holes were found in the airframe so that shoots that theory right out of the sky. Personally I suspect the two aviators were simply physically and mentally exhausted after 37 hours in a confined and noisy space when they fell to earth.

The Military Museum of Vytautas the Great houses an exhibition on the nation's greatest heroes, since because they crashed *after* they had crossed the Atlantic, they were thus sort of successful in their mission. The neat gardens of this war museum come alive with the sound of the city's 35-bell carillon which connects through a series of bells, pedals and keys to concoct an amazing sound, every Saturday and Sunday at 4 p.m. I went there. On a Saturday. At 4 p.m. I waited … Nothing happened. Inside a number of attendant ladies in violent homespun cardigans are in charge of the locked doors, dark stairs and black plastic drapes. They are unable to speak any English and only move to shut the doors to stop a draught. No photographs are permitted. A large room on the top floor is devoted entirely to Steponas and Stasys. Behind a long glass-enclosed wall, the *Lituanica* crash site is painstakingly reconstructed with the actual airplane wreckage laid out before my eyes exactly as it was found 75 years ago, dirt and all. The plane is painted bright orange, much like a modern day easyJet Airbus aircraft. There is a compass, fuel pump, windscreen and sextant in a glass case. No radio. The propeller is twisted. It is an impressive panorama. It's like stumbling upon a multi-car pile-up on the motorway. I feel like calling the emergency services.

Not everything is here since souvenir hunters pilfered items at the crash site but the glass cases contain an amazing variety of items. There are seasickness remedy tablets. There is a bottle of Horlicks Malted Milk (presumably empty). There is the Air Almanac for 1933 (in good condition). There are water bottles. There is a breathing device with an oxygen bottle (which looks unreliable e.g. 'Drain saliva at base of bottle'). There are the Parker pens and business cards of the pilots. There are their two wallets with initials (both are empty). There's a torch with Eveready batteries. There are postcards and letters sent from New York to Lithuanian addresses and presumably eventually delivered by others. There is an emergency flare (sadly unused). There is a pilot's licence of a Stanley L. Girch. One of the aviators was not licensed to fly.

On the opposite side of the room are the uniforms worn by the aviators during the flight. Their clothes make unlikely national treasures but I suspect in a small nation, you have to make do with whatever you can when it comes to commemorating your national heroes. The aviators didn't wear fleece-lined jump suits but black double-breasted suits, with white shirts, black patent shoes and natty flying helmets. There are two folded cotton vests on display ('Made in America'), but no underpants. The two pilots' suits have been sewn back together in several different places and are definitely the suits in which they died. One of their wrist watches is on display alongside, the passage of time permanently stopped at 12.36. Last are photographs of the aviators' bodies lying in repose in wooden coffins, their grand funerals, a memorial built in Soldin, and a Lithuanian Airlines aircraft with the call sign LY-BSD in memory of Steponas and Stasys.

A portable television set with a built-in prehistoric VHS video tape recorder (remember those?) hangs from one of the walls. I read that the two aviators were interviewed by Fox News before they took off. I need to see this video. I walk over to the lady sat in the corner of the room and point at the TV set.

'Video?' I suggest.

She shrugs her shoulders, looks away and then stares down at the ground. She doesn't seem interested so I assume the TV is to be used on a self-service basis. I stand below the TV. A red light is on so there is power. I press Play. Nothing happens. I press Stop, wait and press Play again. Still dead. I look at her and she says something I cannot understand but she makes no effort to come to assist me. I go back to work, switch off the Power button, wait and press Power and Play. Still no joy. She is now warbling away to herself in the corner, 10 feet from me. I try all combinations of the buttons, back and forth. Play, Stop, Pause, Play, Fast Forward, Rewind, Fast Forward, Play etc. Still no joy. Her mad chatter grows louder. Two other visitors walk into the room. I point at the video and I assume everyone here can speak German.

'*Die video is kaput,*' I advise all those in the room.

The young couple stop, listen to the mad old lady and reply. 'She says don't touch the video.'

I wonder whether the distant ancestors of the people who maintain this video recorder 75 years on might have also been involved in maintaining the *Lituanica*. I'm half thinking of asking for a refund but I cannot since admission was free due to some ugly renovations in progress; if I could get some money off them then I would be up money for the day. Before I leave I make do with reading a sign with a quote from the aviators taken from the TV interview. 'Transatlantic flying isn't very difficult if you have the proper equipment and you are well prepared. Our trip from New York to Lithuania shouldn't be very difficult.' When they took off Fox News reported the two pilots were waving goodbye for the whole world. And to it too.

A few hours later I am back in Kaunas International Air Shed where the rain torrents down on the corrugated tin roof. The giant departures weighing machine is popular with locals who check their baggage to avoid excess charges but some of the locals could do with stepping onto the scales in person since it is calibrated up to 200 kg. We enjoy the world's fastest check-in since here they choose to X-ray us plus our baggage before we receive our Ruinair boarding cards and pass through passport control. Airside I sit in a chair discarded from some company head office refurbishment to watch Lithuanians queuing for all of the two hours inside the tiny duty-free shop to buy cheap cigarettes, cans of beer and bottles of alco-pop. They down the alcohol immediately and rip open the cartons of Marlboro cancer sticks to bury them inside hand baggage. Most of my fellow passengers, it seems tonight, are fully-employed tobacco-smuggling alcoholics. One of the guys appears comatose but he makes it to his feet and they let him board the flight and fly.

The Ruinair signs in the Air Shed exhort us to fly from Kaunas to Glazgas (Prestvikas), Senonas, Dublinas, Liverpulis, Londonas

(Stanstedas) and Frankfurtas (Hanas). Every place name in Lithuanian seems to end in -as. We are encouraged by this airline to *Skrisk Pigiau,* which is my first and only bit of Lithuanian lingo and I don't need to be a genius to translate it into English. When the incoming aircraft lands, two of the Ruinair cabin crew join the duty-free queue for Absolut vodka and so delay our departure.

I'm the only passenger buying water in the shop. I go to pay with a crisp 10-litas note. I have used this note a few times in the past two days but now I look at it carefully. I recognise Steponas and Stasys on the front of the note, in their pilots' uniforms. They are as genuinely Lithuanian as the two guys who sat next to me on the way out. The reverse side of the note shows the Lituanica flying towards Ireland and the UK.

Steponas and Stasys never arrived here but they are here in spirit. I take out a twenty note instead and place the aviators back inside my wallet. In a few minutes' time they will be with me and 188 of their compatriots aboard another almost unendurable flight: a midnight Ruinair run back to Dublin. Would they have ever believed that they could have stopped off in Dublin ex New York and flown on to Kaunas for 1 cent?

Customer Service
Ruinair Ltd
Dublin Airport

Dear Sirs,

I would like to complain about my recent return flight from Kaunas to Dublin.

Firstly, whilst the late night flight was adequate and I got home, I was unable to get any rest or sleep at all due to your staff wheeling trolleys of food and drinks up and down the aisles, plus more trolleys of toys, David Beckham fragrances, followed by the hard sell of tickets and scratch cards. At one stage there were so many endless announcements that I thought I might be sitting instead inside a bingo hall. Why was I blasted with endless deafening announcements from the speakers above my head? I know your airline is keen to make more money from us passengers in the form of ancillary services, so can I make an innovative suggestion? Could you introduce a new online reservation option called 'Peace & Quiet' which entitles a passenger to sit in a quiet zone on the aircraft or at least provides them with some ear plugs to use whilst on board. I suspect that myself and many other elderly passengers would be more than happy to pay as much as €5 for this additional service.

Secondly, our flight left Kaunas International Air Shed at 10 p.m. and not at 9.45 p.m. as scheduled. The incoming aircraft arrived on time and the sole reason for our late departure was that two of your cabin crew spent 15 minutes in the queue in the airport duty-free shop buying vodka. Are your cabin crew permitted to go shopping whilst at work since they ruined your famous 25 minute turnaround time? PS Eva is great.

Thirdly, there was a young Lithuanian gentleman (in a pair of white socks) who was completely hammered yet he was allowed to board our aircraft. I saw him knocking back cans of lager and bottles of alco-pop in the Air Shed and when he boarded after me, he sat slumped forward in his seat for the entire 3 hour flight duration. I thought he might be dead but someone resurrected him when we landed in Dublin. He was so obviously 100 per cent drunk and he blocked the aisle for other passengers. Why was he allowed to board?

I look forward to hearing from you in due course.

Yours etc,

Disgusted of Dublin

I am surprised they still bother to reply to my letters. The last few letters that I wrote to them, the ones with their replies saying *Private & Confidential*, were published in a two-page spread in *The Dubliner* magazine.

Dear Mr Kilduff,

I acknowledge receipt of your letter.

We apologise for any discomfort that you endured of your recent flight with us on flight FR 2972 from Kaunas to Dublin. Thank you for your idea on having a quiet zone on board the aircraft, we are sorry that you felt harassed by the amount of announcements made on board during your flight. As such we have forwarded a copy of your letter to our in-flight manager at Kaunas to ensure that the amounts of announcements made are kept to a reasonable amount.

In relation to your comments about the passenger who sat near you during the flight we have strict guidelines for the carriage of passengers who are disruptive or under the influence of alcohol. For the most part, passengers who are creating a disturbance at check-in are not permitted to board by our ground staff. However, if a passenger appears to behave in an unacceptable manner during the flight, the Captain will be informed. Our staff will then assess how to deal with the passengers bearing in mind not to inflame a potentially volatile situation. Passengers who become disruptive during a flight will be cautioned, by the crew or Captain and if the disturbance continues the police are alerted and meet the flight on landing.

The flight was delayed for 15 minutes not due to cabin crew buying duty free but by the airport having air traffic flow management restrictions.

I hope, despite your experience, we have not entirely lost your goodwill and that you will afford us the opportunity of serving you more successfully in the near future.

Yours sincerely
For and on Behalf of
RUINAIR LIMITED

'... *the airport having air traffic flow management restrictions?*' Kaunas International Air Shed is used by one airline, Ruinair, and there are never more than five flights daily. More *Bolloxology*.

Mick's Plane Speaking (1)

So how's Ruinair boss Mick O'Leery doing these days? 'Not well at all,' he moans. 'Someone's just frozen my 'effing pay.' Has he told Mrs O'Leery? 'I'm trying to keep it quiet,' he adds. 'I might have to tell her that we've got to cut back, that she'll have to start shopping at Lidl or Aldi rather than Tesco.' O'Leery's convinced all airlines are in for a rotten year, but he trots out the usual mantra that however much he's suffering, Willie Walsh at the much flabbier British Airways will be hurting more. 'The major sufferer here will be Mrs Walsh,' predicts O'Leery. 'Mrs O'Leery may suffer as a consequence but she'll just have to tighten her belt for a year or two.'

THE TELEGRAPH

Ruinair boss Mick O'Leery just could not help himself yesterday when we had all witnessed the spectacle of the Taoiseach, Mr Ahern, handing over the Powers Irish Grand National trophy to him at Fairyhouse. 'I don't get much off Bertie Ahern, but I'll take the cup for the Grand National off him any time,' said Mr O'Leery. Mr O'Leery was as taken aback as anyone on the course when his horse, Hear The Echo, won the big race. The 33/1 shot has surprised everyone, including the Taoiseach. 'I suppose if Michael had known it was going to win, he would have told me,' said the Taoiseach. O'Leery seemed genuinely surprised that his horse had taken the big race. 'We had no money on him. Two people asked me earlier should they back him and I told them no way. I thought he was going out for a run to keep himself warm,' he said.

IRISH TIMES

£179,332|828

Flights should be free but the sky's the limit—say €42,000—for pedigree farm animals. Or so goes the logic of one Mick O'Leery who splashed out the bumper sum on an Aberdeen Angus bull at a cattle mart in Perth, Scotland. The purchase made the no-frills Ruinair tycoon the flashiest buyer of the day, as his farm manager romped home with the appropriately named Mr Elevate. Mr O'Leery's fascination with bulls, cattle, et al, dates back to his farming roots in Mullingar, and he claims to be at his happiest when tending to his Gigginstown herd. So dear are the herd to his heart that he even served them up for his all-frills wedding to Anita Farrell some years ago. Mick O'Leery's passion for bulls has also yielded some wonderfully ironic moments, most notably when one of his herd seized the 'Best Bull' award in 2000. Asked about the latest purchase, Mr O'Leery replied: 'As you know I have a long standing policy of not commenting on rumour or speculation—regardless of how much bullshit is involved.'

IRISH INDEPENDENT

Angry residents opposing the expansion of George Best Belfast City Airport have hit back at comments made by Ruinair boss Mick O'Leery. The flamboyant airline chief executive said it was vital that plans by City Airport's owners to extend the runway by 600 metres were implemented in order to enable Ruinair to open up new direct services from Europe. He urged the business community to press for the runway to be lengthened in order to help boost tourism. 'We would like to do more and base more aircraft here and are working with the City Airport to get the runway extended,' he said. 'Let's get the planning permission through and let's ignore the mewling and puking from local residents which is a load of nonsense.'

BELFAST TELEGRAPH

Cathal Giomard, the man who regulates Irish aviation, has a press article pinned to a board above his desk. The article is about Mick O'Leery having yet another go at the regulator. Your eye is immediately drawn to the sections highlighted in yellow in which Mick calls Giomard 'a wanker', an invective the Ruinair boss later repeated in an RTÉ interview. Giomard used to adopt a stoical attitude but when

his nine-year-old daughter asked him 'Why does that man hate you?'
his philosophical resolve was tested. He said 'It should be possible to
argue about policy without descending into abuse.' Like most observers
Giomard attributes Mick's language to his desire for publicity. 'I will
be happy to match or surpass Mick word for word as soon as I have a
cheque for 25pc of the free publicity it would generate for Ruinair.
Otherwise I don't propose to join him in the verbal gutter he inhabits.
Let's just keep to the facts. I think I'll have to wait until he has chil-
dren old enough to understand this language. Maybe then he'll stop.'
Instead of climbing down, O'Leery sent Giomard a copy of the
Ruinair Cabin Crew Charity Calendar which is an unapologetically
saucy publication. The accompanying note, which has fallen into our
possession, expressed Mick's wish that next year's calendar 'will give
you something interesting and uplifting to hang over your desk, and
to look at, as you and your 20 colleagues while away the many idle
hours between now and the next Airport Charges Review'.

IRISH INDEPENDENT

The war of words between two of Ireland's top airline tycoons has
taken a bitter turn with the head of regional airline Aer Arann claim-
ing Ruinair boss Mick O'Leery told him: 'Fuck off back to Connemara
where you come from.' Aer Arann boss Padraig O'Ceidigh says the
abusive remarks were made during a meeting which he called with
the Ruinair chief to try to sort out the increasingly hostile situation
between the two airlines. Mr O'Ceidigh also alleged that Mr O'Leery
pretended to play the fiddle on several occasions during the meeting
when the Aer Arann boss asked him why he was trying to put his
comparatively small airline out of business. 'What really hurt me was
the way he pretended to play the fiddle. The Connemara remark
didn't damage or hurt me but the fiddle thing was crazy.' Asked how
he felt about Mr O'Leery's comments on a personal level, Mr
O'Ceidigh said, 'I was taken aback but you have to have a tough skin
in this business. I want Mick O'Leery to know that you can take the
man out of Connemara but you can't take the Connemara out of the
man. And I ain't giving up easily.' When asked about the controver-
sial meeting between the two airline bosses, Mr O'Leery scoffed at the
idea it was a sales pitch for Ruinair to buy the third Irish carrier. 'I

don't think he could even give it away. I mean he has tried to sell it to just about everybody and nobody will even take a present of it,' he said.

IRISH INDEPENDENT

'I filmed Tuesday's Ruinair press conference for the Press Association in something of a fluster. My dilapidated and wonky tripod was giving viewers the false impression that Ruinair's chief executive, Mick O'Leery, had presented his company's annual results on a hill. I was also pressed for time. So just half an hour in, I had to leave the press conference early. I clambered across the floor on all fours to retrieve my microphone, trying desperately not to interrupt those journalists still at work. O'Leery was mid-sentence but he stopped what he was saying when he saw me. The combination of a woman, on all fours and in a skirt had proved too much for him. 'If you want to stay on your knees, by all means, I'd encourage you,' he said in front of the gathered, mostly male, journalists. 'Sorry, I've forgotten the question ... there was a very pretty girl on her knees there in front of me.'

THE GUARDIAN

Ruinair boss Mick O'Leery has flown into a storm after boasting about low fares and free sex on a new service. The airline chief told a stunned audience that his transatlantic business fliers would pay for 'beds and blowjobs'. Answering a question during a whistle-stop tour of three airports in Germany, O'Leery said: 'In Economy it will be very cheap fares, we say about €10. And in Business class it will be beds and blowjobs. In Business, it will all be free—including the blowjobs.' His comments shocked Anja Seugling, Ruinair's sales and marketing manager for Germany, Switzerland and Austria, who was translating his answers. She began to choke on her glass of water when O'Leery asked: 'Surely you have a word for blowjobs in German?' O'Leery, who has a fiery reputation, then poked fun when told there was no word for 'blowjob', saying, 'Terrible sex life in Germany.' An airline spokesman yesterday confirmed O'Leery's comments. He said: 'The working title for the Business class service is "Beds and Blowjobs".'

DAILY STAR

Latvia

Flight FR1976 – Tuesday @ 9.20 a.m. – DUB-RIX-DUB

Fare €15 plus taxes, fees and charges €54

The highlight of any visit to Dublin Airport is the Dubs who drive the buses from the airport to the long-term car park, as they call out the various parking zones and passengers push the bell if they wish the bus to stop at any zone. On my last visit the driver called out 'Zone G' but no one rang the bell. Zone G is a popular zone so the driver was surprised. 'Zone G, folks. Anyone for zone G?' Still no one wanted to get off. 'Zone G … G as in George.' No one got off so we moved on. Soon he announced, 'Zone J, folks. Anyone for zone J?' Again no one wanted to get off. 'Zone J, folks. J as in George … the other George.' The baffled bus driver soon turns to face us. 'Where are yez all?' A lone male voice from the back of the bus replies, 'In de bus.'

I park today in zone K, specifically in K9, as in 'This place is going to the dogs'. Parking remains an expensive luxury. The daily rates for short-term parking went up from €30 to €40, which only Mick can afford, and the daily rates for long-term parking increased from €6 to €9.50: proof that the annual increases are still determined by officials at the Ministry of Finance in Zimbabwe (where the 100-billion-Zimbabwean-Dollar bank note is worth €3). It costs €12 to sit in your car in the short-term car park for three hours, but it can cost only €1 to sit in one of Mick's aircraft for three hours. *The DAA has jacked up the passenger charges by 100 per cent in four years. The car parking charges have gone up by 200 per cent in four years.*

The *Irish Times* reported that the DAA earned €52 million in revenues from its car parks in Dublin, Cork and Shannon in 2007, most of which I feel that I personally contributed. The motto of the Dublin Airport Authority is '*Helping you on your way*' but they omitted the words '*to a larger overdraft*'. I used to spend the majority of my income on my mortgage but now it goes on long-term car parking. The DAA are great. Do you know they have various internal departments and one of them is called *Terminal Services*?

There is a boy on the car park bus who screams repeatedly at his father, 'Look Daddy, a plane. Look Daddy, a plane. Look Daddy, a plane.' I suspect it will be a very long day for this family. Then the father asks his son, 'What zone are we in?' The seven-year-old responds with 'K, Daddy.' The father is not done. 'Red or green car park?' The seven year old obliges: 'Red, Daddy.' My fellow passengers on today's Ruinair flight will likely be the Dublin family with the matching set of lovely leopard-skin print suitcases.

The future alternative to driving to the airport might be the planned Metro, if it comes to pass. '*It is a €6 billion white elephant that should never be built. If there is one good thing to take from a restraint in Government spending or a recession, it is that the white elephant that is metro north to Dublin Airport might be scrapped. It would be the best saving that this Government would ever make. It will have no function whatsoever for the airport. Tourists travel on* CIE *and Aircoach. No one in Foxrock, Mullingar or Kildare will get up and drive into St Stephen's Green at 5 a.m. to connect onto a white elephant that will lose money forever in order to connect to Dublin Airport. Inbound passengers are perfectly well served by competitive bus services and a quality bus corridor that runs the whole way in. It is a €6 billion hole in the ground.*'

We pass the signpost that encapsulates everything you need to know about Dublin Airport, with its signs for the IALPA pilots' trade union office, the SIPTU trade union office, the mortuary and Ruinair's head office. The latter building is where Mick's taxi still collects him from work for the trip back to Mullingar in the bus lanes. I know this for a fact because a rather irate (and genuine) taxi driver told me he has seen Mick's taxi leaving the airport environs. Mick has a black 07-D Mercedes Benz s500 which would set you back €155,000 in Ballsbridge Motors. It's not your average taxi. The taxi driver even emailed me a photograph of Mick's taxi. *'I have a taxi because it's a good investment. I have a Mercedes 500. Not because I like the Mercedes 500, but because it's a big, comfortable fucking car. A helicopter would be a little over the top. I was always a transport innovator. I always like to be at the cutting edge of transport solutions.'*

The DAA are spending €2 billion on a 'transformation' and to date this money has been spent on lime-green paint and signage telling us that they are building a new terminal, which is nice to know. The signage photographs of the new terminal includes Aer Lingus check-in desks but none for Ruinair, which is a little ominous. In the absence of the signage I might have assumed that the levelling of the listed buildings and the laying waste of acres of land might have happened in a world war. The wasteland extends dangerously near to the ugly white Ruinair head office building but to date this has not been demolished. The new construction rising weekly before our eyes is a skeletal frame of curved iron girders. They may be building a new airport terminal or they may be building a land-locked P&O cruise ship.

The DAA have demolished half of the salubrious Pier C, which was built only seven years ago for €150 million. Mick will be delighted. *'Where in the legislation does it say the DAA can subsidise the fat cats waddling down to Pier C to board their British Midland morning business flights to Heathrow? Pier C was designed by Aer Rianta to win an architectural competition rather than serve the needs of airlines.'*

Mick really doesn't like the Dublin Airport Authority. *'It is widely known that Dublin Airport is the second most expensive of our 28 bases. It is a regulated Government-owned monopoly. The costs associated with the airport are escalating rapidly. Two years ago, the Dublin Airport Authority announced that Terminal 2 would be built at a cost of €170 to €200 million. We supported that development. What they are currently building are two buildings, one of which is for deep queuing check-in spaces for people who have already checked in on the website. The second building is five storeys high, three storeys higher than one will ever need in an airport terminal building, and the cost is €850 million. They are planning to waste approximately €2 billion on facilities that should cost one tenth of that sum and they have a regulator that rubber stamps cost increases as if they were going out of fashion. Dublin Airport would have one believe it is a sophisticated capital city airport whereas we just fly to fields some-where else in Europe.'*

'Dublin is more expensive than main city airports in Rome, Valencia, Madrid, Alicante, Milan, Pisa and Marseilles. There is no justification for a small airport in a small peripheral country like Ireland having such an expensive airport infrastructure. We do not need it. Dublin Airport is not the same as Charles de Gaulle or Heathrow Airport, much as the Dublin Airport Authority would like us to believe it is. The demand is there as long we offer very cheap seats but we cannot keep offering cheap seats to an airport monopoly like the DAA *which is trying to screw us for €15 per passenger. We wrote to the* DAA *and told it that we will maintain the flights and deliver this traffic if it gave us a discount on those flights and that traffic for this winter period. It wrote back, as most monopolies do, and said the second word was "off". If I were the Minister for Aviation, the Dublin Airport monopoly would not bloody exist. It would be gone 30 seconds after I took office.'*

23 million of us make Dublin the eighth busiest airport in Europe and the 14th busiest airport in the world. I am amazed at the number of people who still holiday overseas, rather than staying at home. Paris, Madrid and Berlin will always be there, but with a credit crunch, falling property prices and a recession, your home may not. So enjoy your home while you still can. Mick is not one of the frequent flyers. *'I don't like to go abroad on holiday. I don't like sunshine. When I can stay at home in Ireland what the hell would I want to go away for?'*

Inside the terminal building there are long queues at Ruinair's ticket desk. This is one of only two man-made features on earth which can be seen from outer space—the other being the Great Wall of China. There are two places in Ireland which have a licence to print money. One is Ireland's Mint in Sandyford which produces notes and coins. The other is this Ruinair ticket desk in Dublin Airport where the desperate buy tickets. Some of these are funeral-goers: *'They book late because they don't tend to have much notice, and they tend to be price insensitive because they have to travel.'* Mick has his favourites. *'Green protesters are our best passengers. They're always flying off to their demonstrations.'*

The security guy who checks my *Check N' Go* boarding card today is chatty. 'How are you today?' he asks.

'Fine,' I nod, taking the bait. 'And how are you today?'

'Great,' as he hands me back my folded A4 page. 'Sure, didn't I win the Lotto this week.'

'Very well done,' I reply. 'And you're still working here.'

It is the first time that I see Customs officers in the security screening area bring a sniffer dog up and down the queues of passengers. Young lads with shaven heads and Man Utd kit remain very anxious as the spaniel wags beside their carry-on baggage. The dog comes close to me but it suspects nothing. No one knows that I am a user and that I am addicted ... to flying on Ruinair.

On the way to the gate we run the gauntlet of two girls selling Ruinair credit cards. 'Do yez live in Ireland?' they ask us. I do but I do not want a free flight worth 1 cent but have to pay the taxes, fees and charges.

I divert into the Hughes & Hughes bookshop to annoy their staff, to sign 'Ruinair' stock and to sell a few copies to people who will buy any book once it's signed by the author. I signed a copy here once for a husband and wife who told me their daughter worked for Ruinair and they asked me to add a dedication to the book for her of 'Hard Luck'. 'Ruinair' has slipped to number 3 in their sales charts, behind *Ma, He Sold Me For A Few Cigarettes* and *Not Without My Sister*. Sometimes I almost wish that I had suffered an horrendous upbringing so I could write a book about it. I don't know who buys these depressing books—they are about human angst, trials and tribulations, horrific family experiences and man's inhumanity to man. Just like flying frequently on Ruinair, I guess. I learn that the shop staff remain puzzled by the 1 cent price sticker on 'Ruinair' (plus taxes, fees and charges of €12.99) and some have tried to ring up a sale for 1 cent, which would be a disaster, not only for Hughes & Hughes, but for myself, my agent and my publisher.

Today a Polish traveller, named Anna, is about to buy the book so I offer to sign her copy.

'Do you like flying on Ruinair?' I ask.

'They are cheap,' replies Anna.

The airport's Portakabins have been replaced by the Pier D departures terminal. To get there we must walk along an elevated undulating glass corridor that takes us via all of north County Dublin. I circumnavigate the plastic rubbish bins and floor mats which impressively catch the rain water from the year-old leaking roof. This hike takes us along three sides of a square when it would be have been simpler, quicker and cheaper to take us along one side of the square, past the old airport building. There is an elderly couple ahead of me who take faltering steps and I doubt they will make it to any gate this side of their departure time. Another mother encourages her three small children to follow her. 'Will we ever get there?' I used to arrive at the airport one hour before departure time. Now I allow two hours to hike. I don't know why the DAA don't provide complimentary orienteering maps and set up some water stops, Portaloos and rest stations for us weaker passengers. Personally speaking, I'd sooner climb Lugnaquilla (3,035 feet) of a Sunday afternoon. *'We oppose Terminal D. It should not be in place, it is in the wrong place.'*

But once there it's worth the hike. Pier D is a destination in itself. No wonder Mick was hopping mad when the Dublin Airport Authority spent €120 million on this facility. *'In the Dublin Airport Authority you have the masters of waste, inefficiency and incompetence.'* Several hundred Ruinair aircraft come and go outside the floor-to-ceiling plate glass windows. Do you know that every second, somewhere in the world, a baby arrives on Planet Earth, a child dies in Africa, a metre of ice cap melts, something is sold on eBay and a Ruinair plane takes off? This is no low fares terminal. It has acres of space, light, seats, chrome, marble, glass and peace. Although brand new, one of the WCs is closed to 'upgrade' the facility—which is fine for us blokes, but the ladies are queuing out the door of the one remaining WC, in a long line somewhat reminiscent of the queue for take-off at JFK Airport at 7 p.m. on a Friday evening.

There are not many free seats so I hobble over with a pronounced limp and sit down in a *Reduced Mobility Seat*. No one has
ever asked me to move from such a seat and I am only keeping it
free, if a really reduced-mobility type of person comes along who
is about to keel over. The shops in the terminal are busy because
there are several delayed flights. A manager in WH Smith in
Heathrow once told me that airports, which are essentially retailing operations, love to see delays. Once a delay of an hour or so is
announced, all the passengers head off to the shops to stock up on
books, newspapers, magazines, sandwiches and drinks before they
run out. In Ireland, however, we react differently to delays. I see
groups of passengers head off to the bars to return with pint
glasses of creamy Guinness and chilled Bulmers. Their worst fear
is that our delay will be short and they won't get a second round in
before we board. Meanwhile the German passengers like to stand
in the queue for another hour and the Japanese take more photographs of each other.

An Aer Arann plane appears a little shy about coming to a halt.
Perhaps it competes with Ruinair on the Dublin to Cork route. *'Aer
Arann has been on a campaign—I presume born out of desperation
—to the effect that we are trying to put Aer Arann out of business. I
assure you that we do not think about Aer Arann from 1 January to
31 December in any given year. It is too small for us to worry about.
We operate over 700 routes in Europe while Aer Arann operates
40 routes. We compete against each other on one route. Apparently,
that is enough for us to damage Aer Arann or put it out of business.
If Aer Arann is going out of business—and we do not know its financial position because it does not publish accounts—it is not because of
our entry on the Dublin to Cork route, it is because the 39 other routes
it operates do not make money. We operate a 189-seat aircraft and if
we tried to treble our fares to match Aer Arann our load factor would
be approximately 25 per cent. The people of Cork, of whom my
parents mercifully are two, have more sense than to fly to Dublin on
expensively high air fares on flights that almost never leave on time.
The only beneficiaries of our entry on the Dublin to Cork route have
been the people of Cork and the occasional person from Dublin who
wants to go down to see how hurling and football should be played.*

*I am sorry if Aer Arann does not like the fact that Europe's largest low
fares airline is operating on the route but it should just get over it. As
regards whether we want Aer Arann off the Cork route, we do not. We
wish it well on that route. Apart from the fact that it makes us look
very low-cost and low-fare, that is Aer Arann's only achievement on
the Cork route. Every day a couple of thousand passengers choose how
they want to travel between Cork and Dublin, CIE, buses, Aer Arann
or us. I cannot help it if two thirds of the passengers choose us over
Aer Arann. I believe they are good, sensible people, but I would say
that.'*

I have it bad when it comes to looking at aircraft at airports all
around Europe but I am nothing to the guy seated close by who
produces a pair of binoculars to closely examine the successive
take-offs. I survey the scene outside. One Ruinair aircraft has a
faded painting of a flattened Leinster rugby player with a Brown
Thomas shopping bag. '*Up Munster.*' I bet this aircraft is really
popular amongst all the Leinster Lions supporters in Dublin. On
another nearby Ruinair jet, a crew member stands at the top of the
steps with a plastic beaker of fresh Costa coffee, and she looks
blankly back at me. Another aircraft passes the windows with a
large slogan on the fuselage, '*Bye Bye Latehansa*', proof that
Ruinair's aircraft are still an insult to all other European airlines.
There are three Ruinair aircraft parked on a distant apron, destined
to spend this winter flying to nowhere. That's about 150 million
dollars of Boeing's finest hardware going to waste. Outside also is
the most beautiful aircraft of all their Boeing 737-800s. EI-DCL was
specially painted in light and dark blue to mark delivery of their
60th aircraft. The reason the paint job is so smart is because it was
designed by Boeing, not by Ruinair. I have been on this aircraft and
regret to advise that despite the exterior, the interior is still disgusting. Maybe someday when Mick retires they will christen an aircraft
EI-MOL. It will be their noisiest aircraft. Once Mick collected a
Boeing 737 in Seattle: '*It will be christened EI-DAC, short for 'Driving
Airbus Crazy'.* Next to us they announce a departing flight to
Birmingham. It is flight 'FR triple 6'. Surely this is the Devil's flight
and is a bad omen? They make an announcement at gate D61 that
another Ruinair flight is famously 'boarding shortly'. The passengers

are standing up in two queues but there is not even an aircraft parked below on the stand.

I consider myself to be an experienced frequent traveller on this airline but today I am shocked at the behaviour of one of the Ruinair flight dispatchers. A guy dressed in black with a red fluorescent jacket and a walkie-talkie appears to be conversing directly with paying passengers, who are concerned at the delayed flights on the screens and come over to ask him a question. Worse still he seems to be genuinely answering their questions to their satisfaction, thereby encouraging other passengers to approach him tentatively. This man who works for this airline is delivering customer service. This sort of thing has to stop.

We are all sitting calmly and quietly until some fecker gets up to stand in one of the two queues. Someone else arises to stand behind him and then a couple join them. Feck. Soon we are all on our feet to stand in line for the next 40 minutes despite the absence of an aircraft outside. There are the faces of those who survived the Great Depression of the 1930s, the faces of those who realised there were not enough lifeboats on the Titanic, the faces of those who saw the horrors of World Wars and then there are the faces of those who stand in a Ruinair *All Other Passengers*' queue. Some of the people in that queue are moving their feet about to avoid the premature onset of Deep Vein Thrombosis, and they are not even airborne yet. Some of the people standing in the Priority Queue seem more anxious than the rest of us because they have paid to be first onto the aircraft but they are not at the very top of the rather long Priority Queue. What's that quote from Mick in the Bible, as in Matthew, 18:20? *'For where two or three are gathered together in my name, they shall form an orderly queue for priority boarding...'*

We do not board at the scheduled departure time. The two Ruinair staff at the desk don't feel the need to announce any explanation to us. They prefer to see us stand in line and wait, and to chat to two of the passengers whom they evidently know, and who have Ruinair IDs with them. Naturally the two off-duty staff board first to sit in row 1 and chat to the crew in-flight. Imagine spending your working days on board Ruinair aircraft and then on your day off work deciding to spend the day ... on board a Ruinair aircraft.

There is a lone Ruinair employee with a money bag who is selling Priority boarding and amazingly some folks are actually buying. The rest of us checked in online earlier and so we have an A4 page from our home computers. We are asked to fold the page at the dotted line to speed up the boarding process as this airline continues to strive for even greater efficiency and speed. I am reminded of the Irish woman who received a new driving licence but when caught speeding along the centre of a road by a Garda, she told him, 'Sure, officer, when the driving licence came, it said at the bottom: *Tear Along the Dotted Line.*'

Boarding rules, like all rules, are there to be broken. When we begin to board, three agitated pikies on their first trip away from a tin caravan on a remote halting site push their way into our queue.

'Pat, I can see your Ma up there at the front? Should we go join her?' shouts Pikie # 1.

I am fairly convinced that their 'Ma' is not even in Dublin Airport. I ensure I stay ahead of them until we reach the two bored Ruinair staff who check our boarding cards. Pikie # 2 offers up his boarding card.

The tiny timid Ruinair girl examines the card carefully and slowly realises that today is her worst nightmare. 'This is the queue for Priority boarding only. Do you have Priority boarding?' she stutters.

Pikie # 2 is not fazed. 'Right, I did it on the computa at home, but sure, didn't it not print out right.'

This is what's known as a *bollocks explanation* and everyone knows it, including the Ruinair girl. There are 100 passengers behind and we wish to board within the 25-minute turnaround time. It remains a sad fact of life that a tiny timid Ruinair girl will never stop three determined pikies from boarding an aircraft whenever they so wish. She tears the cards. 'So there's three of you. There you go.' They all board. You don't need to buy Priority boarding to board first. All you need is a *Hard Neck and Balls*. The same girl who checks my boarding card and my passport hasn't the strength to look at me and averts her eyes. This time it is a pointless check. I could look like my passport photograph or I could be Osama bin Kilduff.

Outside it is raining hard. You don't need a boarding card to board a Ruinair aircraft—you need a rain coat. Latvians are the world's fairest folk when it comes to queuing to board aircraft. They all refuse to join the Priority boarding queue since this would be unfair to those in the non-Priority queue. Two queues is an alien concept. It must be all the practice they got under the Soviets. I see a family of six beat the system—one of them has paid for Priority boarding and they keep seats for the other five. Another person, an Irish lady, sits in a window seat and places coats on the next two seats. A Latvian passenger stops beside.

'Can we sit here?' he asks.

'I am keeping them,' she replies.

'For who?'

She stares him down. 'For two people.'

'Are you allowed to do that?' he persists. She looks away. Evidently you are. A young couple stop near me, seatless. She soon sits beside me in a middle seat. He sits in an aisle seat on my other side. I am surrounded. There is no alternative but to be a gentleman.

'Are you together?' I ask. He nods. 'I don't mind swapping seats.' He nods again. We get up and swap our seats. He thanks me. 'No problem,' I say. 'That'll be another €5 please.'

I would like to write about the wonderful in-flight service, food, drinks, etc. but on this occasion Ruinair forget to bring along food and drink trolleys so the *self-loading cargo* remain unfed and unwatered. Latvians are less experienced airline passengers; they accept this news with quiet resignation; they allow children to roam the aircraft freely looking for treats from other passengers (biscuits and chocolate suffice). They attend the wc in pairs once they work out where the wc is hidden and how the wc door cunningly opens outwards. They remain the nation most likely to pray before landing and to make signs of the cross after landing (presumably only when successful). Despite departing somewhat late we arrive early. This is Europe's most punctual airline. It's so punctual that they delay their departures so as not to be *too* early. Trumpets play within the cabin at the beginning of the pre-recorded announcement. 'Congratulations. Your flight has landed on time. Surprised? You shouldn't be. Last year over 90 per cent of

Ruinair flights landed on time, beating every other European airline. Outstanding.' The announcement concludes with wild cheers.

I take the airport bus number 22 to the city which at 0.20 Lats, or 30 cent, is the epitome of low fares travel. Beat that, Mick. Only he does. Later I learn there is another sort of airport transfer. The *Strip-Limousine* ride from the airport to the city takes a 'minimum of thirty minutes' so as a paying passenger all you can do is pray for a significant traffic tailback along the way. The advertising says the stripper 'goes all the way'. And they don't mean to the main train station or to the hotel of your choice.

I gravitate to *Vecriga*, or old town, which tumbles down to the banks of the Daugava river in a dizzy warren of cobbled pedestrianised streets and pretty romantic squares. Riga is the capital of the Baltics, seven miles from the Baltic Sea, home to 800,000 attractive and youthful inhabitants. The old town is traffic-free because the city charges €5 per car to enter via one of the many road barriers. In the new Riga drivers of BMW X5s and Lexus SUVs (socially unacceptable vehicles) stare enviously at the many Porsche Cayennes, the latter being the only car to date to be named after a food ingredient.

I am 200 miles from Russia, as close as I have ever been. Ladies in their seventies clear mounds of snow from the streets and they are good at their job because when I walk back that way six hours later, they are almost finished their shovelling. The *Centraltirgus* market near the train station is still a shock. At first sight the five giant warehouses look like former Zeppelin hangars and that's because that's exactly what they are. In 1930 when the nearby Zeppelin base shut down post-WW1 the cavernous buildings were moved to the city. One hangar is devoted only to meat products and walrus-whiskered peasant crones sell unrecognisable knuckle joints in what is the world's largest butchers' shop. There is also a shop which sells only fake plastic carrier bags of leading stores and brands. Locals who come to buy pork and spuds prefer to carry their provisions home in a Gucci or Boss bag so as to impress Boris and Inga, the neighbours. The interior is cold, the prices are miserly, the produce is of poor quality and each stark counter is significantly over-manned. Or over-womanned. I realise this is what the Soviets meant by having a market economy.

The Latvians have been sacked, occupied, reoccupied, then sacked again by everyone from the Teutonic Knights to the Swedes, from the French to the Poles, and more recently by Stalin, and then Hitler in 1942, whom they welcomed with open arms and flowers on the basis that he couldn't be any worse than Stalin, and having got rid of Hitler, along came the Soviets again who stayed until ultimate independence in 1991. In the same way that German TV is obsessed with WWII and Hitler, so Latvian TV is obsessed with gulags and Stalin. Elderly former inmates with white Santa beards recount their truly terrible experiences. When Stalin died, many thousands filed past his open coffin, to make sure he was completely dead.

I am increasingly convinced that if I was a small European nation in the twentieth century, the one location I would not wish to be is stuck somewhere between Germany and Russia, because I would have the neighbours trundling through my peaceful country, pillaging and ravishing, every 20 years or so. The 42-metre Freedom Monument in Riga city centre was always something special to Latvians, not because the 1935 monument was paid for and erected by the citizens (a cunning ploy by any city council) but because up to 1991 laying flowers at the foot of this memorial meant a guaranteed one-way ticket to Siberia. The Soviets never dared to demolish this potent symbol during five decades of Communist rule. Now soldiers stand guard for tourists, so be sure to come and go on the hour, as they do.

The Museum of the Occupation of Latvia is housed in an ugly Communist-era shoe-box building. Inside the exhibits are of atrocities committed against the people of Latvia and the systematic destruction of their nation over 51 years. The darkest hour was on 13 June 1941 when 15,000 Latvians, including 1,200 children under seven years of age, were rounded up by the Soviets at an hour's notice and deported in cattle trains on a journey of several weeks to Siberia. The Soviets took the leaders, the intelligentsia and intellectuals, but I learn one mother and her child were taken instead of their neighbours who were on the Soviets' list but who were not at home. In the following few weeks handwritten notes were found strewn all along the train tracks to the east. One man wrote to his son to say he would return and to continue to water the plants in his study. On the same night 11,000 Estonians and 21,000 Lithuanians were taken eastwards. At the time nothing about these events was published in a newspaper and officials were unable to answer any questions. To this day Russia has never condemned these deportations.

There is a walk-in replica of a Siberian labour camp barracks with wooden beds and an oil drum for heat in temperatures that dropped to 50 degrees below. Inmates' hair sometimes froze to the wooden planks in the night. Latvians were placed in barracks with Soviet street criminals who terrorised them. It was so overcrowded that if you got up at night, you lost your space. Only the newest or hardiest inmates had the energy to clamber up to the top bunks at night. Inmates could write two letters home a year, penned in Russian, often on bark. Food was so scarce that when inmates died their bodies were hidden in the barracks by others so as to continue to receive their food ration. The personal keepsakes here testify not only to persecution and inhumanity, but to defiance and resistance. A handkerchief is hand-embroidered with the names of 100 women in a forced labour camp. Thousands of women were deported simply because of whom they were married to. Latvia lost 550,000 of its citizens in the Soviet and German occupations: killed, exiled, disappeared. What impresses most is that 30 animated school children sit on the hard wooden beds beside me to learn all there is to know about totalitarianism.

Tourism numbers are on the up despite the fact that following EU membership in 2004, Russians can no longer hop across the border at their leisure, with or without their army. Up until 1991 only Aeroflot was permitted to operate at Riga Airport. Passenger numbers flying through Riga Airport have trebled in three years and there are plans to transform the airport into a transit hub between Europe and former Soviet states. The airport authorities plan to welcome 10 million passengers per annum by 2013 so for the first time in their nation's history, Latvians are looking forward to an invasion of foreigners. I missed a visit by Queen Elizabeth and Prince Philip but the *Baltic Guide* reports that during the visit to a school, Prince Philip pointed to the assembled children and was clearly heard to ask the headmaster, 'Any sign of intelligence?'

There's a different sort of EU tourist in town and many of them arrive on Ruinair. The first evidence are the groups of English male rutting stags I see falling out of bars and clubs in the night, closely pursued by bouncers and owners, shouting and screaming back at their none-too-pleased hosts, giving them upturned middle fingers from a safe distance. Local guys hand me cards and flyers for their premises. 'You want some sexy action tonight, mister?' The Hotel Riga is the world's first four-star hotel with an in-house strip club, called *Dolls*. I pass what looks like a restaurant since it is named *Restorans*—but inside, past the glass windows, men sit at tables while ladies in white lingerie dance on the neon bar tops, and others dance at the entrance to entice me to enter and to be ripped off. Outside two black BMW 7-series with smoked windows pull up and six bulky locals alight and enter, wearing black shirts, black suits and black leather trench coats. The owner of the premises has arrived to check on his sexy investment. We don't have restaurants like this anywhere in Ireland. Inside there is no eating, only much salivating and drooling.

It gets worse. Websites offer stag weekend options such as Lesbian Dinner Parties, VIP Sauna Strip Shows and Soviet Nurse Banquets, although I am not sure what's so special about Russian nurses and their native culinary skills. Other packages include mud fighting where women will wrestle men and prices vary based upon the number of ladies and whether they will wear teeny bikinis or their birthday suits. Ladies' options for hen parties include spa days, wine tasting and for the brave, pole-dancing lessons for budding amateur strippers. Mick has a view. *'If the worst the locals can complain about is a couple of hen or stag parties, how bad is it? We'd like a lot of ballet-loving opera-attending visitors.'* Shortly after my visit, police in Riga arrested a British national after he urinated on the Freedom Monument on what happened to be the Latvian national day of remembrance for a World War I battle. The British Embassy cited the growth of low fares airlines when it issued a notice on its website warning travellers to behave themselves. *'Do not urinate in public—always use a toilet. It is not worth going to jail. Do not use abusive language.'*

Alcohol is part of the attraction. Beer is €2 a glass, and 200 Marlboro are €15 in the airport. There are no licensing laws so 'Flames' *nightbar* beside my hotel is open from 7 p.m. to 7 a.m. In the news a drunken bus driver crashes into four cars in Riga and his breath alcohol test shows he is over the limit despite the fact that blood alcohol tests are compulsory for all bus drivers here before, during, or after their shifts. Latvia has the dubious honour of holding the record for the world's drunkest person, when a vagrant was found unconscious by the police and a hospital blood test revealed he had 7.22 parts per million of alcohol. Before this local find, the established medical opinion was that anything over 4 parts per million was a lethal dose for any human being. Newspapers report that villains smuggle vodka from Russia to Latvia through underground pipelines. Why would anyone want to import illegal alcohol when they can go to the shops and purchase *Riga Black Balsam*, a bitter black herbal liquor whose recipe contains 24 plants, flowers, buds, juices, roots, oils and berries, and which was first made by a home-brew pharmacist? Locals do not like to, or do not dare to, drink it neat but have it with tea, coffee, redcurrant or blackcurrant juice. Legend has it that Empress Catherine the Great of Russia, having fallen ill during a visit to Latvia, was cured after drinking *Black Balsam*. No wonder she enjoyed such a recovery. It is 45 per cent proof.

Not content with stag tourism, locals now offer gun tourism. *'There sure is something mysteriously satisfying about letting loose with real shooters and live ammunition.'* The *Regro S* shooting gallery across the river in Pardaugava is the optimal venue. The action takes place in a former KGB bunker constructed for Communist party chiefs to hide in case of a nuclear attack. *'Used as a bomb shelter during the war, this imposing bunker features long corridors, thick metal doors and a vibe that will have you thinking you're a legit vodka-swilling Russian soldier.'* There's a variety of guns to choose from such as pistols, pump-action shotguns, semi-automatic and automatic rifles and the great Soviet beast itself, the deadly accurate Kalashnikov assault rifle. Transfers, professional instructors, translators, safety instructions, rent of guns and the shooting range, targets and refreshments are all included. *'This is the big daddy of Soviet shooting experiences; go out and bust some caps with some of the Soviet bloc's finest show-stoppers.'*

The various gun-toting packages on offer are amazingly detailed. *The John Wayne* gives you the use of 3 guns: a Glock Pistol (10 shots), a Bereta Revolver (6 shots) plus a Winchester Pump-Action Shot Gun (6 shots) or a 'Spas 15' Heavy Gun (6 shots) or a Kalashnikov 'Saiga' rifle (6 shots). Price: €58. Also on offer is *The Clint Eastwood*—the use of 4 guns, being the three aforementioned plus a 'Spas 15' Heavy Gun (6 shots) or Kalashnikov 'Saiga' rifle (6 shots). Price: €82. Lastly there is *The Arnold Schwarzenegger* (the use of all 5 guns). Price: €96. Clearly Arnie remains top of the pops and he will make your day in Riga. *'Personalised targets are available at extra cost of £2 per person. A picnic with* BBQ *can be arranged.'* 'Hello, I am coming to your shooting range. Do you have a large picture target of Mick O'Leery? You do.'

'Fully automatic UZI *(25 shots in two seconds) is an option depending on availability.'* And when would the UZI not be 'available'? When one of the owners left it at home with the kids or lent it to a neighbour so he could let off some steam or the wife went shopping with it slung over her shoulder? *'A golden bullet will be rewarded to the best marksman in your group and you can take home and frame your mutilated target.'* The winner of the shoot-out earns a diploma and the losers go back to their hotels alive. Sadly I cannot participate myself since the minimum group size is six and I cannot find five other psychopaths.

Why stop at stags, beer and guns? *'Enjoy the attraction of terror.'* Stag parties book kidnappings. A guy once told me his stag party mini-bus was overtaken near here by a car in a remote area. The car stopped and three burly blokes in balaclavas with guns forced them off the bus, tied them up and threatened them. Only the best man knew it was a set-up. One of the stag party thought it was real and ran off into a forest where he hid for a day in freezing conditions and only reappeared next day at the Ruinair check-in desk in RIX. And there's the Australian special forces guys who run an ex-Soviet prison/hotel in Liepaja which proudly boasts: *'You will be having a tour in a remote town of Latvia leisurely checking out the historic and interesting sights when you will be arrested and taken to a 100 year old prison. Here you will be processed for two hours. You will be locked in a cell, interrogated, photographed and basically treated like the scum you always wanted to be. No mummy here to save you. This is a well documented tour where you will have a photograph of you holding up your number. There will be video footage of your whimpering and protesting your innocence. The impact is best if all participants are not aware what is going to happen. Price includes tour of soviet military base, prison experience, transport to and from Riga, lunch (scraps) and beer. Our hotel is not heated, not air-conditioned, not friendly, not comfortable, with unhelpful staff and impolite treatment.*' So what's so original about this? Have they ever flown on Ruinair?

After Ruinair launched flights to Riga from Liverpool's John Lennon Airport, an MP from Latvia's First Party named Oskars Kastens announced to the BBC that Liverpudlian holidaymakers who come to Riga were *'savages'*. When the Merseyside backlash followed he neatly corrected himself by saying he didn't mean to single out people from Liverpool, but his statement applied to British tourists in general. *'I am sure that cheap drinks are not the only attraction in Latvia—we have beautiful architecture of Riga, white beaches at the Baltic Sea, unspoiled nature and many other things, but if tourists are coming only for hard drinking and picking up local girls, they cannot win the sympathy of local people, and it is not a secret that British tourists with their behaviour are considered as the rudest tourists in Europe. It is not my subjective opinion, but according to a survey done by the magazine "Caterer and Hotel-keeper".'*

In the same week of Oskars' outburst, the Merseyside Tourism-owned *Magical Mystery Tour* bus, packed with visitors from Japan, Italy and the US, was trundling around the Beatles sites in Liverpool when a brick was hurled through a window of the same coach, showering everyone inside with shards of glass and terrifying the international visitors. One-nil to Oskars.

I send Oskars an email before my visit. He agrees to meet to discuss Ruinair and Riga. I locate the government offices on *Elizabetes iela* and recognise Oskars immediately from last night's

TV news. Parliament has reconvened after a general election and he is a minister in the government. The mood is euphoric because it's the first time a sitting government has been re-elected in any former Soviet state. Oskars has excellent English from a stint in Brussels, which is fortunate because my Latvian is not good. I choose my questions carefully and marvel at how easy it is for a loony to meet a government minister.

We sit at a conference table in his spacious yet virginal office. 'What brings you to Riga?' he asks.

'Ruinair.' I don't think Oskars gets it. I move on undeterred. 'Is Ruinair good for Riga?' I open.

'It's a two-sided coin. Yes, because they bring tourists who spend money in our hotels and in bars and on car hire. But they also bring a special category, these English stag parties, who behave badly in our old city. Maybe only three or five per cent of the visitors are English youths but they ruin our bars and harass our ladies. They are only a small number of people but they have a much bigger impact. The Finns are bad too. I know of locals who won't go into city bars. Girls pretend not to speak English when these English men talk to them. I have seen some of the stag packages on the internet and I was astonished at the things they are offered. I know of stories of men being charged €100 for a drink with a girl in a club or bar.'

'Are they *savages*?'

Oskars smiles. 'I used that word as a sort of joke but it seems to have stuck with the BBC.'

I am in pseudo-journalist mode. 'Is there a solution?'

'We have taken some action. When passengers arrived at Riga Airport there were advertisements in the arrivals hall for girls and bars but we asked the airport not to renew such advertising. We don't want visitors to have this as their first impression.' Oskars phones the head of Riga city council and checks some facts in fast Latvian. 'And we are considering banning these clubs near places like schools and churches.'

'We used to have stag parties invading Temple Bar in Dublin until the bars barred them.'

Oskars nods. 'Some bars have done that here. They put up signs. Stag Parties Not Welcome.'

'Have you flown on Ruinair?' I ask.

'No.'

'Would you fly with them?' I persevere.

'I use easyJet. I go to Berlin with them when my wife and I go on holidays.'

I sense urgent ministerial business. I rise and we shake hands. 'Will Riga survive Ruinair?'

Oskars nods. 'We survived the Soviets and the Nazis. We will survive the stag party invaders. In ten years' time there will be a display in Riga's Museum of Occupation dedicated to Ruinair.'

Customer Service
Ruinair Ltd
Dublin Airport

Dear Sirs,

I wish to complain about my recent flight from Dublin to Riga. Shortly after we departed Dublin we were advised by the cabin crew that there would be no drinks or food available for purchase since there were no catering trolleys on board the aircraft. We spent three parched and starving hours without water or food, no better than cattle on their way to the abattoir. The crew did not know how to pass the flight so one of them spent the time doing her hair up in a very nice bun and the rest hid behind their curtains and read a 'Hello' magazine together. We were reduced to scratching our heads rather than the cards which you normally sell to passengers. I would like to know why this basic customer service omission occurred? Your airline remembered to bring other essentials such as the engines, fuel, wings, two pilots and even an ample supply of Ruinair in-flight magazines, so why not remember the fairly obvious catering trolleys?

Yours sincerely,
Disgusted of Dublin.

PS This was my most enjoyable flight ever on your airline because no one did, or could, sell us anything.

Dear Mr Kilduff,

I acknowledge receipt of your letter. I do apologise that there was a lack of refreshments on your recent flight. As you will appreciate, the food/refreshments service is discretional i.e. not every passenger will purchase food, therefore we have a limited amount of stock on board. However, we will have occasions whereby there is a high demand for food on the previous sector which results in a shortfall on the next flight. Due to our very quick turnaround it is not always possible to re-stock the trolleys, as to do so would risk the flight being delayed. We do apologise that such an incident would spoil your flight, however we do not at any stage guarantee that there will be a full complement of snacks and refreshments for sale.

With renewed apologies,
Yours sincerely
For and on Behalf of
RUINAIR LIMITED

More Bolloxology.

Mick's Curriculum Vitae

Name:	Mick Gerard Joseph Mary O'Leery
Address:	Gigginstown House, Mullingar, Co. Westmeath

'I'm an Irish peasant at heart. I grew up on a farm in the Irish countryside, and now I live on a farm in the Irish countryside. You would impress fucking nobody if you drove to the paper shop on a Sunday morning in your Ferrari. They'd think you were a gobshite. And you probably would be. A big tractor, now, they might be impressed. But it doesn't get to the shop fast enough for me.'

Date of Birth:	20 March 1961
Marital Status:	Married to Anita, 2 sons

'I never thought about selling my wedding to Hello! That's for the ones who can't afford to pay for their own weddings.'

Telephone:	n/a—ex-directory
Email Address:	n/a—*'My inbox just fills up with shite.'*
Pay:	€595,000 plus €560,000 bonus

Education:

1968–1974	Christian Brothers School, Mullingar, Co. Westmeath

'I was pretty good at school but without having to try that hard.'

1974–1979	Clongowes Wood College, Clane, Co Kildare

'I left Clongowes frankly with no ambition.'

1979–1983   Trinity College Dublin, Bachelor of Economics &
                 Social Studies 2.1
                 *'Without a doubt the best fuck-up years of my life
                 were in Trinity.'*

Work Experience:

1983–1985   Trainee tax accountant at KPMG Stokes Kennedy
                 Crowley, Dublin
                 'Accountancy was fucking dull.'

1985–1987   Owner of three newsagent's shops in Walkinstown,
                 Crumlin and Terenure, Dublin
                 *'Being a greedy little bugger like I was at the time,
                 we decided to open on Christmas Day.'*

1987   Personal Assistant to Dr Tony Ruin, founder of
                 the airline Ruinair
                 *'The job was anything from hunting cattle, running
                 errands, doing tax returns.'*

1988   Director of Ruinair
                 *'The place was a shambles yet it was still amazingly
                 sexy.'*

1991   Deputy Chief Executive, Ruinair

1993   Chief Operating Officer, Ruinair

1994   Chief Executive, Ruinair
                 *'My role in making Ruinair succeed is to interfere as
                 little as possible, try to stay out of other people's way
                 and then claim the credit for all the success when it
                 comes along.'*

Interests:

Bulls: *'I spent one week on a course about Low Cost
                 Artificial Insemination Techniques for Angus
                 Heifers.'*

Horse-racing: *'The trainer and the jockeys make all the important
                 decisions, I just pay the bills.'*

Manchester   *'When I was younger I dreamed of playing football
City: for Manchester City. I'm a bit rebellious, and when*

*I was a kid everyone else was supporting Man Utd
and the like so I chose Man City.'*

Taxis: '*The taxi was the best six grand I ever spent.'*

Likes:

Favourite book: '*Elizabeth Longford's biography of Wellington'*
Favourite film: '*Patton, Lust for Glory'*
Favourite gadget: '*An old-style Philips Dictaphone'*
Last holiday: '*Algarve'*

High-flying tastes:

Rugby shirts or striped shirts?   '*Rugby shirts.'*
Guinness or Champagne?   '*Champagne.'*
Oysters or chips?   '*Chips.'*
Riverdance or U2?   '*U2. Riverdance is for tourists.'*
Yeats or Joyce?   '*They're both rubbish.'*

Estonia

Flight BT311 – Saturday @ 7.30 a.m. – RIX-TLL-RIX

Fare €45 plus taxes, fees and charges €23

Before I book my first flight with airBaltic they send me an email: *'Christmas and New Year's Eve is a time for presents. airBaltic has prepared presents for all our friends. Travel through ten airBaltic flight destinations, correctly answer ten questions and receive a 20 per cent discount on all airBaltic direct flights.'* I do not usually indulge in quizzes and competitions but I need to save as much as possible on my air fares.

1. *Which of these beer brands is not Irish? Guinness, Kilkenny or Budweiser?* Easy, Bud. I am amazed that these questions are so easy.
2. *The duration of the airBaltic flight from Riga to Baku is 1 hour, 4 hours or 6 hours?* Not a clue. I guess one hour. I am amazed that these questions are so difficult.
3. *The capital of Kazakhstan is either Astana, Almaty or Baikonur?* All look to me more like typographical errors. Only Borat would know the correct answer. I guess Astana.
4. *When the British say 'Hello', the French answer with what?* Easy. *'Bonjour'.*
5. *Which river flows through Belarus and Latvia?* Choice of Daugava, Volga or Danube. I guess Daugava.
6. *Brussels is the headquarters of OPEC, UN, or NATO?* Easy. Nato. OPEC is in Vienna. UN is in New York.

7. *Which type of aircraft does airBaltic use on the Vilnius to Chisinau route? An Airbus A380, Tupolev TU-154M or Fokker F50?* I guess that it's a Fokker.
8. *Which of these bands are not from Sweden?* Abba, Boney M or Roxette? Easy. Boney M. *Daddy Cool.*
9. *How many direct flights does Air Baltic operate from Vilnius?* 7, 18, or 30? I guess 30.
10. *Which of these cities is not in Uzbekistan?* Almaty, Samarkand or Tashkent? Where? I guess Almaty.

I get 8 out of 10 correct. Not bad for six guesses but not good enough to earn my 20 per cent discount.

AirBaltic Corporation was established in 1995 and is jointly owned by the Latvian government and that Scandinavian high-fares airline, SAS. It is based in Riga and Vilnius and uses 26 aircraft to fly two million passengers to 50 destinations in Europe, Russia and several former Soviet republics in the Caucasus and Central Asia, which are so unknown as to ensure that no one will ever succeed in the above quiz. They fly to Moldova which sounds similar to the destination of the excellent Central European spoof guide book which was published a few years ago: '*Molvania—A Land Untouched by Modern Dentistry*'.

This is a smart-casual sort of airline so the youthful management team are always photographed in open-necked shirts. Their German-born chief executive is Bertolt Flick, not to be confused with the chap of the same surname in BBC's comedy '*Allo, Allo*'. When Herr Flick became chairman of airBaltic's board in 1999, the airline was small, ill-defined and without a regular customer base, and was unsure whether its identity was as a posh Baltic version of SAS, a small budget airline like Ruinair, or an old-fashioned, flag-waving, inefficient national carrier. Herr Flick oversaw a complete reorganisation of the airline, with a new eye-catching lime-green colour scheme for the airline. Best of all, airBaltic even makes money.

It's so deserted at Riga Airport's boarding gate 12 that I think my flight might be cancelled. There are six passengers. I am baffled at only six passengers because I researched the options for getting from Riga to Tallinn. Option one was to take a *Eurolines* bus, which would be a five-hour journey. I have never been on a bus to anywhere in my life for five hours, bus depots are not my natural habitat and I have visions of sitting with my legs crossed very tightly for five hours or queuing for the single chemical toilet at the rear. Option two was to take the train but trains around here are slow and there is no direct service. Passengers have to leave a Latvian train, trek across the border and get on an Estonian train, which is nonsensical. It's not as if there is a huge choice of flights between Riga and Tallinn. Today there are two flights and both are on airBaltic. Estonian Air do not even fly this 45-minute route between two capital cities—the same distance as Dublin is from London or London is from Paris. Do people from Riga and Tallinn not like each other?

We six intrepid travellers are shuttled to the far reaches of Riga Airport, all looking apprehensive, wondering why no one else is taking this Marie Celeste flight. There are three Americans who talk incessantly, perhaps because they are as nervous as I am when we see the size of our tiny little Fokker. They are a Senior Executive, a Middle Ranking Manager and a Young Keen Girl Who Does All The Work while the two men talk and talk. The Senior Executive tells an unlikely story about a flight he took in the USA on a tiny aircraft owned by Pilgrim Airlines, where the same airline employee checked him in, boarded the flight and sat in the co-pilot's seat for the duration of the flight. I meet, or overhear, the two American men two days later in the Old Town and they have been talking for two days. I soon learn that the other two passengers on board are a demure French couple. The only locals on this flight seem to be working on it.

Onboard the Americans are confused because they have been given new boarding cards and are now sitting in rows 12 and 14 at the very rear of the aircraft. They still look terrified but evidently have other things on their mind as the Senior Executive shows his new boarding card stub to the cabin crew. 'Is this still business class?' We six sit in a cluster at the rear of the aircraft, like ballast. We are all so terrified of moving and plunging to Mother Earth that the Senior Executive asks permission from the crew before he walks to the toilet at the front of the aircraft mid-flight. The French couple produce nice chocolate wafer biscuits but, being French, they do not share them. The aircraft is ancient and the hot water dispenser near me still has the logo of Polish airline LOT on the chrome tap, as in 'This aircraft has been used a LOT'.

A Fokker 50 has 42 seats and two cabin crew but this is the first flight I have been on where the ratio of cabin crew to passengers is 1:3. The crew are smart and pleasant. They wear dark uniforms with lime green scarves and navy ties. They change into aprons with lime green piping and drawstrings. They have exotic Baltic names such as Arita or Zane, names that Swedish designers might give to new pieces of stylish über-furniture. I would not use the words 'style' and 'Ruinair' in the same sentence. Unless I could be allowed to add a 'No' into the sentence. Below we hug the coastline as we journey northwards. I see deep blue water and sandy beaches which would look inviting were it not for the foot of deep snow elsewhere on the deserted landscape. At this time of the year the frigid climate in these parts is absolutely bloody Baltic.

After 45 minutes we plummet and get a wonderful first view of Tallinn, perched on a hilltop, all snow-topped roofs, medieval castle walls, russet tiled turrets, pointy clock towers, Lutheran church spires, bulbous Russian Orthodox onion domes, red brick chimney stacks and as many building cranes as Dublin once had. There are avocado-green, salmon-pink and primrose-yellow gabled residences on cobbled streets. Nearby are neat green parks, newer bank skyscrapers and a dockside port area with ferries plying back and forth. As I exit the little Fokker I speak to a member of the somewhat under-worked cabin crew.

'Why are there so few people on the flight?' I ask.

'It's the weekend.' What's wrong with the weekend? In Ireland that's when we all travel.

The Baltic region features in an aviation news item which I cannot omit to mention. An online travel agency announced details of the first nudist flight, which will take clothes-free passengers to the Baltic Sea islands from Erfurt in Germany (where else?). '*The flight can be enjoyed as God intended,*' said the travel agency boss. '*I don't want people to get the wrong idea. It's not that we're starting a swinger club in mid-air or something like that. We're a perfectly normal holiday company.*' Yeah, right. This surely represents the ultimate in no-frills flying. It was confirmed that on the flights the crew will remain fully clothed 'for security reasons', which is a huge disappointment. Nevertheless the flights sold out in record time but later the charter company pulled out of the arrangement. Rest assured that if these flights ever take off, then your intrepid aviation correspondent will brave all and show on the first flight. Now mind those seat belts please.

EasyJet fly to Tallinn. Ruinair do not. I know why Ruinair do not fly here. It's because at 4 km the airport is too near the city centre. This is an airport where if I was fitter I could most likely walk into the city centre. Ruinair staff probably visited here before me but are still looking for a former Soviet nuclear missile base/airfield 100 km away from the city centre, as per their normal preference. But ultra-modern Tallinn Airport represents the ideal Ruinair destination, since much like the Olympic Mile, I can stride from aircraft door to taxi door in a sub-four-minute record time. Former Estonian President Lennart Mari once said that you can tell how good an airport is by how quickly you can get out of it and he's not wrong. Before the redevelopment the President once did a press interview in the toilets here, to prove how dire they were.

Today it is quicker than normal because a momentous event has just occurred. Estonia has joined the Schengen Zone, which allows the citizens of 25 EU countries to cross borders without needing to show a passport to a miserable guy in a grey uniform. The Zone is named after a village in Luxembourg (where else?). The immigration control booths are empty, the doors near them are open and the signs above the booths have red sticky tape over the EU and non-EU wording. Some airport officials welcome us with open arms and beaming smiles and wave us through with glee. Most here view this as the last step in pulling back the heavy drapes of the Iron Curtain. The only unimpressed officials are some immigration staff who now seem to be out of a day job, but given the amount of grief I have got over the years from passport checking staff, this day has been coming for a while. Ireland, the UK and

Switzerland remain outside the Schengen Zone (and vast expanses of water are not an impediment to entry to the zone because Iceland is a member). So while the rest of Europe are hopping back and forth using no more paperwork than a Post-It note, the rest of us still prefer to stand in a long line and show complete strangers our passport containing our worst ever mug photograph in which we look like we're seasick. And if many EU nations no longer require a passport to enter their territory, why do Ruinair still require my passport when boarding? The only reason they ask for it is so that I cannot buy cheap tickets and sell them later to someone else.

Estonia does not like to see itself as small despite the fact that former Prime Minister Mart Laar wrote a book about his country called 'The Little Country That Could'. Estonia is still larger than Denmark, Belgium or Holland. If Estonia could be a square country, and it is, then the Baltic Sea lies to the west and north, Latvia lies to the south and Russia lies to the east. Obscure Tallinn with 400,000 inhabitants is on the middle of the northern side of the square. It is 330 km west of St Petersburg (so it was never too far away for a phalanx of Russian tanks), an hour and a half by jet-foil from Helsinki (50 per cent of tourists here are booze cruise Finns), or 20 minutes from Helsinki by helicopter—although in 2005 one plunged into the Baltic, taking 14 passengers to a watery grave. Tallinn already feels like Europe's smallest big city. I immediately exit my 500-room city-centre hotel, which was built for the 1980 Moscow Olympics when the yachting events were held in Tallinn. The hotel is a former converted property of Intourist, a Russian hotel chain where every room had bare floor boards, cold running water, a single woollen blanket and a KGB listening device.

Estonia is on an economic binge with GDP growth of 10 per cent but it comes with house price rises and 10 per cent inflation. Their current claim to fame is that Estonia is the most technology-friendly country in Europe. 70 per cent of the population have the internet at home. Estonia is the only Central European country with broadband penetration above the EU average. Few people visit banks. 80 per cent pay bills over the internet. People think that a cheque book is a literary work from a nearby Central European country. 90 per cent of citizens do their tax returns online and they receive tax refunds, if they are due, within five days of filing. The government conducts cabinet meetings using a paperless web-based document system. The entire voting population is able to vote online, the first such country in the world. Skype, a company that offers free telephone calls over the internet, was founded here. The internet is free unless you stay in the Hotel Sokos Viru, where they charged me 10 EEK. This is E-Stonia. The city's next claim to fame will be as the European City of Culture in 2011. Even Liverpool won this title.

Tallinn Town Hall Square is an architecturally intact legacy from the Middle Ages yet it's wired for WI-FI. The first ever Christmas tree was placed here and the square boasts Europe's oldest working pharmacy: it dates from 600 years ago, when herbal potions and tasty bat wings outsold aspirin and condoms. A few metres away from the pharmacy two long cobblestones make a distinct 'L' in the ground. This is where Fr Elias Panicke was beheaded. He walked into an inn here and ordered an omelette. What he got was 'hard as the sole of a shoe' so he sent it back. The next two omelettes that the waitress brought were worse so the priest made an example of her by killing her with an axe. For this extreme crime, the priest was hauled out to the square and beheaded and the spot was marked for the convenience of future diners and all local tour guides. I can confirm that the service in Tallinn's restaurants has since much improved.

I walk around the old city walls which have 26 impressive towers, most with their own name. There is the politically incorrect Fat Margaret tower, which is the stoutest of them all. There is the Ropemaker's Tower, so called because the streets here were long and straight so ropes could be laid out. This area was also the old red-light area because where there's ropes there are sailors, and the rest follows on logically. There is the Sauna Tower, which has a hollow brick interior because even in times of war, pestilence or famine in these parts, there was always time to go for a sauna. The Peep Into the Kitchen tower is so called since soldiers had such a good view from the top that they could see into kitchens of nearby houses. There's the Virgins Tower, which inappropriately was formerly used as a prison for local ladies of ill repute. Nearby is St Olaf's Church with the tallest spire in Estonia, and which legend surprisingly says was built by one man. I walk along wide streets that were once the city moat, past the poignant steel memorial to the more recent sinking of the MS Estonia ferry in the nearby sea in 1994, where 852 passengers and crew lost their lives. Finally I make a particular point of giving the Mine Museum a wide berth, despite the fact that the tourist office literature confirms that the dozens of mines dredged from the sea bed 'are now safely deactivated'.

Underneath the city wall ramparts little old ladies with 10 layers of clothing and moustaches sell home-spun clothes, mostly woolly jumpers, hats and gloves. The clothes are so authentic that in between a rare sale, they knit at speed, manufacturing their products. In the past these motifs were designed so that the bodies of drowned sailors could be identified by their knitwear. Now designs on the output are typically Arctic and feature a single prominent animal in all its guises in red, white and blue. 'Looks like Rein, deer?'

There's a fantastic bustling sociable vibe to a city which has come in from the cold. Estonians is even an anagram of Sensation. Yet I haven't seen one stag party. I take the opportunity to ask Tomas the multi-lingual tour guide if stag parties come to Tallinn and what the locals think of the beery invasion.

Tomas shakes his head. 'We don't get many stag parties here. Because Ruinair do not fly here. Only easyJet fly here from the UK. EasyJet bring a better class of tourist. That's what I think, anyway.'

I also ask Tomas why only six people fly from Riga to Tallinn at the weekend.

'People take the bus. That's what the young people do.' Meaning I am not young.

When struggling for independence most angry citizens turn to street protests, mass strikes, civil disorder, culminating in much bullet-dodging, pulling down of razor wire and the storming of radio stations and parliament buildings. But the Estonians are different so they did something unique. They could have martyred themselves in the streets but instead they took the tram out to a place called Lauluaukio. I could take the no. 1 bus but a tram

journey always seems safer. Trams can only go on the tracks whereas buses can go anywhere. I always feel that I can only get half as
lost when on a tram as when I am on a bus.

First stop is the Russian War Memorial straddling the beach on
the coast road to Pirita. I walk up an inclined banked valley of
concrete paving to a square concrete area which is surrounded by
concrete steps and a solid concrete monument with two giant
open hands set into the concrete. There is a nasty echo as I walk
around the concrete paving, such as might suit stomping soldiers.
Around the grassy areas lie clusters of concrete crosses. Two completely pointless trough-like concrete structures sit on the edge of
the beach road, facing towards the sea. Yes, here there is a lot of
concrete but most of it is chipped or grafittied or was removed—I
suspect for a better use on people's back garden patios. There are
no wreaths nor flowers nor guards of honour. There are flagpoles
but no flags fly. There is much neglect evident with weeds, rubbish
and broken glass. Free and independent Tallinn is clearly visible in
the distance. Today is a dry and sunny spring Sunday, it is midday,
yet I am the only visitor here. Enough said about what they think
here of the Russians. The locals refer to the 40-m-high concrete
obelisk as Pinocchio's Nose.

Close to this coastal highway is where it all happened in the
great struggle for independence and freedom. A small side gate is
open and unguarded so I walk in unopposed and towards the
curved building from the 1950s, which on first inspection looks
like the giant spacecraft from the final scenes of *Close Encounters of
the Third Kind*. I take a detour around it to the rear and step inside
a vast amphitheatre at the foot of a natural grassy bowl. The stage
is made again of Russian concrete and has 40 levels which can hold
up to 20,000 singers. These are the Song Festival Grounds. Song
was their weapon of choice.

Estonians have always loved to sing and song festivals have been
organised regularly since 1869 and they draw big crowds. In the
Soviet era, Estonians sang songs here in their native tongue, albeit
under huge posters of Lenin and Marx. Singing festivals were held
to celebrate wonderful occasions such as Stalin's birthday. The
festivals always ended with a song that was never listed in the

official programmes, *My Dear Fatherland*, based on an Estonian nineteenth-century poem. Tears would well up in the eyes of the singers. They wouldn't sing the forbidden song once, they would sing it over and over for the Russians.

The so-called Singing Revolution began in 1987 when 10,000 unsung heroes packed into these grounds to protest at the Soviets, who could not stop the music. In 1988 300,000 Estonians sang loud and joyous anti-Soviet anthems here and they flew Estonia's then-banned blue, black and white national flag. And that's some crowd to draw to a single place in a nation with a population of 1.4 million people. Political leaders attended and made speeches for independence to public acclaim. Then they sang some more. One critic said, *'Imagine the scene in 'Casablanca' in which the French patrons sing 'La Marseillaise' in defiance of the Germans, then multiply its power by a factor of thousands, and that was Estonia.'*

One song led to another and so it continued for four years. The Singing Revolution was an extended period of passive musical resistance in A-minor, modest protests and little acts of defiance. In 1991, as Soviet tanks attempted to stop the progress towards independence, the Estonian Supreme Soviet proclaimed the restoration of the independent state of Estonia. Through these actions Estonia regained its independence without any blood on the streets. The fat lady had sung. The Russians finally went home.

There is a movie about it all. In the traditions of Hollywood the trailer for The Singing Revolution is slightly over the top. *'A Single Nation. A Million Voices. The Fall of an Empire. A nation brutalised by two empires and abandoned by the world. Whenever you give free speech to people, then things get out of hand.' 'This singing together… this was our power.' 'This revolution was about hope … and the music.' What role can singing play when a nation is faced with annihilation by its neighbour? Can culture hold a people together? The small country of Estonia has faced these questions. This is the story of how culture saved a nation. 'I think that to have freedom through singing was the most important thing … maybe in my life. If 25,000 people start to sing one song then you just cannot shut them up. It's impossible.'*

I have seen clips of recent Song Festivals and they are inspiring to behold. Usually there's a sort of James-Last-type lead vocalist in a white suit, pushing 80 years old, who begins the verses. As soon as the drums start his fellow performers start a mass hand clap and sway rhythmically. He is never going to die on stage because his refrains are repeated by the 20,000 backing vocalists, most in traditional garb. The girls wear garlands of flowers in their hair and the guys wear forage caps with medals and badges. In most of these clips there are more people up on the stage than there are watching the performance. It's the sort of show that makes those Last Nights at the Proms in the Royal Albert Hall look like a bad karaoke show. In any other country 20,000 people would do something sensible and attend a soccer match or a rock concert but here they practise to join what is the world's largest choir.

The singing madness continues to this day. Estonia was delighted to be the first former Communist nation to host the infamous Eurovision Song Contest. When they won in 2001 locals took to the Tallinn streets, waving flags and blaring car horns. Some say winning the Eurovision is the most important event here since independence. And even in my hotel room I cannot get away from this vocal nation. They don't have Pop Idol here on ETV. They have Choir Idol, or something quite like it. Three choirs contest the programme each weekend and a group of judges (no Simon Cowell) pick the winners, who do an encore.

History is full of lessons but the Tallinn Song Festival Grounds are unique. When Estonia joined the EU, the then Prime Minister enthused, 'We demolished the Russian empire by singing, now we are not knocking on the door of Europe but will simply walk in singing.' If you are ever a tiny little country occupied by a much larger world nuclear super power, there is really only one course of action to take. Get singing.

Tony Ruin

On 14 October 2007, an elite group of people gathered in the grounds of Lyons Demesne in Celbridge, Co. Kildare. They included politicians and businessmen, sporting figures and celebrities. They came to mourn the passing of one of the leading figures of the global aviation industry. No, not Mick. In his 71 busy years on God's earth, the deceased made one fortune, lost it all, and made another fortune. Those gathered came to pay their respects to Dr Thomas Anthony Ryan. Also known as Tony Ruin. Mick spoke: *'Tony was one of the greatest Irishmen of the twentieth century. His many achievements in business, education, sport, the arts and heritage preservation leave an astonishing legacy to an extraordinary man.'* At the end of the funeral, to the strains of *Nessun Dorma (None Shall Sleep)*, and with annoying punctuality, a Ruinair Boeing 737-800 flew low over the graveside of the man who brought us all low fares.

Tony Ruin was born in 1936 near Thurles, Co. Tipperary. He had a history of transport in his family, his father being a CIÉ train driver and his grandfather being a station master. A ride on the footplate of a steam engine from Thurles to Limerick Junction as a small boy with his father triggered his obsession with travel. Tony was so bright at school that the Christian Brothers told his father they thought he wasn't doing his homework properly because he always finished it so quickly. One of four children, he had ambitions to go to university, but when he was 18 his father died of a heart attack and Tony became the family breadwinner. His first job was working at the sugar factory at Thurles, determining the grades of sugar beet. He joined Aer Lingus, Ireland's original national airline. He worked as a management trainee in Shannon

Airport until he applied for, and was awarded, a job as the airline's station manager in glamorous JFK, New York. He later returned to work with the airline in Dublin where he leased out their surplus aircraft.

In 1975 after 20 years' loyal service with Aer Lingus, Tony spotted a gap in the aviation leasing market and founded Guinness Peat Aviation. He liked to say that his inspiration to go into business on his own account came to him on one evening in SouthEast Asia when he watched the painstaking care with which a Bangkok street food vendor went about the preparation and selling of his products. *'He was a banana-chip-maker. His business was to slice, cook and sell banana chips to passers by. I felt it a pity that such marketing, technical talent and energy was devoted to a process which produced a mere penny. Then and there I determined that when I went into business on my own account, I would apply my energies to developing and marketing a big-ticket product which could sell for vastly more.'* So aviation it was.

Aer Lingus and Guinness & Mahon Bank stumped up 90 per cent of the capital and Tony invested £5,000 of his own cash. GPA was based in the tax haven of Shannon and it grew to become the biggest airline leasing company in the 1990s. It was worth about €4 billion, owned 400 aircraft worth €7.5 billion and had orders for €20 billion's worth of new aircraft. At its height GPA was buying one in ten of all new aircraft built worldwide. Tony roamed the continents, managing this immensely complex business from a foolscap notepad in a battered ostrich-skin briefcase, stuffed with airline tickets and wads of foreign currencies.

Tony gathered the great and the good together in GPA. Nigel Lawson, the ex-British Chancellor, joined the board, as did former Taoiseach Garret FitzGerald, Peter Sutherland (now of Goldman Sachs) and the UK management TV guru and ICI boss Sir John Harvey Jones. GPA was to be floated on the stock exchange in 1992 with a price tag of $2 billion but the Gulf War combined with last-minute wrangling with bankers over the share price led to the total collapse of the flotation. *'My father had an expression—the best deal goes through the hottest fire. You'll never have character, my son, without pain.'*

GPA was soon sold to General Electric for a song. Tony said that Jack Welch, the boss of GE, had 'raped' GPA, to which Welch replied: 'What do you expect when you're walking around with no clothes on?' Tony lost many millions in GPA's demise. *'I sleep like a baby— I wake up every ten minutes screaming.'* When asked by Pat Kenny on RTÉ if he was 'devastated' by the collapse of GPA, Tony replied, *'There must be a stronger word … I was knocked off my ass, if I can use a crudism like that.'*

In 1985 Tony had founded a small airline called Ruinair with £1 million of his own money. The intention was to fly from Dublin to London Lootin' Airport, and to ultimately take on Aer Lingus. But Ruinair remained small and unprofitable. With GPA's divestment, Tony turned his attention to developing Ruinair. One weekend a young tax accountant from KPMG Dublin named Mick called him up to advise that he could save him some tax. A few years later Tony sought out Mick to become his personal assistant, told him to oversee his investments, including Ruinair, and he sent Mick to look at Southwest Airlines in the USA. He told a friend: *'I have found the man who will be the best airline manager of his generation.'*

Mick says, *'I started to work for Tony in 1987 and that is how I got into aviation. Tony was working at an international level, I had been working at a newsagent in Walkinstown. I had already worked at KPMG, so I'd seen a lot of big Irish business. But here was a guy who was going across the UK, across the US, across Asia. He was the guy who started with nothing and was going all the way across the world. Tony is a genius. I learnt an awful lot from him. You get few opportunities in life to learn from someone so rich and successful. I just wanted to see how somebody at that level operated.'*

'I couldn't get a real job. It just sort of fell out of the sky. My title was bag man. I was based on the farm in Tipperary. I was brought along as the gofer. I was very impressed by Tony because he was rich, successful and was running a company that had terrific mystique. Nobody knew what the hell aircraft leasing was. He was the first businessman I'd met who had this global ambition. Everybody else was worried about the cost of women's knickers and the cost of this, that and the other. He had maps of the world looking at where he

could lease aircraft. It was revolutionary in the mid-1980s because Ireland back then was very insular. He was one of only a few businessmen putting an Irish stamp on the world. By the time I started there was a crisis at Ruinair and I was sent in.'

'When I first arrived at Ruinair it was like you'd arrived at the pearly gates. There was a gorgeous blonde chick at every desk. The place was a shambles yet it was still amazingly sexy. They lost the run of themselves. Tony has never been a great man to focus on cost. He wanted it to be elegant, to deliver a better service, business class and frequent flyer club; I mean complete bloody nonsense, to serve nice china mugs and slippers but charge ten quid. You can decide to either be Marks & Spencer or be Fortnum & Mason but you cannot be something in between.'

'Ruinair was set up originally to take on Aer Lingus and British Airways on the Dublin to London route and offer low fares but they kind of lost the plot a bit. They were opening routes fucking left, right and centre, the route network was nuts. They had no fucking schedule at all. It was madness. It was all planes, planes, planes and no airline. We were trying to do what many other airlines were trying to do in Europe, which was to be a slightly lower fare 'me too' carrier to Aer Lingus or British Airways. But the fares were about 20 per cent cheaper, which meant we just lost more money than they did. I was begging him, shut it down, close it down, it will never make money. It was doomed. Tony was the only person who said no, partly because his name was on the side of it but also partly, I think, because he didn't like being beaten. He wasn't going to be beaten by the Government and the State monopoly. He had great balls.'

'The accounts were rubbish. There was nobody collecting cash. We didn't know how much money we had, except that we had nothing in the bank. The bottom line was that if Tony didn't give us a million quid by next Friday we couldn't pay the wages. There was a hole in this fucking company. Where the fuck was our money? We actually came to a point one night where we bounced a cheque to Aer Rianta for £24,000. They said if the cheque didn't go through on Friday they were going to put a yoke on the front of the plane and seize it. My role in Ruinair from 1988 to 1991 was to stop it losing money—it wasn't looking to make Tony money.'

'It was all about putting some order on it. I was doing a lot of ripping and burning and slashing. There wasn't any great foresight on my part. Over two or three years three of us together did turn the airline around and put it on the footing it is on today. I get far too much credit for being the turnaround artist. I didn't particularly want a job in the company that I was recommending should be closed down. I said close the fucking airline because it's a basket case. Eventually we made a £10 million profit and they had to write me a cheque for £3.5 million at which point they said 'hang on'. I get on with Tony half the time and I fight with him the other half.'

'We followed the Southwest model, but we have taken it way beyond Southwest. Much of that was down to Tony. We were the first to take the food off the planes and the first to charge for drinks. This was revolutionary stuff and every time Tony said: 'Go for it, providing you reduce air fares.''

Tony later set up a low fares airline in Singapore named Tiger Airways (owning a 16 per cent stake) and another airline in Mexico named Vivo Aerobus. When asked about his enduring passion for the rough and tumble of business he said: '*One is dead long enough. My father used to say that it is better to wear away than to rust away.*' When he died, according to the gospel *Sunday Times* Rich List, Tony was Ireland's seventh-richest man with an amassed fortune of €1.5 billion. '*There are three ways to win wealth, you can steal it, fluke it, or earn it. Some people have to get rich first, otherwise we will all remain poor together.*'

He found time to sit on the Court of Governors of the Bank of Ireland, acted as Ireland's honorary counsel to Mexico, invested in works of art and a portfolio of property, restored a country estate in Kildare, had homes at various times in London's exclusive Eaton Square, Monaco and Ibiza, owned a share in the Château Lascombes vineyard in Bordeaux, bred horses at his 1,000-acre Castleton Lyons stud farm in Kentucky, and owned Kilboy House, a 300-acre estate in Co. Tipperary replete with stables, a trout pond, Irish wolfhounds, and a herd of Blonde d'Aquitane cattle. He loved hurling, rugby, a pint of stout, a good bottle of wine and time with his 10 grand-children. '*I don't have any hobbies,*' Tony once said. '*I don't think I would like spending all my days trying to find interesting things to do.*'

Nicknamed 'Jumbo' and permanently sun-tanned, Tony had a chauffeur-driven Daimler and a $22 million two-bed private jet at his disposal. For his sixtieth birthday Tony asked Mick to lend him a spare Ruinair aircraft and he flew 100 friends and family from Dublin to Marrakech. Onboard the lucky passengers avoided the airline's usual no-frills policy and were each handed a fez, drank champagne, ate Turkish Delight, and watched a Moroccan belly dancer sway through the aisles, but presumably only when the *Fasten Seat Belts* signs were switched off. Tony once told a journalist: *'I am not a humble man.'*

Tony was married once to his childhood sweetheart Mairéad, the mother of his three sons, Cathal (who died eleven weeks after his father's death), Declan and Shane, but they separated early. He dated Lady Miranda Iveagh of the Guinness dynasty. He had a relationship with Louise Kennedy, of fashion designing and Tipperary Crystal fame. Tony received an honorary doctorate from Trinity College Dublin, he founded the Martin Ryan Marine Science Institute in NUI Galway (named after his father) and he founded the Tony Ryan Academy of Entrepreneurship at Dublin City University with a €10-million donation.

Mick told the Irish Times that Tony had bluffed his way into his first Aer Lingus job at Shannon: *'In the space of a month or two, Tony went to the personnel department and said that he'd had an offer of a job as a teacher in London. Because he was a traffic officer with Aer Lingus, he had skills that they couldn't replace easily and he eventually negotiated a full-time contract there. He was just bluffing. If that personnel manager in Aer Lingus in Shannon had said: "Well, bugger off to London", the history of Irish and European aviation would have been entirely different. He has changed the lives of millions of people. Ruinair started the low fares revolution in Europe. I think and hope that Ruinair would be the lasting and enduring legacy.'*

Mick told RTÉ radio about his final conversation with Tony. *'Every week, or maybe twice a month, I'd pop down to Lyons for a cup of tea. I met him last week for a couple of hours in Lyons. Despite the fact that he knew he was dying, he wanted to discuss the strategy, not for next year, but for five and 10 years. He thought we're not growing fast enough and he thought we shouldn't confine ourselves to Europe. He still thought I wasn't doing a good job.'*

The Czech Republic

Flight FR206 – Tuesday @ 8.10 a.m. – DUB-STN-BRQ-STN-DUB

Fare €44 plus taxes, fees and charges €77

The queues at Stansted Airport are long. There are six people ahead of me in *Costa Lot Coffee* so I give up but not before I hear a security announcement on the airport's PA system. 'Would the person who left a black suitcase in Costa Coffee please return to collect it? Unattended luggage may be removed and destroyed.' The suitcase is 10 foot away. I move closer to it. I might as well go painlessly in one fell swoop than be far enough away to be maimed, disfigured and crippled but still be able to fly frequently on Ruinair.

There are no queues at the Ruinair check-in desks since we can no longer afford to check in. The Ruinair staff in their blue Smurf uniforms sit behind the counters, bored rigid, knowing that their jobs are on the line. For the first time I see the Ruinair self-check-in kiosks dotted around the departures hall. I go up to one kiosk and try to break it by punching the screen. A nice man from Ruinair, not Mick, approaches me to ask if he can help. He tells me that the new self-service kiosks are 'on trial'. I turn to him and say, 'Guilty.'

The former grease-monkeys selling MBNA credit cards have been replaced by the *Lovely Girls* dressed in black who flutter long eyelashes at older men at the end of the ever-dwindling check-in queues (I blame online check-in) but they prefer to spend their time with Lee from Bishop's Stortford at Left Luggage because he minds their handbags and purses (no safer place) whilst they ply their trade. Lee has a beer gut and thick bi-focals and he knows all there is to know about baggage, especially if it is oversized, and he is one of the few people who is happy to have a lot of baggage in life, albeit at £5 per suitcase.

There are 10 people ahead of me in WH Smith so I check out. There is a veritable credit crunch at the only functioning ATM so I cash out and go immediately to security control. The queues here are very long. *'Yes, but that is not the airport's fault. That's the noddies in the Home Office because they decided they'd got some incredible intelligence that lipstick was the new weapon of mass destruction: that Osama bin Laden had spent years in a cave in Pakistan developing a range of lipsticks unknown to Estée Lauder or anyone else, which were clearly the new weapons of mass destruction. It's insane. We are already trying to get them to change it. We are the only airline that came out, even a year ago, and said that these security provisions are absurd. It makes no difference to a terrorist whether you can bring your liquid explosive in one 200ml bottle or in two 100ml bottles. The secureaucrats have determined that you're all somewhat safer because you can bring two 100ml bottles. None of the ridiculous procedures they apply to airport security apply in the Underground. What was the last thing to be bombed by terrorists? The Underground—where they still let you take as many bags on board as you want. When I say this, I'm told we don't care about airport security. We do care, which is why we should call these secureaucrats idiots when they come up with these idiotic regulations such as lipstick is a weapon of mass destruction. It's been a weapon of man's destruction for a couple of centuries, but that's another matter.'*

Once on a Sunday afternoon only seven out of 14 security check points at Stansted were manned so Mick complained: *'The only explanation was that Arsenal and Tottenham Hotspur were both playing football on the television and there were huge no-shows among security staff because many of them live in North London. We have written to the Football League asking them not to schedule Arsenal and Spurs matches on the same Sunday afternoon.'*

I go through security control. It amazes me how the staff can also carry on so many important conversations about each other's social lives, holiday plans, shift working etc. I have been through so many X-ray machines in the past 12 months that in the event of any personal medical emergency, my usual doctor will simply have to ask various European regional airports for the latest black-and-white picture of my vital innards. I ask the nice security lady if she would like me to remove the belt on my jeans.

'No need, we will leave you with some clothes today. But you need to take your shoes off.'

I have been travelling since morning. It's a hot day. 'You really don't want me to take my shoes off.'

Those who do not make it through security control go to the Security Repacking Area near WH Smith. Here I can watch Ruinair passengers trying to repack an infinite amount of items into a finite space in their quest to avoid those nasty excess baggage charges, currently a chunky €15 per extra kilogram.

There are cheapskates who, despite being able to afford to binge-fly for one penny on Ruinair, insist on bringing their own packed lunch, comprising his and hers matching hard-boiled eggs, napkins, sandwiches in tin-foil and the *pièce de résistance*—chicken drumsticks. They have more plastic bags than a branch of Sainsbury's and even utilise a separate plastic bag for any rubbish which they neatly discard. There are pairs of Japanese girls who are *Lost in Translation*, as they periodically look at their boarding cards, nod politely to each other, annoy nobody, return to mutual silence and wait for a flight which apparently never departs. They may have been here for days. Perhaps they should be at Heathrow. I am always amazed at how meek and mild-mannered Japanese tourists are. How did they ever form an army?

There's a '*Krispy Kreme*' family where the mother has bought a box of twelve assorted donuts at the concession stand and passes them out to her daughters, who in turn race about the airport at jet speed and the parents wonder why the kids are hyperactive and why they won't sit down. Worst of all they don't offer me the last donut with the hundreds and thousands topping. We are all watched over by *Pump Action Men*: pairs of Essex cops in full battle gear, one tall and aggressive looking, the other small and squat (but both evidently frequent the police gymnasium daily), sporting peaked caps, walkie-talkies and mobiles and lugging menacing black Heckler & Koch sub-machine guns. I have always wanted to go up to these guys and shout *Rat-a-Tat-Tat-Tat* and see how quick they are on the draw. But never try anything funny here.

The last time I was here I had an interesting encounter on the flight back from Stansted to Dublin. Before we took off the cabin supervisor made an announcement asking, 'If Michael Cawley is on the aircraft, could he make himself known to a member of the crew?' Cawley. This guy is the joint Deputy CEO in Ruinair and he works for Mick. I looked around the plane excitedly. A young guy sitting two seats away from me pushed his call button but he was not Cawley. He told the cabin supervisor, 'Mr Cawley did not travel over this morning. He won't be on this flight.' This Ruinair colleague gave her the comfort she needed. She knew that Cawley was a no-show but she needed to be sure, otherwise it could be a P45 for her in the post if they left without the boss. When we landed in Dublin I gave a signed copy of *'The Little Book of Mick'* to the colleague. 'Give that to Mr Cawley tomorrow morning.' He said he would. But my question is whether no-show Cawley got a refund? I doubt it. *'The way I see it is when you book a ticket in the uci cinema and cancel it you don't get a refund so why should we offer refunds on "non refund" flights?'*

Stansted has gone downhill. Last time the prize car draw featured a Bentley but now the prizes are a mere Audi TT and a BMW 3-series. Sure, these sorts of cars are ten a penny in Dublin. I make the mistake of sitting outside Hamley's toy store for 10 minutes until I can endure it no longer. Their toy display features an oinking pink pig, a yapping cuddly puppy and a drum-beating beef-eater bear in Union Jack costume, who all play incessantly while their batteries still have life. I while away the connection time looking up at the revolving advertisement for Visa credit cards and marvel at the creative copy-writing genius who wrote that *'Travel flows better with Visa—it is €£$¥'*. Outside several hundred Ruinair aircraft come and go like a swarm, they queue up to take off, and land to taxi back to us at near take-off speed.

Mick tells *The Telegraph* today that Ruinair would like to acquire Stansted Airport. *'We'd be in like a bandit.* BAA *knows we're interested. We'd pay probably around £2bn. I'd take it up from 24m passengers today to more than 40m by halving landing fees for all. You could have a second runway for £150m and second terminal for £250m, instead of the £4bn Taj Mahal* BAA*'s planning and we could bury Harry Bush [the Civil Aviation Authority's economic regulator] under the concrete on the ramp. It would be very hard not to improve any of the London airports. We'd staff security queues properly, and passport controls—which are a joke at the moment. We have people being delayed one or two hours just to get back into their own country.* BAA *would have you believe that people want to spend half their holiday at their wonderful airport buildings, spending money at their wonderful duty frees. Do you realise that people actually want to spend 20 minutes at an airport? Park. Go through. Get on the plane and get the hell out of the place.'*

On the next day when asked about how serious Ruinair is about buying Stansted Airport, Mick tells the *Irish Independent* of his change of heart: 'We're not serious. Were Ruinair to get into the business of airport ownership approximately 20 French and 20 Spanish regional airports would be throwing themselves at us tomorrow morning—our job is to run an airline. We have no interest in acquiring airports, we will not be acquiring Stansted Airport, but clearly we will be happy to work with anybody who buys it. It's the same offer we made to the BAA five years ago. We've offered to build a second terminal in Stansted in the past and double the traffic. But the BAA told us to go away. The only way airports make money is to build passengers numbers. BAA stands for Britain's Awful Airports.'* But Mick garnered his free press coverage about high airport landing fees so it's PR mission successfully accomplished as usual.

Mick is so much better at PR stunts than his airline industry peers. *'Richard Branson will bore you to tears at a press conference. For all the PR, he is not the most entertaining man in the world. Apart from doing a photo-op with girls with big boobs, he is not that exciting.'*

I stride to the departure gates and pass the Ruinair girl with the worst job in the airline. Yes she too sells Priority boarding passes. I pass the Ruinair Customer Service Desk—ho ho. The restaurant/café still doubles as a Ruinair staff canteen because I guess they don't have one of their own. Now we will play Ruinair's favourite game at Stansted, called *Musical Gates*. First they tell us we will board from Gate 53 so we all stand or sit there. Next with no sign of any aircraft they tell us we will now board from Gate 49. This is because of 'the late arrival of the incoming aircraft'. Whose fault is that? The nice Ruinair staff smile and grin at us we all rush off to the other gate where those at the head of the queue now find themselves stuck at the end of the queue, and much like getting into heaven, the first shall be last and the last shall be first. I am sure there are Ruinair flight dispatchers who sit there and say, 'Will we make them move gates again? Will we send them to Gate 60? Let's pick a gate a long way away. Ah go on, let's.' Today there are a mere 11 passengers in the Priority queue, proof that we will no longer stand for their fees. As we wait they hurry us and announce that 'as soon as the passengers have disembarked from the aircraft' then we will board. What a surprise. I always assumed we would rush them while they are still on board and that we would fight them for the best seats as they all tried to get off the aircraft with their carry-on baggage.

I receive a glare from the Irish Ruinair girl at Gate 49, which to be honest is what I usually receive when I board. The girl makes a boarding announcement for the 'flight to Bruno', as in Frank, the boxer. I am not sure that she has the right pronunciation. Our destination is pronounced as Brrrr...No. Czech it out, girl. When I told others I was going to Brno they looked at me oddly. 'Borneo? That's a very long journey.' When I am in Brno I plan to continue the search for the second missing vowel in the city's name. I have a vague suspicion that it may have surreptitiously been stolen by the capital of Mongolia, one Ulaanbaatar.

My preference for the best seating has evolved into a near science. I still aim for an aisle seat but which row is best? Rows 1 to 3 are usually blocked off for various spurious reasons, such as 'balance purposes', ease of selling and feeding, and to keep passengers out of cabin crews' faces. Rows 4 to 6 are very popular amongst the ABC1 types who can fool themselves that they are sitting up front in Aer Lingus' old Premier or British Airways Club class, but that's where the similarity ends, and they are great rows for getting off the aircraft quickly. Rows 7 to 8 are very popular amongst plane-spotters since they can take unobstructed photographs of views below and can have the engine and wings in or out of shot. No one sits in row 13 because there is no such row on a Ruinair aircraft, it being deemed unlucky. Rows 16 and 17 remain highly desirable since these emergency rows have extra leg room. Children (and people of reduced mobility) cannot sit here, which is a bonus. The downside is that you are last to leave the aircraft. Rows in the twenties are the worst since you get all that jet noise and you are the last to get anything going in-flight, whether it's scratch cards or the last Bullseye Baggie. Row 29 is the worst of all since you are back by the wc and people will stand beside you all during the flight, with their legs tightly crossed if there is a queue.

My seating is a disaster due to my own stupidity. I board the plane too early and so sit in a window seat without realising my error. Soon an Australian girl stops by the row of seats. She is a virgin. I can tell. Since she asks if she can sit in the aisle seat or has to sit somewhere else. She seems nice so I tell her it is fine to sit in my row. All goes well until about five minutes later as the plane fills up when a tall guy stops beside her and she voluntarily engages him first with eye contact and then commits the ultimate 'keep the middle seat free' crime by asking him if he is planning on sitting between us. She is so nice that he needs no second invitation. And she is 20 and he is 60 so it's the best offer he has got all week. He plonks himself down between us and for the next two hours tries to insert his elbows between my ribs. He also has a nasty habit of displaying the general location of his wedding tackle. Meanwhile the virgin next to us is so unused to air travel that she will hold her passport in her hand for the duration of the entire flight, as if the cabin crew or someone from immigration control in Brrrr...No. are about to ask her for it.

From my window seat I watch the pilot walk around outside, chat to the guy who refuels us and then sign the paperwork to con- firm receipt of the fuel. I am reminded of pilot Cathal Ruin, son of Tony Ruin, who worked for Ruinair when times were harder and the airline had little cash to pay airports, or anyone else for that matter. Once Cathal was queried when refuelling as to whether the airline would settle the account; he threw them his American

Express gold card and told them to charge the fuel. On another occasion Cathal signed some paperwork for a girl who was despatching the aircraft but she queried his name as she could not decipher his signature. 'It's Ryan', he said. 'Like the name on the side of the plane.'

I'm lucky to be flying at all today. When I made the reservation it took ages since that dreaded website was playing up again. That's not my opinion but it's what Ruinair say on their website about their own website. *'Due to system problems, access to our flight booking system is currently slow. Please note, that it may take up to 30–60 seconds to move from page to page during the flight booking process. Although the booking process is slower than normal, bookings can be completed, but the delivery of the confirmation travel itinerary may be delayed. As we are experiencing some delays with our payment authorisation system, if the flight confirmation number displayed on your* PC *has the words NOT CONFIRMED written underneath, then you should wait several minutes.'* This is what is known as The Slow Fares Airline.

It is now appropriate to write a little paragraph about how little everything is when we fly. We board and we depart a little late. The pilots sit in a little room with a little door and little windows. We sit in little seats with a little tray and little armrests. The crew sell us little cans of soft drinks, little slices of pizza and little hot dogs. The toilets are little rooms with a little hand basin with tiny little taps. We arrive a little early in a little airport but the pilot stops the plane a little short so we have to wait a little while he moves it a little forward. Even the air fares are little. Everything is little except the taxes, fees and charges and the size of the bloke who usually sits beside me.

We land on time and I take the 76 bus to town, ignoring the nasty billboards on the airport road for xxx strip clubs and the Samsung billboards near the city centre for the most famous Czech person ever—goalie Petr Cech. It was almost impossible to book a hotel room (I don't know why yet) so I am staying at the four-star expensive Grand Hotel, but it is still a surprise to see signs for a Ruinair event in the lobby upon my arrival. A cabin crew assessment day is in progress and they have kindly attached their schedule to the door of their meeting room so that all of the public can see what they put their future cabin crew through.

DAY 1	9.30	Meeting time for students
	9.30	Entrance Exam (no wasting time here)
	11.00	Lunch (early enough, surely attendees bring their own lunch?)
	11.30	Induction Day
	16.00	Results of Entrance Exam (very quick—close to a 25-minute turnaround time?)
DAY 2	9.30	Repeat Exam (surely no one will have failed the prior day exam)
	9.30	Results of Repeat Exam (quite a feat, no hanging about here either)
	9.30	Ruinair Language Assessment (needs much more work here I believe, Que?)
		Collecting Missing Paperwork (sounds ominous, missing passport?)
		Uniform Fitting by Ms McDaid (needs more time to get the measurements right)

Brno is the second largest city in the Czech Republic; it is the metropolis of Moravia, and lies in the southeast corner of the country, such that it is closer to Vienna and Bratislava than it is to the capital, Prague. With a population of 380,000 I am sure there is lots to see and do. I make first for the tourist office, collect plenty of free brochures and ask the nice lady at the counter for some extra assistance.

'Is there anything on in Brno this week?' I hazard.

'Such as what?' she replies somewhat suspiciously.

'Maybe a sporting event, a concert, a show, a celebration or something.'

She gives the matter some thought. 'Pyros.'

'I don't speak Czech.'

'Pyros. It's on for three days.'

I am vaguely interested. 'What is it?'

'It's the international trade fair for fire-fighting equipment. It is targeted at all professionals and business people operating in the fire fighting and rescue services.'

'Thanks anyway for your help.' I exit faster than a tender on a 999 call.

I walk the city centre, firstly along the pedestrian Masarykova Street, where bookshops sell a book by an Irish author called Cecilia Ahernova, and I take a detour to Vegetable Square, where the daily market also sells fruit and flowers. The main problem with the expansive Freedom Square is that it is not square; rather it is triangular and as such it funnels people through at great speed. Few choose to linger at the monument to a plague. There are pavement cafés but they are used by solo Japanese businessmen who play it safe with pizzas while they read Japanese-language Czech guide books and nod effusively at under-utilised waiting staff. I cannot imagine that there is a huge demand for Brno guide books in Japanese. I suspect they are reading a Czech Republic guide book where Brno is a footnote on the very last page. This city is sparsely populated and is a rare opportunity to explore a city without Boeings of tourists.

I climb the hill to the Cathedral of Sts Peter and Paul where I hear the midday bell ring at … eleven a.m. This is a legacy of a battle in 1645 when the Swedes besieged Brno for three months until one day the Swedish general told his troops they would take the city by midday. The defending general inside Brno learnt of this boastful claim, he had the bells rung an hour early and when the Swedish troops heard the bells they left. I do not wish to visit St James' Church, St Thomas' Church, the Red Church, the Old Brno Monastery or the Cathedral of the Assumption of Our Lady because there is so much to see and do here.

I waste no time in visiting this city's prime attraction. Villa Tugendhat is a monument to modern architecture and is only the fourth such worldwide which has received a prestigious UNESCO designation. The building is named after Fritz Tugendhat, an owner of a Brno factory, who had this jewel of inter-war functionalist architecture built for his family by the famous German architect Ludwig Mies van der Rohe. Mr and Mrs Tugendhat plus kids moved in in December 1930. However, they lived here only till 1938, when they had to flee the Nazis. It was the location of the meeting which decided the separation of the Czech and Slovak republics in 1992. The villa is open 10 a.m. to 6 p.m., Wednesday to Sunday, and I am here on a Wednesday so I am in luck. A tram runs from the city centre to the villa and there is a guided tour on the hour. I check the villa's website before setting out full of excitement. The website advises that the villa is closed for the next six months for construction work. And this in a building which was 'completed' in 1930.

Spilberk Castle is a fortress but was also used a prison. People were tortured here from all around Europe. I have no wish to join them. The casemates in the prison are said to have dark grim rooms but I have one of those in my hotel. The Technical Museum has steam engines, cutlery, metallurgy and a technical playroom for keen kids and backward adults. There's the Mendel Museum of Genetics and the Museum of Gypsy Culture but I am struggling. Brno Circuit is the largest motor racing circuit in the Czech Republic and it is one of 17 circuits which host the World Motorcycle Championship, but it's in August. At the Automotodrom they hold a 12-hour endurance race modelled on Le Mans, called Le Brno. I check their brochure. Nothing on this week. There is the festival *Brno—Town in the Centre of Europe*, with a fireworks competition, but it's on in June. FC Brno is one of the leading soccer clubs in the country and lies fourth in the league. Their 8,000-seater Mestsky stadium is located convenient to the city centre. I check online. There is no game this week. There is Brno Zoo but who wants to look at wild animals caged behind metal bars and wire fences. I visit some, but not all, of the 130 shops in the spanking new Galleria Vankovka shopping mall. A popular day trip from the city is to the nearby Austerlitz battlefield where Napoleon triumphed in 1805, but I have visions of being taken to a large empty field and having to take their word that something happened here. There is a coalminers' cycling route through the former Rosice-Oslavany coal fields. There is the Asparagus Festival in nearby Ivancice in a few weeks' time but I have seen asparagus before in Tesco. Jesus wept. It's 11.30 a.m. I have done Brno. I return to the nice lady in the tourist office.

'How do I get to the Pyros trade fair?' I implore.

I take the No. 1 tram. I don't know why it is but invariably if you wish to go somewhere in a Central European city, you need to take tram No. 1 and invariably it will drop you exactly where you need to be. Congress tourism is big here. Brno is the biggest trade venue in Central Europe. The campus is 650,000 square metres and it has been hosting fairs, mostly for Communists, since 1928. The trade fair grounds have their own shuttle bus, bank, radio station and TV studio. It's sunny enough to suggest that the trade fair even has its own microclimate. They play classical music outside, *Rhythm is a Dancer* and *Pump up the Volume*, both classics from my era. I take great care to bypass other fairs which are being held here simultaneously, including the *International Plastics, Rubber & Composite Fair,* the *International Surface Technology Fair* and the *International Welding & Engineering Fair.* I can see inside one of these fairs and there are men in cream suits with red shirts and comb-overs looking at large nuts and bolts.

I expect to be stuck in some cavernous warehouse looking at shelves of hoses and ropes but the Fire Fighting fair is a red-hot revelation. There are thousands of fans here and we are all in the outdoors to admire rows of polished fire engines, fire-fighting helicopters, fire cars plus more hoists, lifts, winches, pumps, lights, axes, extinguishers, reflective vests, helmets and fire-retardant suits than would ever be needed at the greatest ever natural disaster. The fire engines are so impressive that hardened fire-fighters leave their own engines to take photographs of other bigger engines, a sort of male fire engine envy. There is a stand selling flashing blue lights for use by the emergency services so I order a set for my car back home so that I will be able to speed along Dublin's bus lanes, like Mick does in his Mercedes Benz taxi.

Other fire trucks drive about the fair, their sirens wailing, announcing upcoming demonstrations. A siren of another sort draws a large crowd at another stand. She has cropped hair, much make-up, sunglasses, jeans and industrial gloves and most of us guys have never seen such a girlie use an angle-grinder to cut such large bolts before with such expertise. I see the Holiday Inn hotel inside the trade fair and learn that the hotel is fully booked for the annual fire-fighters' *Pyromeeting*. Now I know why it was so hard to book a room in Brno. But I do wish I was staying at this Holiday Inn. If the fire alarm does go off at 4 a.m., I will be safe in the knowledge that everyone else staying at the hotel will know exactly what to do.

The highlight for the fire-starters are the demonstrations. Members of the *Hasic*, not a fundamental Islamic sect but the Brno Fire Service, light up a few bales of hay and put out the flames—but we are all waiting for them to torch the 20-year-old Toyota, which they duly do in a huge oily blaze. Burn, baby, burn. There are so many men and machines from the Brno Fire Service here that I would seriously worry for the safety of the town if a fire breaks out now. The flood prevention demonstration is provided by a company called Noah. The skies buzz as a fire-fighting heli-copter swoops down like a scene from *Apocalypse Now*, hovers and discharges spray and water in a communal adrenaline rush over a sky-high tower which marks the eightieth anniversary of this the largest trade fair complex within Central Europe. Wow.

It's probably a bloke's thing but exploring new destinations doesn't get much better than this. You can keep your Gothic cath-edrals, occupation museums, old towns, market squares, shopping malls and town halls. This is what tourism is all about in modern Central Europe. Brrrr...No? Yes, please.

Customer Service
Ruinair
Dublin Airport

Dear Sirs,

I wish to complain about my recent flight STN-BRQ. My specific complaint is that you flew me to Brno.

I don't know if you have been to Brno but frankly there is very little to do in Brno. Despite being May, many attractions and events were out of season or were shut. Sadly I had to do what most others there did and attend a trade fair in the city about Fire Fighting. I would much rather visit museums or sit on a beach.

Can you please provide some assurances that in future you will fly to places that are more interesting.
Yours etc,
Disgusted of Dublin.

Nothing happens for a week and then I receive a letter in the post. Not an email. Which is very unusual.

Ref SON/5124

Mr Paul Kilduff
Stillorgan
Co. Dublin

Dear Mr Kilduff,
I thank you for your delightful letter. We are thrilled that you flew with us recently to Brno and more importantly that you did so for just £15 out and £8 back (excluding taxes, fees and charges). Isn't it great that you can now fly across Europe for less than a tenner. What can you buy for ten quid these days? It wouldn't buy you a good book or come to think of it a crap book either.
As someone who has travelled frequently with us over the past 12 months, I am surprised by your complaint that there is very little to do in Brno. We did a brief search this morning and enclose herewith three pages of exciting things to do in Brno, which include churches, castles, town halls, street lights, museums, Freedom Square, monasteries, central station, markets, Brno lake, Brno Zoo, Capuchin's Crypt, the Mahenovo Theatre and Zderad's Column (whoever the hell Zderad was). This excludes obviously the numerous restaurants, bars, clubs where you can check out Brno's active nightlife. Pubs and clubs are never 'out of season' and if the churches were closed, you can always pray directly to the Lord.
If all else fails and you are truly bored, why not bring a couple of good books to read. If you can't find any good books, bring some bad ones. There are some great works of fiction available at present, not least of which is you own recent tome. Better still if

you're bored reading that, why not make a start on volume two?
With the speed of our new route development (adding new bases
and destinations on a weekly basis) this should give you plenty of
scope for your next magnum opus.

Finally as an airline that started off in Dublin and developed at
'interesting' places like Luton and Stansted, we couldn't care less
whether you find our destinations interesting or not. As long as the
flights are cheap, I am sure we will continue to carry millions of
passengers to and from these destinations.

If our unbeatable combination of low fares, high punctuality,
great pilots and cabin crew and our charming Chief Executive
leave you bored with life, then why don't you simply stay at home
in somewhere interesting and exciting like ... Stillorgan. After all
you are at least close to a beach in Stillorgan (well Booterstown at
least?), whereas if you were looking for a beach in Brno, you were
clearly mad, sad or a couple of hundred miles away from where
you should have flown to.

I hope we will have the pleasure of welcoming you on many
more low cost, on-time Ruinair flights and that you will continue
with your wonderful writing, which helps keep us entertained and
spreads the gospel of Ruinair's lowest fares across Europe from
exciting places like Stillorgan to uninteresting places like the Czech
Republic!

Best wishes
Siobhan O'Neill
Deputy Head, Customer Services.

Siobhan has indeed kindly enclosed three pages of material from
the *Yahoo! Travel* website.

It's a nice enough letter and they evidently get the joke but overall I am disappointed.

I had hoped that the *Head* of Customer Services would reply.

Or maybe even Mick himself would reply.

Perhaps he did.

Job Application

'*Do you want to be really famous ???*'

'*There is no such thing as bad publicity. Tell us about it. Ruinair is the only low fares airline in Europe. What we need now is a Head of Communications. Reporting to the Chief Executive, you will be responsible for all of Ruinair's external communications. If you are ambitious and can show us that you can deliver an outstanding communications programme, then we want you.*

Position:	*Ruinair Head of Communications*
Start Date:	ASAP
Package:	*Up to €100k*
Requirements:	*Hardworking and Committed*
	Ambitious to succeed
	Write Well
	Speak/Interview Well
	Good in a Crisis
	Be able to handle negative PR

Send your CV today to Ruinair.'

Human Resources Dept
Ruinair
Dublin Airport

Dear Sirs

Firstly, I should advise that I am already '*really famous*' yet I am applying for the advertised role.

Secondly, as the author of 'Ruinair' I know slightly more about your airline than the average punter.

Thirdly, let me say that I was surprised to see Peter Sherrard leave you to join the Football Association of Ireland (I guess it was for the free match tickets). He seemed happy enough with his job at the last AGM.

I believe that I meet the various requirements for the Head of Communications role as set out below:

Hardworking and Committed—You cannot visit all 27 countries in Europe on low fares airlines over a three-year period and write two books and not be hardworking and committed. In fact some of my readers tell me that I should be committed, preferably to that institution in Dundrum near the fancy Town Centre.

Ambitious to Succeed—Believe it or not some publishers madly declined 'Ruinair', but I persevered.

Write Well—Me book wot I wrote was snapped up by an Irish and a UK publisher.

Speak/Interview Well—I can speak clearly in 'South Dublin' English and I interview reasonably well, or so my publicist tells me. In the last few months I have done about 20 interviews; mostly they were with A-list celebrities like Ray D'Arcy (Today FM), Derek Mooney (RTÉ) and George 'Ruggerby' Hook (Newstalk FM). I almost made it (but didn't) onto the Ryan Tubridy TV show, where I planned to ask Ryan if his rather fashionable and distinctive haircut would be referred to in Dublin's barber shops as *Ryanhair?*

I will be committed to maintaining the existing sound-bite communications culture, i.e., the European Commission are *'Communists'*, airport operators are *'overcharging rapists'*, British Airways are *'expensive bastards'*, environmentalists are *'eco-nuts'*, all other airlines *'gouge'* their customers, the Irish Aviation Regulator is a *'wanker'* and travel agents are *'fuckers'*. As Mick says: *'We prefer to dole out bon mots at regular weekly intervals. If you have low fares, you have to shout your mouth off a lot more. All we do is go around, create a bit of controversy, do silly things, get our photograph taken in silly places and reduce the advertising money, and like that we can afford to keep the prices down. We specialise in cheap publicity stunts. Usually someone gets offended by our ads, which is fantastic. You get a whole lot more bang for your buck if somebody is upset. Bookings peak for big advertisements. And they'll peak even more if somebody reacts badly to the advertisement.'*

Good in a crisis—I was left for 10 hours in Malaga Airport by a low fares airline but I'm over that now.

Be Able to Handle Negative PR—I can deal with negativity, e.g., one 'Ruinair' book review in the Irish Times. As Mick says, *'As long as it's not safety-related, there's no such thing as bad publicity.'*

I am willing to perform other additional communications related tasks, e.g., I would be happy to personally assist with the selection of the various female cabin crew for next year's *O'Leery's Staff Charity Calendar.*

I am already familiar with your corporate culture so I will attend the interview in jeans and an open shirt.

I am interested in free staff travel on your airline since I travel often in my current job as a travel writer.

I look forward to your favourable consideration of my genuine application in due course.

Yours sincerely,

Paul Kilduff

PS I will be able to start the job in approx three months' time when I have finished the sequel, 'Ruinairski'.

PPS Some people rather unkindly, and unfairly in my view, said that 'Ruinair' does not paint a favourable picture of your airline. On that basis it would be better for your airline to have me on the inside pissing out, rather than on the outside pissing in. Rest assured, Mick will understand this type of racy terminology.

PPPS Considering my choice of language in this application, I think I'd be fucking excellent in the role.

I never received a reply. I wonder why?

The Czech Republic (Again)

Flight FR1021 – Monday @ 7.45 a.m. – DUB-PRG-DUB

Fare €3 plus taxes, fees and charges €41

Ruinair is a fantastic airline. Where else could you book a €3 flight to a glamorous city on a Bank Holiday weekend? There is one snag. While the rest of the nation departs Dublin on Friday or Saturday and returns on the Bank Holiday Monday, I must depart on the Bank Holiday Monday. Otherwise it's €199. *'I grew up in Dublin in the early 1980s when it cost £208 to fly to London. If we did not exist, that figure would now be somewhere between £500 and £600 and we would all still be crossing the Irish Sea by ferry.'*

'It is like some Russian analysis, like the five-year plan. You pay for what you get. I will sell you a seat today on an aircraft tomorrow. There will be passengers on board that aircraft tomorrow who will have paid me €1 and there will be passengers who will have paid me—probably at the top end—€129 or €149. They have each paid for what they got. Are our fares fair? Yes. There is only one test and that is whether consumers support what we do. We have the support of many consumers. We will take all the brickbats we get from the press or anybody else because the competition does not like us. The acid test will be when passenger traffic will be up on the previous month. Price is the best form of loyalty. We own price. I see no reason why fares don't keep falling for 10 years. I don't see why in 10 years' time you wouldn't fly people for free. More than half of our passengers will fly free.'

I have seen flights on this airline's website, mostly from Ireland to the UK, which have a €0.00 fare out and a €0.00 fare on the return trip. Added to this however are €10's worth of taxes, fees and charges out and the same €10 on the return trip, plus a €10 credit card fee. This is the miracle of how €0 can easily become €30, in the same way that Jesus changed water into wine, and fed 5,000 with five loaves and two fishes.

So because this is *Conair* I must once again pay the usual after-thought of taxes, fees and charges on top of my €3 fare. I object to the aviation insurance levy of €5.92 each way. This charge was introduced following higher insurance costs for all airlines post-9/11 in the USA. 60 million passengers paying €5.92 each way is €355 million per annum. I don't know how much Ruinair pay to insure their aircraft each year (they do not disclose that) but easyJet have a similar size fleet and they pay £20 million per year. That makes sense. A plane costs $60 million and airlines rarely lose one. In fact Ruinair has never lost a plane in any accident so they have a 20-year no-claims bonus on their insurance policy, as I have with my car.

I object to the legacy wheelchair levy of 50 cent. Firstly, I have taken 50 or more flights on Ruinair in three years and I cannot recall ever seeing more than an occasional person who needed a wheelchair to get onto a flight. What right-minded wheelchair-bound passenger would choose to fly on such an airline when they could fly on a caring airline instead? Secondly, Ruinair charge me this fee despite the fact that since July 2008, those with reduced mobility are entitled to assistance free of charge at all airports in all EU member states and the airport operators have full responsibility for providing all services to reduced-mobility passengers on the ground at airports. Yet the Ruinair website still shows: '*Wheelchair Levy—This charge is 33p/50 cent per passenger/per flight.*'

Does Ruinair dislike the disabled? '*We don't. We carry more than two million of them every year. There's a lie being perpetrated here all the time. We happily get wheelchairs on the aircraft, always have, always will. But we don't believe that the airline should be paying to get wheelchair users through buildings that we don't own. Now we ask every passenger who flies with us to pay 50 cent or so to defray the cost to us of paying someone to come out with the wheelchair and put them on board the aircraft. If you don't like the wheelchair charge, don't fly with us. But you can't expect all these services to be provided for nothing. We're not some bloody government institution. We're supposed to be making a profit.'* 60 million passengers at 50 cent each is a nice €30 million per annum.

I object to paying €5 each way to use my credit card. This charge is levied per passenger per trip, not on each credit card payment. While I pay €10, a family of five pays €50 but uses one credit card. Ruinair claims that it is charged a handling fee by banks for every passenger included in a single credit-card transaction: *'All of those processes go to Visa 10 separate times as well so we have to make sure that we are covered in order to cover the costs.'* The banking industry told *The Sunday Times*, however, that airlines are charged a set percentage of the total payment irrespective of how many passengers or tickets are booked. *'The credit card is an ad valorem charge, it is a percentage of the value of the transaction that is chargeable,'* said AIB, one of Ireland's three merchant acquiring banks. Ruinair would be charged no more than 2.5 per cent of the transaction total to process the payment, and due to the bargaining power of the aviation giant it is likely to be less than 2 per cent. I should be paying €1 but instead I paid €10. But why does the fee exist? Does anyone else charge us a fee to use our credit card? Dixons don't, Dell don't, IKEA don't, Wal-mart don't. Imagine paying your weekly shopping bill at Tesco of €100 and the check-out girl adding on an extra €5. We'd walk out. 60 million passengers paying €5 a trip is €300 million of more easy money.

I object to the baggage charges, so much so that I never check in baggage on this airline. They would probably lose it on me anyway, once they saw my surname on the luggage tag. It's only the ultra-high-net-worth people like property developers, IT millionaires and airline chief executives who can afford checked baggage. The average length of a passenger trip on this airline is only two and a half days and Ruinair have stated that they plan to keep increasing their baggage charges until only one in four of us checks in baggage. The way to avoid these charges is to pack whatever you want into your 10 kg of carry-on baggage. With online check-in you never meet anyone working for Ruinair who is near a weighing scales so you will be fine with 20 kg.

Mick hates all this baggage. *'What other form of transport does someone stand there and take your bag off you on departure and hand it back to you on arrival? You don't do it on trains. You don't do it on buses. Checking is the most useless activity known to man. You queue up to hand in your bag and to collect it afterwards—if BA hasn't lost your bag, which, 50 per cent of the time, they probably have. Don't complain about checked-in bags. You're the one who checked them in. Pay it. If you don't want to pay for check-in, use web check-in. If you don't want to pay the baggage charges, travel with hand luggage: we allow you 10 kg. I can live happily for three weeks and change my clothes every day with 10 kg of luggage. It just needs educating passengers away from this notion that you're going to Klagenfurt for a week and you have to take five bloody suitcases. The purpose is not to make money from checked-in luggage—the purpose is to get rid of it altogether. Will it piss off people who are going on a two-week holiday to Ibiza? Yes, it probably will. But we don't fly to those charter holiday destinations anyway.'* The time has come to stop messing about with baggage charges and to start weighing lardy passengers.

So insurance levies, wheelchairs and credit card fees earn Ruinair €685 million per annum. But they are so kind to us travelling passengers because they have not, unlike other airlines, introduced a fuel surcharge to reflect the cost of oil. *'It's the best thing that's ever happened to an airline like us because you have airlines such as BA not just increasing their fares but scamming up the fuel surcharges. The gap between BA with their fuel surcharges and ourselves with low fares plus a guarantee of no fuel surcharges is getting wider—which is why BA's short-haul traffic is falling by 3 per cent and ours is growing by 19 per cent. Now, with oil coming back from $140 a barrel to $110, there has been no sign of BA reducing its surcharges. Not a hint. They won't give it back because they are just a bunch of dishonest rapists.'*

Ruinair don't, and never will, charge a fuel surcharge. Why would they need to when they have so many charges they can increase whenever they feel like it? Ruinair is not an airline. It's an insurance provider, wheelchair rental, credit-card-processing and freight-carrying operation. It's more like an AXA Insurance/ Health Service/AIB Bank/Federal Express industrial conglomerate. *'Yes, we charge for bags, check-in and credit card payments. The difference is that these charges are all avoidable. We encourage our customers to travel with hand luggage only, pay by debit card and use the on-line check-in facility. If they do, they can avail of a €1 fare, 1 million of which are on sale today. The €1 fare includes all taxes, fees and charges. Whatever fare we advertise, and there is continuous claptrap from the consumer agencies, that is the fare. As long as one does not have to check in a bag, and checks in on the website, one can get that fare if one wants it.'*

Ruinair change their many rules often, so that we don't know what to do, then we make mistakes and they can charge us. They charge us €5 to check in. I have not suffered this embarrassment yet. I don't know if they utilise a wicker collection basket such as used at Mass or whether they ask us to pay by credit card and then charge us another €5 for the privilege of paying the €5, but if you have to pay them to use a check-in desk, here is my best suggestion. Go around your home before you fly and gather all those annoying one-cent coins you keep in jam jars and desk drawers, and do check behind the sofa, until you can find 500 of the little copper blighters. Take them to check-in, tell Ruinair that they are legal tender and they must accept the coinage. Tell them you might be one or two coins short so they should count them out one by one in front of the long line of passengers. If we all do this, they will soon tire of lugging all this copper to the bank every night, in what perhaps represents the ultimate in petty cash.

Onboard I am delighted to receive my copy of Ruinair's in-flight magazine, now on issue 17. I have the previous issues except for issue 12, so if anyone has a copy please send it on to me. And what a great magazine. Seriously. Once again the cover features a lady in a bikini. Inside there is nice piece from Mick, confirming how fantastic Ruinair is on a variety of fronts. Gone is the accompanying photograph of Mick in his tall green stage-Irish Shamrock hat where he amusingly gives all his passengers a two-fingered salute. Now they use an old photograph of pious Mick in a church where he is dressed in white papal robes with his hands joined together to prey. Sorry, that's the incorrect word. I meant to say pray. This photograph is from the old publicity stunt where Mick uttered the immortal words: *'Habemus lowest fares, my children.'*

This magazine contains travel guide essentials such as, on this occasion, the *Top 10 Stag Night Destinations*, and unsurprisingly enough, they are all Ruinair destinations. In another edition they carried this essential travel article: the *Top 10 Places to Blend In if You Have a Beard*. Plus there are fashion tips, tech tips, foodie tips and health tips. There are many adverts for what is known now as dental tourism in Poland and Hungary. The worst advert has to be the one for Saile & Sabga products which features a bloke in bulging trunks lying with his head in the crotch of a bikini-clad babe on a speed boat as she pours champagne down his chest. The Advertising Standards Authority since banned this lewd advertisement for linking alcohol with seduction. There are property advertisements too. One advises us of 'Croatia, Closer Than Ever' when I am thinking it has always been the same distance. Another advises us to 'Invest in Plock' which looks like it is a large petro-chemical refining town. There is an advertisement for The Beacon Hotel, which is 'A slice of Miami in Dublin's Southside' and there I was thinking that the Beacon Hotel is located in Sandyford Industrial Estate near a Woodie's DIY store and Alo Kavanagh motor car sales.

This edition contains the infamous Hertz advertisement which was reported in the press. *'Ruinair's geographical incapabilities were dramatically highlighted when an airline hostess noticed a critical mistake on a map in the in-flight magazine and became enraged. The Czech stewardess was reading the Ruinair in-flight magazine and looking at the map of Hertz rental locations across Europe when she noticed something was wrong with the map. On the Hertz map, Prague, a landlocked city, was located on the banks of the Baltic Sea and Poland had taken the place of the Czech Republic. "I've told them before," the attendant fumed. "If they can get France and the UK in the right place, why not the Czech Republic?"'*

Each month the magazine features one of the lithe cabin crew girls from the prior year's charity calendar. This month there is a photograph of my favourite, Magda, sitting on a suitcase in an airport in her bikini. I learn that 'Minxy Magda', from Poland, usually only wears her bikini on the beach. She confirms the true value of buying scratch cards on Ruinair flights. *'One handsome guy bought some scratch cards from me and when he handed over the cash he also handed over a romantic note, too. Now he's my boyfriend.'* Now why didn't I think of that ploy? To think I used to share Mick's opinion. *'Scratch cards for are morons.'*

I still have issues with the *'Buy as You Fly'* brochure, because I have not found anything that I need or want. This month I can choose between the Infra-Red Pocket Helicopter 'ideal for relieving stress', the wooden Shoe Stretcher 'expand the leather within the shoe where needed most', the Ear Cleaner 'no poking, no prodding, no risk', the Telephone Ringer Amplifier 'ever find that you miss a call because you can't hear the telephone ring?' (er, no), the Ceramic Posture Support 'do you often get back or neck pain?' (only when sitting in these non-reclining seats), and the Now & Then Music Centre, which plays cassettes and 33/48/78 rpm vinyl records. And where would I be in life without owning a Jean Patrique 15-Piece Professional Stainless Steel Cookware Set? I have never seen anyone take this *'Buy as You Fly'* brochure off an aircraft, except perhaps to use it later to start a fire in a grate at home of a cold winter's evening.

We have a food and drinks trolley today and I am feeling so well-disposed to this airline that I will offer them my custom. The back pages of the in-flight brochure show an appealing selection of soft drinks.

'Apple juice, please,' I ask the Polish crew member with the shaved eyebrow, darting eyes and hyperactive manner. How do I know that he is Polish? Because he wears a Polish flag pin in his tie. That's below the open collar of a well-creased off-white short sleeved shirt.

He passes me a sandwich. 'Ham and cheese.'

It's not exactly what I asked for. 'Apple juice.'

He still holds out the sandwich. 'Ham and cheese.' Maybe it sounds the same in Polish.

'No, an apple juice drink.'

He nods and swaps the sandwich for the drink. '€2.50.'

Now I am not that tight but I checked the price in the magazine because I only have € 2 of spare change in my pocket, and we both know I am not spending it on those infernal scratch cards.

I hold out my €2 coins. 'It's €2.'

'No, it's not. It's €2.50.'

I shake my head and show him the page in the in-flight magazine.

He is not bothered. 'They're always changing the prices. Sometimes the prices go up. Sometimes the prices go down.'

I have been a frequent flyer on this airline for three years. 'The prices only go up.'

When the perfumes and cuddly toys are wheeled past me and the seat belt signs are switched off I decide to visit the forward wc. It is 'Engaged' so I watch and wait for about 10 minutes but no one emerges. I am fairly terrified about what might be happening inside but I need to visit so I walk up, stand and wait. A woman immediately stands in line behind me. Then a crew member nods to me and tells me the wc is empty. I point at the 'Engaged' sign but they open the door and it is indeed empty inside. I see a wad of paper has been stuffed into the door latch, which means that the 'Engaged' sign is on constantly.

I am horrified to say that when I enter the wc I find the person before me has trashed the place and if I don't clean it up the woman next up will think I have an appalling aim and will tell everyone else. So I do the work of the cabin crew and clean up the interior as best as I can. But I have a solution to this eternal problem. Why not have separate ladies' and gents' toilets on aircraft? The ladies' toilet will have soft carpet and fluffy towels, flowery paper and bright lights, plus complimentary moisturising lotions and sweet scents. The gents' toilet will be a hole in the side of the aircraft and it will operate on the vacuum principle. Mick? '*We can't charge for a pee because Boeing hasn't made a toilet door to take coins.*'

We land. I've been to Prague before, for work, but it was hardly work. My job was to check out the operations of a tiny 10-person banking office in the city. The work ethic there was not strong. I was told to arrive at 9.30 a.m. because the office doors would be opened then and by 4.30 p.m. there was much nervous coughing and slamming of old filing cabinets in case I did not leave by 5 p.m. The office had one English-language newspaper delivered daily: the *Financial Times*. No one ever read it during the day so as I exited after a gruelling day's work, I always nicked the copy and took it to some outdoor cafés in Wenceslas Square where I would digest news, beer, steaks, cakes and the local inhabitants till dusk. At the end of the toughest week ever I took the Friday afternoon off to sightsee in the castle grounds before my Czech Airlines flight back to Heathrow, which cost my employer £700 but I got a free salad and a glass of plonk.

So I naturally gravitate back to the now significantly commercial hub of Wenceslas Square and it is not as I recall, comprising all things authentic Czech, including Debenhams, Marks and Spencerski and the Sham-rock Irish bar. Groups of police stand around by their parked cars and keep an eye on the hobos and winos loitering by the greasy hot-dog stands. Restaurant owners attempt unsuccessfully to hustle me into their roadside eateries. All this local colour is not sufficiently compensated for by the majestic sweep of the boulevard, which is like the Champs-Elysées, but lying further east. At the top of the Square the grand and dirty National Museum towers above, with a statue of Prince Wenceslas on horseback. History can often be kind. This Prince was subsequently upgraded to the 'Good' King Wenceslas of Christmas fame.

I walk along the picturesque streets to the *Stare Mesto* old town but I have to circumnavigate the Sex Machine Museum on Melantrichova, which is a very popular place for tourists to take photographs of each other with a dirty grin, but none, myself included, dare to venture inside. Souvenir shops sell naff T-shirts with *Prague Drinking Party* or *Czech Mate*. The expanse of the town hall square opens up in front of me and I cannot fail to be impressed. Every building around me is decorated with wonderful details and painted in a rich palette of colours. There are turrets and spires, flags and banners, clocks and sculptures, awnings and canopies. This may be the most well-presented city square in all of Europe.

I sit on a bench and unfortunately five youths soon sit on the next bench. Four of them are stripped to the waist and are as white as a flag of surrender. The fifth wears an Eircom national soccer strip. They get chatting and they are from Dublin. Tallaght, I deduce, and they are effin' and blindin' about everything. They appear to be hungover after a night of debauchery. 'If that's what you get when you pay a few bob, imagine what you would get if you paid for a cracker.' They discuss one missing member of the group. 'Shano would blend in with anyone. You could stick him in a room of Chinese people and he would blend in.' They seem bored by Prague. 'Jaysus, what else can we do here?' Excitement comes when they see, as I do, a nearby Arab gentleman using a lit cigarette to burn off grey hairs from his bushy beard. 'Jaysus, your man is burning the feckin' face off himself.' They are loud, loud enough to attracted the unwelcome attentions of a few wandering guys in the English national soccer strip. My peace is also disturbed by a group of vocal German female tourists with bulging *Bohemian Crystal* shopping bags. The bench is made for a maximum of five people but about ten of the ladies progressively squeeze on at the other end. They need to sit down because they all wear their stilettos today for a city centre of medieval cobblestones. Eventually I am pushed so far along the bench that I balance precariously at the other end on only a single testicle.

I move on to another part of the square but all the seats are taken so I have to sit on a kerbstone. Then another couple of tourists sit close to me and more follow until there are maybe 40 people all sitting on my kerbstone and I wonder why they won't leave me alone. The visitors wear yellow stickers and they are part of a tour. Their guide appears with a balloon up on a stick, so he won't lose his tour group and vice versa. Like a herd of cattle they stand up and trundle off, almost trampling me in the stampede. It takes a superhuman effort on my part not to join their 12-hour *Prague Explorer Walking Tour* which includes the Old Town, the Jewish Ghetto, lots of castles and bridges, a traditional Czech lunch with drinks, a free map of Prague and a free CD with 500 pictures. And worst of all the tour is given in Russian.

I have not seen so many tourists concentrated in one place since St Mark's Piazza in Venice or all of Barcelona any August. I walk about to a cacophony of digital cameras. The Asian tourists are still taking photographs in unusual positions, as if standing on one leg and contorting your body like an inverted gymnast is going to make a huge difference to the end product. Why do the Japanese take photographs with their free hand held up in the air? Is this for balance purposes? I am in lots of other people's photographs. I am sure there are US couples who return from their month-long Grand Tour of Europe to their home in Iowa, and who upload their hundreds of digital pixel pics to their PC. The wife will tell everyone that this is a photograph of her in that magnificent town hall square in Prague. The husband will stare at the photograph and complain about the Irishman in the Gant shorts and the K-Swiss runners who strolled between the couple just as he was snap-happy. The wife will say she saw me in Riga and Tallinn.

At the duly appointed hour, one thousand people arise and walk to the astronomical clock in the southern corner. The clock is so-called because of the average price of a cappuccino in the cafés in this square. We wait as Indians try to sell us sets of postcards and bouncy spiders on wire coils. A hush descends. Expectation is high. Like for any great event we generously allow those in wheelchairs to sit in the front row. On the hour the clock predictably springs into life. A sea of mobile telephone cameras and Sony handy-cams are held up. Twelve wooden figures pass by overhead at speed. It is a very short performance. The crowd scatters afterwards and there are growing mumblings of discontent, maybe even of refunds.

'Is that it?' asks a nearby American lady. 'This happens every hour? Wait, I don't get it.'

My earliest memories of the Charles Bridge are from a video on MTV in 1988. Michael Hutchence of INXS strolled through Prague's streets until he crossed the bridge in a big furry coat, occasionally turning to sing to the camera ... *'and they will never tear us apart'*. I felt then that a band from Oz had shown us the mystery of a part of our continent, albeit with some artistic help. Prague was an incredibly glamorous destination in a far-away behind-the-Iron-Curtain sort of way. Now there are three daily flights from Dublin to Prague, it is a €3 sort of destination (plus taxes, fees and charges). In the video the bridge was deserted because we had no low fares airlines or because it was filmed at 7 a.m. INXS was a low fares homage: *'I told you that we could fly, cause we all have wings, but some of us don't know why.'*

It seems that everyone from the town hall square has followed me here. If there is a greater bridge in all of Europe, then I have yet to cross it. Charles Bridge is alive. Locals sell wooden arts and metal crafts. Cartoonists will draw caricatures of Will Smith, Mick Jagger or you. There are oil paintings and charcoals, bracelets and jewellery, photos and posters. A blues band plays tunes. Cars have been banned since 1950. Tourist sightseeing boats and pedalos for hire (like in the Costa del Sol) traverse the Vltava river underneath. This stone bridge has endured the centuries, perhaps because construction was purposefully begun in 1357, on 9 July at 5.31 a.m., a so-called lucky number sequence of 1-3-5-7-9-7-5-3-1. The bridge is definitely not straight and it meanders to the left and right, so much so that I wonder if it was designed by the same architects who designed the elevated walkway to Pier D in Dublin Airport.

I walk the bridge, unimpressed that the 30 statues of saints are grubby but impressed that the Italian tourists know the saints. These saints were canonised by Popes but were christened by pigeons. The biggest crowd-pulling saint is St John of Nepomuk since his is the oldest statue and has been rubbed golden by those who make a wish. In contrast St Anthony of Padua next door has no female admirers. At one saint a tour guide announces it is lucky to rub the saint. An American replies, 'We already did that.'

On the other side of the river I struggle uphill to the funicular railway and jump inside a carriage which hangs at a 45-degree angle from the steep slope. The 10-minute trip slowly reveals Prague below. At the summit lies the Petrin Lookout Tower. It was opened in 1891 and it is a copy of the Eiffel Tower but is one fifth of its height. There are a hundred wooden steps but I spy an elevator which will be easier. The entrance to the elevator is guarded by a small rope hung across the entrance and by an elderly man.

'Can I use the elevator?' I ask.

The elderly man looks me up and down. 'Are you handicapped?'

It looks like the elevator is reserved for special cases. 'No. I am not. But I could be.'

He shakes his head. 'It's only for handicapped or old people.'

'How old?'

'Older than you are.'

I resign myself to my fate. 'How long does it take to climb the steps?'

'Five minutes.'

Fifteen minutes later I ascend to the highest point of the tower. I stick my head out of the window to be buffeted by the wind, such is the altitude. The view is spectacular, a maze of densely packed cream buildings with terracotta or copper roofs. No two buildings are alike. There is a quiet calm over the city. There are parklands and forests and a hundred spires according to legend and the local tourist office. The Vltava river twists and bends through the city and I count all 13 bridges. I can make out the town hall square and the Charles Bridge, plus people walking its 500-metre span.

Suffice to say, Brno this is not.

Lidice

I take the metro from the centre of Prague to the end of the A line. Dejvicka station is the last stop and is a transit hub where buses and trams meet the metro system. I have done the necessary research and wait by a bus stop opposite the Diplomat Hotel. The timetable on display confirms that the number 22 bus will leave here at 11 a.m. I check this fact by gesticulating at the timetable to an old lady with shopping bags who confirms the departure. At five minutes to eleven o'clock a number 56 bus stops at the next bus stop. The lady points the bus and advises me to take this bus. 'Lidice,' she says. I take her word and jump onboard, knowing that I have yet to work out how the buses operate in most Central European countries.

Thirty minutes later and 20 km west I alight at a rural cross-roads, next to a services area with farmers selling produce to passing families and pseudo-chefs selling burgers to passing truck drivers. My destination is well signposted and I walk through wooded parkland towards a tall and prominent circular sandstone colonnade. The site opens up as I enter, with low buildings on either side of an open plaza. Below lies an undulating grassy meadow with copses of trees, some monuments, a narrow river and tarmac pathways. This was the village of Lidice. I find it hard to believe that a thriving community once lived here.

Off to my right is the Child Victims' War Memorial. This is a monument not only to the children of Lidice, but to all children who died in World War Two. A Czech sculptor spent 20 years creating this sympathetic life-size work comprising a cluster of 82 standing children of various ages. I stand opposite the children and all of them seem to make eye contact with me. At the foot of the memorial other visitors have left candles, toys, small bears, cars, scarves, even a single admission ticket for Prague Zoo, many of which seem to be impromptu gifts left by other children who saw a greater need for their own favourite toy.

On the morning of 10 June 1942, Nazi troops arrived early in Lidice and forcefully removed the villagers from their homes. All 105 children were transported away. Nine children were considered to be suitably Aryan and were sent to live with families in Germany. 82 other children, excluding babies under 1 year old, died later from exhaust fumes whilst locked into a specially converted truck in Chelmn. Their mothers and other womenfolk of the village, 184 women in all, were sent to a concentration camp.

I descend into the valley and stop by a single stone lintel which rests on the ground. This is all that remains of the Dolezals family home. Further on I stop at the excavated foundation of the Horak family farmhouse, which now lies below ground level. After the women and children had been taken away from the village, the Nazis arranged rows of mattresses from the homes up against the barn wall to prevent bullet ricochets. They stood the menfolk of the village here in groups of five at a time at first when they began at 7 a.m. but when the process took too long, they changed to groups of 10 men at a time. The men were left where they fell for the next group to see, and after each group was shot, the Nazis took two steps backwards and continued. 173 men were shot here without a blindfold, without being bound and without any explanation being offered nor any sentence being passed. Nineteen men of the village were elsewhere at the time, working nights. They were identified, rounded up and shot on the following day. In all 192 men were shot. They were farmers, tradesmen, workers, miners and civilians. Innocent too.

Further along the path is the common grave where the executed men were interred. A cluster of tall trees surrounds a small square burial site. Nearby I can see the footprint of St Martin's Church. The Nazis destroyed and levelled this church. Next door is what is known as the old cemetery. The Nazis destroyed this cemetery, uprooted trees, dug up human remains and desecrated the graves. They took film footage of the destruction for subsequent propaganda purposes, but this film later fortuitously served as document No. 379 at the Nuremberg trials of the Nazi leaders in 1946. The specific orders of Hitler were carried out in this brutal and arbitrary act of revenge: Send all women and children to concentration camps, shoot all men, raze the village of Lidice to the ground. The site was marked by notices forbidding entry. A report in the Reich press on the next day confirmed that *'the village of Lidice has been erased from maps'.*

But why? In 1942 the Czech government in London decided to assassinate security police chief ss Obergruppenführer Reinherd Heydrich, the so-called 'Butcher of Prague'. A subsequent commando-style operation by Czechoslovak parachutists led to Heydrich being fatally wounded. The vague contents of a letter addressed to a woman employed in a Czech factory roused the suspicions of the Gestapo that there was a connection between Heydrich's assassination and the Horak family in Lidice. They had a son serving in the Czechoslovak army in Britain. Although investigations and a house search produced no compromising material, weapons or transmitter, the Nazis wished to carry out an act of vengeance for the death of 'an outstanding man of the German nation', and for this they chose the 503 people of Lidice.

I walk back up the hill in silence. A small museum off the plaza documents the events which occurred. Inside there is an audiovisual presentation about Lidice, with footage of families at work and at play, farming and mining, fairs and sport, weddings and schools, then footage of a raving Hitler and the Nazis. In the next large room the first items I see are the two tall wooden doors of St Martin's Church, which, despite demolition by blasting, survived intact. In another amazing feat of religious survival, there is a small figure of Jesus Christ, along with a photograph showing that the statue came from the crucifix on the altar of St Martin's Church. The statue is damaged, with arms and legs blown off, but it is resurrected.

There are cameo photographs of the victims, each one looking more ordinary than the last. A Gestapo photograph of the dead bodies piled up against the wall of the Horak farm house is projected onto one entire wall. The stone farmhouse barn is so much bigger than I expect, being two storeys tall and the length of several homes. Realisation is dawning that the village of Lidice was a much more substantial place than I feared. There are four idle German soldiers standing over the bodies, staring at them. I see the crumpled mattresses. The bodies of the men all lie in the same direction, facing their enemies. None of them tried to run away. The projection is life-size and I am conscious that I stand amidst the aftermath of a terrible crime. The collection in the Museum is entitled *'And Those Innocent were Guilty'*.

After the war the Czechs held a memorial service in June 1945 which 150,000 people attended. They pledged to rebuild Lidice. New homes were built in 1949 only 300 metres away and residents moved in. 17 of the lost children returned to the new Lidice. 143 of the lost women returned. Other nations, horrified at the events, renamed their own towns. Today there are villages named Lidice in Mexico, Panama, Illinois and Brazil, squares and streets named Lidice in 15 more countries, and a Lidice Square in Coventry.

I take one last look at the village. Below me workers lovingly tend the lush meadow. The smell of freshly cut grass and the blooms of the rose bushes wafts through the air. Other visitors walk about the site and stop to remember. The acts perpetrated by the Nazis here will never be forgotten. Their plan to erase this village has had quite the opposite effect. Lidice will always be on my map of Europe.

The Low Fares Airline (1)

THE LAW FARES AIRLINE

A mum who gave up her job to go on a budget holiday with a difference has spoken of her life on the hoof living out of a rucksack. Jenni Stevenson, 42, from Dorchester, planned a trip around Europe and North Africa after hearing about Ruinair's offer to fly for £1. When she realised she couldn't get time off from her job as a senior prison officer she threw caution to the wind and resigned. She has planned to take 10 flights and visit six countries over the next few weeks, paying just £1 for each flight except for the last leg which was not covered by the offer and cost £14.99. Continuing the no-frills theme, she is keeping costs down by staying on campsites and travelling with hand luggage. Speaking from France, Mrs Stevenson said: 'It's everything I thought it would be, and more. Because I've only got hand luggage I've had to buy a tent each time I arrive in a new place. I've been thinking of shaving my hair off so I don't have to bother with shampoo and conditioner.'

THE DORSET ECHO

THE LOO FARES AIRLINE

Ruinair may have a reputation for being bog-standard, but even regular passengers on the low fares airline expect to be provided with toilet paper. The basic provision of loo roll was too much to ask, however, on a Ruinair flight from Spain to Dublin earlier this month. Passengers on board the 10.15 p.m. flight from the holiday resort of Malaga in Spain were astonished when cabin crew announced that there was no toilet roll in any of the bathroom cubicles. The flight was packed with holiday-makers, including many small children, who had to endure the three-hour journey without standard toiletries. One passenger said: 'The air steward was making the usual announcements about food and drink being available for purchase and just at the end, she abruptly added at the end of the announce-ment: 'And there is no toilet roll on this flight.' We thought we had heard incorrectly until one of the kids wanted to use the bathroom and we found out for ourselves. There was no soap either, for that matter. I was angry because I felt that having paid for the flight, the least you can expect is to be able to use the toilets and be provided with the basic products to do so hygienically.' Curiously, Ruinair management insisted the company had 'no record' of the lavatory malfunction, despite it being a big talking point amongst all those on board the flight. A spokesperson for Ruinair said: 'We have no record of this whatsoever, but we are looking into it.' She emphasised that the toilet roll budget has not been removed as a cost-cutting measure by the company. 'We would like to let passengers know that there will continue to be toilet paper on Ruinair flights.'

IRISH INDEPENDENT

THE LOW FEAR AIRLINE (1)

To most of the passengers on the Ruinair flight from Sardinia to London, the five black men sitting quietly in the economy cabin were nothing more sinister than fellow passengers. But to the psychology professor seated near them, they could only be terrorists. For one thing, they were sitting apart when they had been together in the departure lounge which could only be suspicious. Worse, one of the group acted as if he was blind but was reading newspapers and mag-azines. After he went to the pilot saying the aircraft was in danger, Captain Sam Dunlop had the men removed from the aircraft. The five members of Caribbean Steel International were awarded £1,116 each in damages yesterday after a judge found that they had been removed unreasonably. Far from being terrorists, they were returning from a music festival in Sardinia. The court heard that the musicians were not sitting next to each other because the flight was full. The band's drummer, Michael Toussaint, was indeed blind and one of the other band members had been reading the football scores to him from a newspaper while they waited for take-off. Captain Dunlop decided to remove the men, the only black people on the flight, after two families and a stewardess said that they would not fly with them on board. Summing up at the Mayor's and City of London Court yesterday, district judge Roger Southcombe said that the five claimants had been scared and embarrassed when Italian police armed with guns boarded the aircraft to take them off. Although they were later cleared by the airport's security, the men had not been allowed to reboard the Ruinair flight. The judge said that Captain Dunlop had adopted a 'zero tolerance' approach, despite being informed by the airport authorities that the band posed no threat. 'Captain Dunlop considered that he must enforce that policy even though the residual fears of a few passengers and crew were, he must have known by then, irrational,' the judge said. 'Just because a passenger was black or someone did not like the look of him or her, it would not be acceptable to offload that passenger.' Ruinair had also lied about the incident to the press. The airline's head of communications had told newspapers that 'airport security were informed and decided to remove the group', and that 'no request was made to our pilot to allow this group to reboard'. This was 'false and misleading', the judge said.

THE TIMES

THE LOW FEAR AIRLINE (2)

A tanned yob sparked a security scare on a plane after he made a gun gesture with his hand and told a woman passenger: 'You are my next victim.' The woman freaked out because she thought he and his 'dark-skinned' mates on the Ruinair flight looked like terrorists. Nearly 30 other passengers also became frightened that the plane was in danger and bailed from the flight before it took off. The captain asked police to board the plane as more and more travellers started to become unsettled. The yob and his two pals—all Brits tanned from a holiday in the sun—were booted off the jet from Girona, Spain, to Doncaster because of the incident and ordered to catch a later flight.

THE SUN

THE LOW FEAR AIRLINE (3)

A family were treated like terrorists when they were banned from boarding a Ruinair flight because one of their passports was 'well thumbed'. Kathy and Kevin Higgins were due to fly to Barcelona with children Ellen, 12, and 15-year-old Jack for a half-term holiday. But check-in staff at Bournemouth airport stopped Mr Higgins, 56, from boarding the Ruinair flight because the laminate coating on his photograph was peeling, apparently posing a security risk. Mrs Higgins said that, when the Servisair check-in representative accused them of tampering with the passport, he just looked at her and said: 'Do we look like terrorists? What are you trying to say?' 'Another supervisor said she would call the police and have us removed from the airport and arrested under the Prevention of Terrorism Act. They used it to frighten us. I was in tears. They treated us like criminals.'

METRO

THE LOW FUSE AIRLINE

An airport had to be evacuated when a woman tried to board a plane with a Second World War bomb in her bag. The 55-year-old was getting on a Ruinair flight at Bergerac when security guards spotted the Second World War shell while scanning her luggage. More than 1,000 passengers and staff had to be evacuated. The woman, flying home to Nottingham from France, said she bought the 37mm explosive it in a junk shop as a present for her husband. Police said: 'She said she didn't realise it would cause a fuss.'

THE MIRROR

THE LOW VOLUME AIRLINE

A doctor is threatening to take Ruinair to court after he claims the airline was heavy handed and threw him off a flight for talking during the safety briefing. Dr Paolo Tomasi, 47, was ejected with his eight-year-old son after a hostess had told him not to speak during the safety briefing and not to lean across the aisle. Dr Tomasi, from Hampstead, London, was flying from Sardinia to Stansted and was talking to a colleague while the plane was taxiing and staff were giving the safety demonstration. He said he was asked to 'be quiet' by cabin crew and then minutes later another hostess appeared to tell him that he had already been warned about talking and that he should not lean across the aisle as he was distracting crew. Dr Tomasi said: 'First they said I was talking loudly. I wasn't. I was talking normally. And then they said I was leaning across the aisle. I said jokingly "Well what can you do on Ruinair as everything seems to be banned." The hostess then stormed off and said she was going to speak to the captain about me. The doors had already closed and the plane was moving and it stopped. The captain came on the Tannoy and said the plane was stopping because of an unruly passenger and I was then told to get off the flight. I had to pay another £500 for tickets.'

DAILY MAIL

THE FARE RIGHT AIRLINE

Protesters plan to picket the far right Austrian politician Jorg Haider when he visits London to promote a Ruinair service to Austria. Mr Haider, infamous for praising Hitler's employment policies and lauding ss veterans, is hosting the press launch to mark the start of a scheduled service between London and Klagenfurt, where he is governor. Although the airline's name appears on the press invitation, Ruinair is not organising the event and a spokeswoman said: 'Politics doesn't make any difference to Ruinair.' But Julie Waterson, national organiser of the Anti-Nazi League, urged the airline to condemn Mr Haider. 'Ruinair should say to him that he's got no right to use their name. By allowing him to use it, they are seen to be endorsing him.' The Anti-Nazi League has dubbed the no-frills airline 'Aryanair' for allowing its name to be associated with the former leader of the xenophobic Freedom Party.

THE GUARDIAN

Poland

Flight CO298 – Friday @ 1.30 p.m. – DUB-GDN-DUB

Fare €10 plus taxes, fees and charges €68

Centralwings is 20 per cent owned by the Polish government via the national airline Polskie Linie Lotnicze SA, otherwise known as LOT, or Cost a LOT. As such they run the risk of being regarded as a political gesture, proof that a state-run airline can go low. They are the baby of the industry, a mere three years old with only five Boeing 737s, flying from seven Polish cities. Centralwings' motto is S.P.E.E.D., which stands for Self-management, Passion, Exceeding Expectations and Delivery, the last buzzword presumably meaning that they intend to deliver me to my destination, which is reassuring, but all in all it's a collection of sound bites best left to waffling management consultants. Their CEO says on the airline's website, 'Every take-off is a magical moment which, in spite of its aerodynamical justification, fascinates me and gives me shivers of excitement', which means that he is amazed yet excited that an aircraft can take off from Mother Earth.

The all-female cabin crew sport dark tailored trouser suits with a scarlet blouse and knotted scarf. The crew are all Central European but this is wonderful because this is a Central European airline. We have assigned seating, which as usual means total bewilderment for those passengers who are unaware row 3 follows row 2, and row 4 follows row 3, and so on. One apparent virgin sits in row 2, reacts sheepishly when questioned as to his rightful place in life and is banished back to darkest pits of row 26.

We take off one hour late and receive the textbook explanation from the captain (a late incoming aircraft) but I don't glean more than this because the captain's English is much like my Polish. The only Polish I know is that *Solidarnosc* means solidarity. Our take-off is terrifying because the captain is in such a hurry that he puts the foot to the floor as the crew are mid-safety demonstration. The cockpit door swings open violently with the thrust so the cabin supervisor jumps out of her seat and slams the door shut. This happens three times as we speed down the runway but each time I have a great view of the pilot pulling the aircraft skywards. During the flight the same supervisor enters the cockpit without using the security keypad by the door, which I thought was designed to avoid a recurrence of box cutters, 9/11 and all that.

It's another flight from hell. We travel in a jaded B-737 with tattered sunken rock-hard seats. Screaming babies sit forward and aft, port and starboard. There is no in-flight magazine. There is a *Café Menu* placed in a rack at the front of the aircraft but I cannot read menus 20 foot away. Ordering a coffee means that I am offered a white Styrofoam cup filled with boiling water plus a sachet of Nescafé granules and a tub of UHT milk and left to brew my own. I learn 1 Polish zloty equals 100 groszy which in itself is enough reason to join the eurozone and get cents. The captain has the air-conditioning set on the Sunday Roast setting. I terrify a small boy when I enter the WC while he is mid-flight, so to speak, and his mother isn't too impressed either. No one else on board is Irish because no one in Ireland has ever heard of Centralwings but I know of them because I am the world's greatest living expert on European low fares airlines. It's my hobby along with philately, numismatics, train-spotting and at the weekend I go mad and play competitive league Ludo. Our aircraft is full so there are passengers all around me shouting in Polish. The girl beside insists on raising the armrest between us which I put back down until she looks at me.

'Have you been to Poland before?' she asks.

We are not bonding. 'No, it's my first time.'

'Is it pleasure or business?'

'A bit of both. I'm writing a book about low fares airlines in Europe.'

No evident reaction from her. 'How long will you stay for?'

'Three days.'

'Such a short time.'

'Long enough for a chapter.'

Still no reaction. I guess some folks don't read books. 'Do you know someone in Gdansk?'

Gdansk has 460,000 inhabitants. 'Nope.'

'Are you being met at the airport?' she perseveres.

'No. I've been away before on my own.'

We continue to fight over the armrest until we land, cockpit door closed. 'Welcome to Poland.'

Poles clap wildly upon landing but also like to unbuckle their seat belts, jump up out of their seats, open the overhead luggage bins and stand in the aisle ready to deplane; this is done at 100 mph whilst on the runway only seconds after touch down. As I blink in row 3 the guy from row 21 stands beside me in his hat and coat, three bags in hand and already on his mobile as we are still taxiing to the airport apron. I grab a taxi outside the airport and feel at home immediately, what with all the Polish-registered cars about.

Of the Polish low fares destinations, Gdansk is the second easiest to pronounce, when one considers alternative destinations such as Bydgoszcz (pronounced 'byd-goshch'), Szczecin ('shcheh-cheen'), Rzeszow ('jeh-shuff'), Lodz ('woodge'), Wroclaw ('vrots-wahf') and Poznan ('poz-nan'—easiest). Gdansk Airport is named after the city's most famous son. My lasting memory of him was not making speeches from the tops of shipyard walls with his fantastic bushy moustache, but it was in the 1980s BBC satirical show *Not The Nine O'Clock News,* which was on at 9 p.m., but not on BBC1. The *'Hollywood Salutes Lech Walesa'* sketch patronised Hollywood attitudes to serious issues in other countries, the main theme of the sketch being a series of brutal name mispronunciations by various US TV news anchors: *'Leech Wurlitzer'* for example.

A complimentary travel guide to Gdansk available at the airport information kiosk opens with the following sentence: 'If you've arrived by train your journey into the old town is straightforward; sidestep any drunks mumbling to themselves, then put your head down and speed straight through the subway full of women selling cut-price underwear, then hey presto you are in the historic centre.' Ulica Dluga is the main city thoroughfare (Polish for Long Street although it's only 300 metres long and it was complete rubble in 1945), and it was formerly known as the Royal Route along which Polish kings and wealthy merchants passed. Sadly the Golden Gate end of the street is spoilt by a bar called Rooster, modelled on the US Hooters chain, where Polish girls in tiny red shorts and low-cut white T-shirts with pictures of cocks dispense pitchers of beer to blokes. Next up are pleasant buildings such as the Executioner's House and the Prison Tower. Further on a cinema features a movie called *Strajk*, or *Strike*, about the events here 25 years ago, which has aroused local controversy because one of the female characters, a sacked shipyard worker, has been given many personal issues to deal with, and we all know that would never happen in reality.

Outside the Town Hall there are not one but three statues of Neptune, a throwback to the city's illustrious maritime past as a great Baltic port in a storm when the once-mighty Teutonic knights ruled. During its Golden Age Gdansk was a wealthy urban republic and a melting pot of cultures and ethnic groups. The old city streets are a fusion of Gothic austerity, Renaissance elegance and Rococo splendour and their waterside homes are richly decorated with gilded statues, ornamented facades, tall gables, pinnacled roofs and decorative stonework, reminding me a little of Amsterdam and attributable to a history of trade with the Flemish. There is so much culture, art and history here that Americans could only dream about it. There are more burgher residences than burger joints. Artus Court is one such beautiful home and its banquet room proudly boasts the worlds largest tiled stove, so there.

Around the corner is the Motlawa river and quays where a small ferry will take you across to the other side for one Polish zloty (no taxes): a low fares ferry. Here too is the symbol of Gdansk, the biggest wooden medieval port crane in Europe, which was set in motion by men treading on the steps inside giant wheels to lift loads up to five tons. The street terminates at the Green Gate, which is actually a grand gatehouse and home to Leech Wurlitzer's office, as evidenced by a plaque at the door with the great man's name, although much like Anne Frank's house in Amsterdam, Leech is not at home when I ring the bell.

Gdansk belongs to the Hanseatic League, a medieval Common Market of towns in Germany and adjacent countries for the pro-motion of trade and commerce. As with most major leagues in Europe, each year the top three cities go through to the Champions' League, the next two cities enter the UEFA Cup and the bottom two cities are relegated to the Greater Baltic Conference League, where matches are played on snowy pitches in front of 100 fans on a Monday evening and can be seen on the Sky Sports 175 channel.

One of the finest Hanseatic buildings is St Mary's Church, the largest brick church in the world. The view from the church tower is of a toy town below but it is 400 steps to the top and I'd rather go to the gym. Inside the church is harsh and austere with un-dulating flagstones, sheer white walls and a sub-zero temperature. The vast interior holds 25,000 people and it was here that Solidarity members once sought sanctuary, although they must have had big coats. A few of us in the know congregate at the right time and take a pew by the 13-metre-high fifteenth-century clock. Reassuringly on cue at noon the clock springs into action, maybe Adam and Eve appear, Jesus appears and does an abbreviated version of the Macarena, Adam or Eve toll a bell and it's all soon over and I want my Polish zloty back, if I had paid any. Far more impressive are the bells at the top of the *Rathusz* which play a merry tune for five jingly minutes or more.

Gdansk was once the match that set Europe alight. Prussians and Russians fought until Gdansk became the independent Free City of Danzig in 1919, linked to what was then Poland by a narrow corridor through German territory. The nearby Westerplatte peninsula is where the first shots of WWII were fired. At 5 a.m. on 1 September 1939, the German battleship *Schleswig-Holstein*, in town on a 'goodwill visit', shelled the Polish garrison. A mere 182 Polish soldiers fought 2,600 Germans plus their artillery, planes and ships, before they surrendered after seven days of hopeless fighting. The irony was that the German ship was built in the Gdansk shipyards yet revenge was sweet when it was well and truly sunk off Gdansk in 1944. There are organised cruise day trips to

Westerplatte but public bus number 106 is a sort of low fares alternative. Another maritime disaster in the Bay of Gdansk was the sinking of the German cruise liner *Wilhelm Gustloff* in 1945, hit by three torpedoes fired from a Soviet S-13 submarine. Freezing temperatures, over-crowding and lack of lifeboats meant that only 500 of the 10,000 civilians, refugees and troops survived, a death rate seven times that of the Titanic—and you don't see Hollywood's Leo and Kate making a movie about this disaster. The Russians awarded the honour of Hero of the Soviet Union to the captain of the submarine.

Amidst weeping willow trees I encounter a steely monument to Polish Post Office Defenders and investigate the true heroics of these usually peaceful workers. On the same day in September 1939 the Germans besieged them in their post office yet they resisted 14 hours of shelling until explosives were detonated in trenches dug under their place of work. The workers fled to the basement, which the Germans filled with gasoline and set alight. Five Poles burned to death and the first two Poles who surrendered waving white flags were shot on sight. The remaining 38 Poles surrendered and were put on trial, denied a defence lawyer, sentenced to death and executed by firing squad, but remained to their very last breath civilians. Outside the post office are brass signs with the names of the deceased and untranslatable words such as 'Hitler ss Bojowkiss' so that whoever comes here to buy stamps or mail a package never forgets. The museum, much like postal services, does not always operate on a Saturday.

A 15-minute walk away along Lagiewniki brings me to much more recent history. It's impossible to become lost because the cranes tower over the city like tenuous skeletal grappling limbs. It's hard too to miss the stainless-steel 42-metre-high tripod Monument to Fallen Shipyard Workers, which commemorates the events of 1970 when 44 people died after the army was ordered to fire at striking workers. The three crosses symbolise the three workers who were killed outside the shipyard gates while the anchors represent faith and hope. Leech has referred to this epic monument as being like 'a harpoon driven through the body of a whale—no matter how hard the whale struggles, it can never get rid of it'.

At the base of the statue there's a dedication by Pope John Paul II, who declared that 'beside this monument, nobody can walk by indifferently'. There's a modest tribute to Father Jerzy Popieluszko, Solidarity's chaplain, who was murdered by the secret police. A glass urn contains earth sprinkled with the blood of shipyard worker Jozef Widerlik, killed here in 1970. Nearby is a statue to King Jan Sobieski which is notable only for being the starting point for many Solidarity marches and demonstrations during martial law. A souvenir shop sells items with the classic icon of the Solidarity logo: chunky red letters crammed together to represent people walking shoulder to shoulder, straightening their backs in defiance. This place is so famous that popstar Jean-Michel Jarre has played here—he's the guy with more lights than music.

Nearby are tough residential areas with broken pavements, filthy cars, blokes wheeling used furniture between apartments and so many people going through bins that a communal garbage collection is unnecessary, but nothing is as tough as the shipyard workers who pass me by as they finish their mid-afternoon shift. They exit through the famed shipyard gates, last seen on TV news bulletins when I worried that the smiling mechanic with the big walrus moustache was on a serious hiding to nothing and was going to come off second best, but which gates now display all the Poles hold dear: their national flag, the Vatican flag and photographs of the Popes Benny and John Paul II. I find Solidarity Square a calm and empty place and it belies its historic significance in redefining the national borders of Modern Europe. There are experts who will argue about the fall of Communism but it all began here.

The 'Roads to Freedom' exhibition chronicles Solidarity. There is a reconstructed Communist-era shop with nothing to purchase but sawdusty bread, lard, vodka and vinegar. The shop has a bacon slicer identical to the one used in rural Ireland, where a grocer once placed a sign on his meat counter advising *'Would mothers please not place their children up on the counter, since we are getting a little behind with the orders.'* There is the red-brick wall upon which an unemployed Leech climbed in August 1980, made an impromptu speech and found himself thrust into the spotlight as the hero of the protests.

Inside the BHP trade union hall I hear they have the same four tables where the trade union versus government talks took place (the official end of talks score per FIFA being Solidarity 1, Government 0), a room so authentic that they include the used ashtrays and the ballpoint pen used by Leech to sign the August Accords. These addressed the strikers' 21 demands which were drawn up by hand on two plywood boards and hung on the gates of the shipyard, and which included free trade unions, the right to strike, the release of political prisoners and uniquely a full supply of food products in shops, kindergartens for the children of working mothers, a decrease in the waiting time for apartments, a reduced retirement age for men of 55, paid maternity leave for three years and a day of rest on Saturday.

The brochure for the exhibition contains striking photographs: the shipyard gates festooned with flowers and religious objects; the massed workers attending a working mass; rows of armoured personnel carriers opposite the gates, later daubed with Solidarity posters; youths with sideburns waving red and white flags, street riots, running battles, tear gas and bloodied civil faces; printing presses; the Pope; a victorious Leech with clenched fists held aloft on the shoulders of comrades; Leech in a new suit sitting in the Parliament beside a not-so-happy General Jaruzelski; a Nobel Peace Prize; Leech becoming Poland's first post-Communist democratically elected president; the fall of the Berlin Wall. I recommend you visit although when I was there the exhibition was shut down for renovations, or that's what the nice lady in the tourist office told me, but others say there's a dispute over who owns the exhibition. More solidarity please.

Leech has seen his influence wane and his party won a miserly one per cent of the vote in a recent general election. He suffered his share of political blunders, such as his decision to appoint his chauffeur and table tennis partner as an advisor. Leech does not work full time and only engages in work that interests him, such as when he welcomed the Miss World girls to the Gdansk shipyards. There is a beer called *Lech*, although I'm told it is no relation. At the grand restaurant called Gdanska, a few steps from my hotel, there are pictures of Leech dining inside with one chair for his wife and another for his moustache (he turned down a million-dollar offer from Gillette to shave off his moustache) and his favourite dish here is Polish Pork Ribs in Sauce. And if anyone ever asks you where Leech met his wife—it was at the Gdansk.

Because of Leech there is full democracy in Poland yet when I visited, the Prime Minister and President of Poland were identical twin brothers and while the President lives in a grand palace with his wife, the Prime Minister, single, 57, lives at home with his mum. He has admitted in interviews that he does not have a bank account and he gives his salary to his elderly mum. And when he lost a general election he had to hand his letter of resignation to his brother, the President.

Ruinair are not popular amongst Polish politicians. First they ran an advertisement following the government's 'laughable' education sector pay rise advising teachers to follow the hundreds of thousands of fellow Poles who have left for Ireland and Britain since Poland joined the European Union and to leave a country 'run by a bunch of comic strip characters'. Later they ran an advertisement suggesting a romance between the Prime Minister and a single blonde 50-year-old female deputy, featuring the two of them under the headline 'Are they thinking of a honeymoon?' A comic book speech bubble showed him asking her, 'Shall we take the government plane?' to which she replied: 'There's no need, Ruinair guarantees the lowest prices.' The Polish media has long speculated about a possible relationship between the premier and deputy. *'I am shocked. This is a scandal. Illegal exploitation of the image of the head of government is a crime. Ruinair must pay for this,'* the deputy fumed. Does she know Ruinair pay for nothing? The Ruinair press machine went into sound bite mode at a threat to sue. *'We always welcome decisions by politicians to sue, but she would save a lot of time and money if she opted instead to take a break with one of our £10 fares.'*

Mick, there's simply lots to do in Gdansk after you've seen the shipyard wall: enchanting streets, Hanseatic sights, maritime museums, city tours, seashore cruises, art galleries, cosy bars, dusty cafés and don't forget about that brick church and the medieval port crane. This is the birthplace of modern Poland where shipyard workers overcame their chains and a world superpower. And Leech Wurlitzer is the man who did most to unfold this Iron Curtain, and without him, no low fares airlines would be flying to Poland, or to anywhere else in Central or Eastern Europe.

Postscript: A few months later I find the following notice on the Centralwings website. *'The management of Centralwings Airlines in cooperation with* LOT *decided to implement a reorganisation program which will allow to achieve profitability of Centralwings. Beginning with the second half of the year the company starts the process of massive increase of charter and charter-mix flights in the general amount of flights. Centralwings aircrafts will operate only the charter routes. The management decided to suspend the unprofitable regular flights until further notice. The suspension is caused by the fact that the present market condition might have imperilled the company's stability.'* Another one bites the dust. LOT's advertising slogan is *'You're under our wing,'* when I would prefer to be sitting alongside the same wing.

Mick will be delighted. *'Three airlines in the United States have gone bankrupt in the last month. Alitalia is teetering on the edge of bankruptcy. Clickair is losing so much money they don't know what to do. Sky Europe will probably go bust. Wizz Air, it's harder to say. As for Vueling, I wouldn't take it if you made a present of it to me. If Vueling was losing money with oil at $65 a barrel then it's bankrupt at $95. Air Berlin is lost. I wouldn't book a ticket on Air Berlin this winter. We'll be very happy to see them all go bust.'*

Annual General Meeting

The unlucky shareholders in Ruinair gather on the third Thursday of every September at 10 a.m. This year we are in the Radisson Hotel at Dublin Airport, which is not a no-frills destination but a rather plush four-star place across the road from Ruinair's HQ. I sneak in past the man on the door and I pray that he does not recognise my surname on the shareholder attendance card. We are a mixture of retired folk, airline industry analysts from Dublin's last few remaining stockbrokers, the media and other assorted loonies, including myself, plus some same faces that I recognise from last year. I grab a free cup of coffee, my first ever from this airline, and note that there are no Kit-Kats this year. It's a sign of the times. I take a non-reclining window seat near the speakers' podium. Outside a few hundred Ruinair aircraft come and go.

Some of the directors arrive and begin to take their seats, dressed in their best suits and ties. The TV crews arrive, then more press photographers. The crowd swells but there are 50 empty seats—more than remain empty on your average Boeing 737-800 flight. A Ruinair PowerPoint slide is projected onto the screen. A name tag for Mick appears on the table and naturally Mick is in the centre of the table. At five minutes to the appointed hour, Mick appears. It's important to blend in with the Chief Executive of Europe's lowest airline so I have donned a blue open-necked shirt and some scruffy jeans. *'People think I do this because I'm some sort of a rebel, but it's not. It's just very easy to get up in the morning and find a blue shirt and a pair of jeans. You don't have to think.'* But my attire is all wrong because Mick has a fashionable pink stripey shirt, two buttons open at the neck, sleeves rolled up, worn under a navy windcheater coat, plus his trademark jeans and glasses up on his head. The ensemble clashes with a rather dire blue check handkerchief which Mick has occasion to use. The photographers immediately snap him up. He hands out a hard copy of his presentation to the other Directors so it looks like he does his own photocopying. He walks to the rear of the room where he even pours his own coffee. The photographers stalk him as he greets a few stockbroking suits on the way back. Forget Bertie (and his daughter), Bono, Roy Keane, Pádraig Harrington and the rest. This is Ireland's greatest living celebrity. Lights, camera, action. Man.

Mick stands in front of the slideshow and holds up the Annual Report, the cover of which screams, '*No Fuel Surcharges. Guaranteed lowest Fares*'. The cover does not mention check-in fees, baggage fees, wheelchair fees, credit card handling fees, etc. Mick grins at the photographers, contorts his face into various poses from sheer force of habit and finishes with the photo opportunity, where he gives us the two fingers.

A chart shows that Ruinair is the world's biggest international airline with 51 million passengers per annum, ahead of Lufthansa's 41 million and Air France's 32 million. They do not add Air France and KLM together, which totals 54 million passengers. A related press clipping shows Southwest Airlines' name but not their 95 million passengers. '*I do not know of any other industry in Ireland where the Irish have an indigenous company that leads the world. We will soon end up with four large airlines in Europe, we will be the largest, then Lufthansa, Air France and BA. We will be the only ones keeping the big buggers honest.*'

In the past 12 months the Ruinair fleet has propagated further by 30 aircraft to 163 of the damn things. '*Approximately 123 aircraft will be delivered to us during the next three years at a cost of just over $10 billion. It was probably one of the best aircraft purchase deals ever done, but one did not need to be a genius to work it out immediately after 11 September 2001 when airlines were cancelling orders left, right and centre and Boeing and Airbus had no order books. Three months after 11 September 2001, we showed up and were able to write a cheque. We bet the shop by writing a cheque for $500 million, but it* *was a calculated bet as the industry is cyclical and the time to buy air-craft is always during a down time. I grew up on a farm in Mullingar and farmers start buying when everyone else is selling. We are all planting wheat because the price of grain increased. It is an Irish trait. It is why we have dominated transport.'*

The aviation fuel bill has jumped to €800 million. *'Fuel prices have doubled in the past 12 months and we have almost no hedging in place. As a result of that we are unlikely to make any money this year. That will be the first time in 20 years that we have not made any money. There's no harm making a quarterly loss once in a while. There is absolutely no harm in losing the mythical horseshit that we can walk on water. The times you test the mettle of a company is when it's losing money. The world is in shite and there's going to be lots more fucking bad news this winter.'*

'Clearly anybody who didn't hedge oil a year ago couldn't possibly claim that they were on top of their game. I screwed up in the last year. The good thing is that if I fuck it up or lose my touch it costs me more money than almost every other shareholder, since I'm one of our biggest shareholders. We haven't a bull's notion of where the price of oil will be tomorrow or next week or next month. But we continue to believe that oil prices will fall. I think they will fall back to below $100 a barrel. I just don't know when. I have no idea and, unfortunately, neither does anyone else. Even people involved in the oil business don't know where the price of oil is going to be. On fuel prices, even if the price of oil rises to €250 a barrel, we will still not levy a fuel sur-charge. However, in those circumstances, we will probably be the only airline still flying in Europe and a one-way fare to Paris will be €22 instead of €16. This is one of the few islands in Europe and we do not have the option of cycling to the Continent.'

The formal meeting begins at 10.03 a.m., three minutes late, which is unprecedented with Europe's most punctual airline. *'We don't 'claim' to be the No.1 on-time airline. The official statistics of the Civil Aviation Authority confirm that we are the No.1 on-time airline.'* James, the meeting chairman and legal expert, speaks to summarise another year of stellar financial performance with passenger number up 20 per cent to 51 million punters, 201 new routes, three new bases, revenue up 21 per cent to €2,713 million, profit after tax up 20 per cent to €480 million, earnings per share up 20 per cent to 32c per share and the average fare fell by only 1 per cent to €44.

But in the past 12 months the Ruinair share price has fallen from €5 to €2.00. Ruinair is only half the airline it used to be. *'I do not worry about our share price as we are a long-term project. I love this. It is much more fun when the world is falling apart than when things are boring and going well. We had been saying fares and margins would fall. What we didn't foresee was that they would come down this bloody quickly.'* Mick owns 65 million shares. Mick has lost €200 million on paper since we last met here. *'I am not losing any sleep over it. The only time you lose money is when you sell shares. And I'm not selling.'*

We pass some quick resolutions, one to approve the accounts, then to approve the re-election of directors. We re-elect David Bonderman of the USA as a director. He is the company Chairman and despite my attendance at three AGMs, I have yet to see him in person in Dublin. He is much like a unicorn—sometimes talked about, but rarely seen. Mick explains David's absence. *'David is in Washington. He has a lot of financial investments. He is a great guy to have on the Board. And we get him for free. Some loons from some corporate governance group wrote to us to say that David had been a director of the company for ten years and that good corporate governance says that he should step down as a director. Feck off.'*

The resolutions tabled at the meeting are all passed because James has 800 million proxy votes in his back pocket and there are about 50 of us in the room and we are only small shareholders. Except for Mick. We pass a technical resolution to allow Ruinair to email us next year's Accounts rather than printing 25,000 copies, which James says is a Ruinair green initiative but I suspect is another cost-saving initiative. James finishes the formal business mercifully quickly. 'Mick will make a short presentation. I suspect that is the reason why most of you are here today. Now for the Mick O'Leery show.' You bet.

Mick remains an expert on hosting these media events. Once when beginning a press conference in London to announce results he said: *'I'm here with Howard Millar and Michael Cawley, our two deputy-chief executives. But they're presently making love in the gentlemen's toilets, such is their excitement at today's results.'* On another occasion he began as follows: '*Welcome to the Ruinair press conference, the only press conference where you can identify the person who is lying because his lips are moving. Everyone at a press conference is telling lies. I thought that was the first rule of journalism school. We had the first press conference since the bank holiday and I thought we'd have the whole day to ourselves. And then fucking Marks & Spencer goes and sacks someone. It's only women's knickers. Relax.'*

Mick launches into his sound bites. 765 routes, 147 airports, 30 bases, 1,000 daily flights. Superb customer service statistics. The Dublin Airport Authority's charges. The uselessness of the Irish Aviation Regulator. The disaster that is Aer Lingus's new Belfast base with its 50 per cent load factors. Aer Lingus's directors who are '*fat cats sitting on their arses*', including the trade unionist '*Brother Begg*'. Airline failure and consolidation all over Europe. Hapless flag-carriers around Europe who couldn't find your baggage if their life depended upon it. Paddy Power taking bets on which airline will be next to fail in Europe and they are already paying out on Alitalia. The price of a barrel of crude oil. The '*regulatory goons*' in the EU blocking Ruinair's takeover of Aer Lingus to create our very own new Irish airline monopoly. The greenest and cleanest fleet in Europe. Mick stops in mid-sentence. '*Oh, what do we have here?*'

A guy walks past my aisle seat and stands right beside Mick. The guy is wearing only a pair of black trousers. At first I think that perhaps it is Mick's birthday and someone has ordered him a male strippagram. But on his chest are written the words, '*Exposing O'Leery's Lies*'. It is a credit to Mick that he does not immediately do a John Prescott and level the guy with a clenched fist to the upper jaw. There's a moment of fear in the room where we wonder if something a little ugly is about to happen. The guy starts mouthing off about the airline's appalling environmental record and that higher taxes will stop the pollution. He claims that the airline flies 12 million passengers a year but he is badly out by a factor of four. There is no security present at the meeting. I am amazed that this guy got inside here. This airline is obsessive about identity. Didn't they ask him for his passport? Others try to usher the guy away but he is not budging. Mick reacts superbly. '*Leave him there. Which bunch of eco-loonies are you with?'* The media sense an event and they rise to their feet and cluster around the two combatants. Let the verbal battle commence.

Mick has said it all before. *'Most people when they are asked the question, 'Do you want a better environment?', say yes. But will you stop buying kiwi fruit in Sainsbury's because they've been flown halfway round the world? No. Talk is cheap—free, in fact. And it makes people feel better. But the reality is ... look out of the window, what do you see? Rain. It's pissing rain. This is the middle of August. The skies are grey and the forecast is continued rain. Those two political leaders, Brown and Cameron, are pandering to the chattering classes, so one of them is taking a holiday on a wet beach in Suffolk and the other is down in Cornwall. They should be flying off for two weeks in the sun like the rest of the population does.'*

'Don't call it climate change, because climate has and always will change. If it's global warming you're talking about, the jury's out. Global temperatures decreased from 1945 to 1975. They rose between 1975 and 1998, and from 1998 to 2008 they have been absolutely flat. Does that mean there is no global warming? I genuinely don't know. But what we do know is that man-made CO_2 emissions account for less than 10 per cent of total CO_2 emissions, and air travel accounts for just 2 per cent of that 10 per cent, which is 0.2 per cent. So get on with it. Go fly and enjoy your holiday.'

'We can put more passengers in our planes, we have a fleet of new aircraft that are more fuel efficient, we take less weight. Entire Brazilian rainforests of waste come off BA's *aircraft with all that extra packaging, the ancient planes, the waste of space in business class. Bugger bicycles—I drive a car and a tractor, I have a herd of 600 cows on my farm who probably make a more damaging impact on the environment than my airplanes do. This global warming nonsense is no different to some of the more lunatic movements you've had throughout history. They were excommunicating Galileo 500 years ago for suggesting the Earth might go round the Sun. Now the nut-bag ecologists say we're boiling the planet to extinction. This is just the crazy idea for the first decade of the twenty-first century. All this climate change stuff is an inevitable by-product of a ten-year period of economic growth and low unemployment. Now we have a*

recession you'll hear an awful lot less about the bloody environment.
We might be talking about a depression. I would be very bearish for
the next four or five years.'

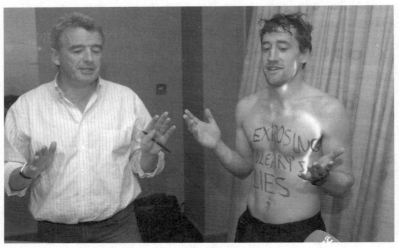

Heated Debate

To be fair, Mr Ray Mac from Lahinch in Co. Clare, who has an
English accent, is never going to win a war of words with Mick. No
one has ever won a war of words with Mick in the 20 years of
Ruinair's rise to global fame. They exchange verbal slings and
arrows but Mick has a sound bite riposte for every old accusation.
'Are you finished yet? If the climate heated up by a couple of degrees
Ireland could have a nice Mediterranean climate. Nice and Marseilles
would be a desert. Tourists would flock to Ireland. Mullingar would
be the new Marbella.' It's game, set and match to Mick in minutes.
The topless Ray Mac makes for the door. Mick sounds a parting
shot. *'Thank you for enhancing the publicity for our AGM. Can you*
organise a female for next year? I'm happy to have a climate change
debate with anyone, particularly if you are female and particularly if
you are topless. Don't get me started on the environment.' Then an
aside to us when Mr Mac is gone. *'He will fly off to join his other eco*
loony friends on holiday in Spain.'

A defeated Mr Mac replies from safety. *'Mick, you're a star. It's*
nothing personal.' True enough. Mick doesn't know it yet but Mr

Mac's pals from the environmental pressure group Plane Mad have hung a large blue and yellow banner on the exterior of the Radisson Hotel with the words *'Lyin'Air.con.'*

Mick follows up this spat later the same day on the airline's website. *'We are sending this semi-naked man a copy of the European Union's Environmental Agency report which confirms that air transport accounts for less than 2 per cent of Europe's CO_2 emissions and is neither the cause of, nor the solution to, global warming. I hope in return he'll send me some of what he's been smoking on the Costa del Clare.'*

The meeting concludes with some questions from the shareholders in attendance. One elderly lady behind me asks, 'Why don't you have a woman on the board?'

Mick replies. *'We would love to have a woman on our board. One of our most senior people, Caroline Green, and I don't mean to be politically incorrect here, is obviously a woman. But we are not putting a woman on our board just to cover our arse.'*

The lady perseveres. 'We could have a former politician on the board. Like Mary Robinson. Or Mary Banotti. Or Mary O'Rourke.' There is no reaction until Mick visibly recoils at the last name.

A studious girl, who may be a pal of Ray Mac, asks Mick about peak oil, which is the technical term for the point in time when the maximum rate of global oil extraction is reached, after which the rate of production enters terminal decline and basically oil is gone and we are all screwed. Mick isn't bothered. *'Peak oil may run out in the year 2150 or 2200. You won't be here. I won't be here. Frankly I don't care.'*

I ask the last question. I spent a year trying to get their website to work since the upgrade. 'Do you accept that the website changeover was poorly executed? Have you fired anyone for the shambles?'

Mick replies as ever. *'We did not fire anyone. We had some initial problems which lasted for four to six weeks. The servers kept crashing. We used to take 12,000 bookings per hour but we were once down to 2,000 an hour. It even affected ourselves. We are the one of the biggest users of the airline and our staff couldn't make bookings. The new website will allow us to take 200 million bookings per year.'* Terrifying.

Six days later that same notice appears on Ruinair's website. *'Due to system problems, access to our flight booking system is currently slow. Please note that it may take up to 30–60 seconds to move from page to page during the flight booking process. Although the booking process is slower than normal, bookings can be completed, but the delivery of the confirmation travel itinerary may be delayed.'* I rest my case.

No one asks when Mick is going to retire. *'Probably never, is the answer. I was very hungry through my twenties to make a lot of money. I thought the first £1 million was going to be like multiple orgasms, the greatest night of your life. But nothing. It's a very unsatisfying experience, because once you've made a lot of money you couldn't care less about the money any more. What are you going to do with it? At a certain point, don't ask when it is, money stops being important. I don't go to work five and six days a week because I want more money. I don't come to work because I need to put food on the table for my family. I come to work because it's fun. I do it because I enjoy it. It's far better than poncing around on a beach somewhere. Since I got married I usually take one holiday during the year but if I can avoid it I will.'*

The annual meeting concludes after an hour. We give Mick a spontaneous round of applause. He hopes to see us all again next year. It's been an excellent and entertaining way to spend a Thursday morning, almost as good as taking a flight. As the elderly lady behind me says to me, 'That was great craic.' If you have €2.50 to spare (that being the cost of one Ruinair share at the time of writing) and you don't wish to take a flight with it, I recommend buying one Ruinair share. Shareholders are guaranteed admission to the Annual General Meeting (you cannot legally be barred even if you have written a book).

In return for your investment you can see Mick in full flight for one hour and there is no greater known comedian operating on the Dublin entertainment scene at present. *'I will trip up at some stage. I'm not God, I might like to think I'm God, but I'm not. I am very humble, shy and retiring. It is my humility that makes me the success I am today and also the fact that I am caring helps too. I'm a genius, but I'm just too humble to say so. Ruinair has been a phenomenal success despite my leadership.'*

Slovakia

Flight NE151 – Tuesday @ 7.50 p.m. – DUB-BTS-DUB

Fare €28 plus taxes, fees and charges €20

SkyEurope Airlines is a rarity in the world of European aviation: it is a beautiful low fares airline. Headquartered in Bratislava, with bases also in Vienna and Prague, flying to 41 destinations in 17 countries, using 15 eponymous Boeing 737s, with 700 staff and four million passengers per annum it has outshone all other low fares carriers by daubing its aircraft fuselages with photographs of stunning svelte Central and Eastern European supermodels. First was blonde bombshell Miss Austria, Tatjana Batinic, followed by Slovak Wonderbra model Adriana Karembeu, who is married to a French soccer player whom she met on a flight. How come I never get seated beside a supermodel on my frequent Ruinair flights? The *Adriana* aircraft was used to transport Pope John Paul II on his pilgrimage around Slovakia, and he was presumably unaware that Adriana's legs from the top of her hip to her heel measure an amazing 126 cm.

The most recent addition to what this airline calls its *'Beauty Fleet'* is Hungarian Benedek Muriel, who was deemed the most beautiful girl at a Miss World Hungary contest and so became Miss *'Face of SkyEurope'*. Ms Muriel, 20, is studying philosophy and communications at the University of Arts and Sciences in Budapest and in addition to her mother tongue, she speaks English, German and French, and she loves travelling. And no doubt she also does a lot of good work for charity, she assists elderly people across the road and she craves world peace. I read too that her very secret dream is to become a flight attendant, which may not be all that secret now, dear. Note that only three aircraft in their fleet are so decorated; any further decoration would be what is generally known as pornography. Based on these representative aircraft exteriors, plus the formerly noted Miss Austria featuring on the airline's website sporting only a red string bikini plus a glitzy tiara, I greatly look forward to my first flight with SkyEurope.

Onboard the welcoming crew sport smart grey and red uniforms with ruffles last seen in *The Three Musketeers*, along with flattering white blouses and red cinch belts. The crew are helpful and personable, enthusiastic and happy: everything that's missing with Ruinair. The CEO, Mr Bitter, says SkyEurope's motto is *'low cost with a human face'* and *'our biggest novelty is not aircraft, it is our people'*. Based on the crew I encounter at 36,000 feet, Mr Bitter is not wrong. Slovaks bring along much cabin baggage; most have bulging Dunnes Stores bags but the better-off display sides of smoked salmon from Wright's of Howth, a pricey shop I can only dream about visiting. I have an assigned seat near the front. This airline is another well-kept secret since I am certain I am one of the few Irish people on board. The interior is pristine with blue leather seats with red trim and natty red seat belts. I learn that the aircraft is only a few weeks old, so new that it emits that new-car smell which we enjoy more usually on a garage forecourt. The *Sky Delights* menu includes caprese sandwiches with pesto genovese, mozzarella and chives, plus they offer smoked salmon. The crowning glory of the stylish menu is a black and white photograph of Mr 'Gorgeous' Clooney downing a Nespresso coffee. *'Coffee, body and soul. What Else?'* The Nespresso caffe leggero (only €4) arrives in a white ceramic cup with matching saucer and a spoon, like something you would receive in a restaurant.

The in-flight magazine, called *Runway,* has a spread on Adriana at a photo shoot. More Beauty. *Q: 'Do you still have any travel dreams—a place you would like to visit, Adriana? A: Maybe Canada and India, because I have never been there. I'm also thinking about Australia.'* Er … dear, you are loaded. Go fly. *Q: 'What do you like to do in your leisure time? A: I would like to learn to sew because I have lots of ideas. I often go to the tailor.'* Er? There is an article on women pilots. SkyEurope employ 166 pilots but only five of the pilots are female. A female pilot opines, *'Female pilots are absolutely normal women who enjoy flying.'* I learn that not content with being beautiful, Sky Europe is also in love and so created a world kissing record on the last St Valentine's Day. With the help of crew and passengers, they broke the world record for the number of kisses in European airspace, being 2,214 kisses on 84 different flights. There is plenty of evidence in the *Runway* photographs of passengers exchanging DNA saliva samples one mile high but it's not clear whether the participants were happily married couples or even happier solo passengers. The magazine concludes with some SkyEurope fun facts which advise that a Boeing 737-700 has 58 km of cables and 367,000 screws, the latter being slightly less than in the United States prison service.

This aircraft has ABS since shortly after take-off there is a severe case of *Angry Baby Syndrome* as the babies seated near me begin to scream in unison. This could be a long flight. I don't know why their parents tolerate this noise since they could have gone to that room in the airport terminal and told the staff there, 'Look, I have this baby but it screams a lot of the time, so could I swap it for a quieter baby?' You know the room that I mean. You will have seen it. It's the *Baby Changing Facility*. Later the babies calm down and begin to totter about the aircraft, as parents converse with other parents. The cabin crew do a remarkable job in calming both the babies and myself. They dispense free packs of snacks to the babies. Now you don't see that too often when flying on Ruinair. If ever. Snacks might cost money.

The two-and-a-half-hour flight flies by and we land on time at M R Štefánika Airport, named after General Milan Rastislav Štefánik, whose aircraft crashed above Bratislava in 1919. Exactly what I needed to learn. Slovaks clap enthusiastically after we land but I suspect it is primarily because we are not flying on Ruinair today. A bendy 61 bus takes 20 minutes to reach the main train station. All is well on the bus until we stop outside an IKEA store. The bus is invaded by locals with bulging brown paper bags and unfeasibly tall green plants which will not fit inside the bus and must be laid sideways. But I am impressed that such a new nation has an IKEA store since the Republic of Ireland, founded in 1922, is as yet embarrassingly IKEA-less.

Bratislava is Europe's youngest capital, established after the collapse of communism in 1989 in the Velvet Revolution, and the subsequent split of Czechoslovakia in 1993 in the Velvet Divorce, where the Slovaks got one third of the land surface while the Czechs got two thirds of the land surface, plus the kids, cats, dogs, family home and the CD collection. Slovakia calls itself the Little Big Country since it is only 450 km from west to east. Bratislava is the Little Big City. It is a young city with eight universities and 60,000 students. All female students on first appearance look rather like Adriana's twin sister.

Bratislava is the place that puts the central into Central Europe, located on the Danube halfway between eminently more fashionable Prague and Budapest, and only 4 km from the Austrian border. I am not the first tourist to come here: the Celts, Romans, Germans and Slavs came long before. The best orientation view is from Bratislava castle, originally built by the Romans at the very frontier of their empire, where I climb high so I can survey the three countries of Austria, Hungary and Slovakia. I am one hour's drive from their ex, the Czech Republic. The castle is a square building with tall towers at the four corners, resembling an upturned table with legs akimbo. I am lucky to be standing here because this castle suffered the indignity of being accidentally burned down by drunken Austrian soldiers stationed here during the Napoleonic Wars. It lay in ruins until it was rebuilt in the 1950s so it's not as ancient as it first appears.

I take a peek inside to prove that the castle stairs are very wide with a shallow gradient because the Hapsburg Empress Maria Theresa, too heavy to climb the stairs herself, insisted on riding her horse up and down the steps instead. I don't begrudge her this luxury because in her lifetime she had 16 children. George W. Bush met Vladimir Putin in this castle and Bush later told the White House press corps that he had been in Slovenia, which sounds similar enough to Slovakia, but nevertheless is an entirely different country. I don't stay long because inside there is an exhibition of Ancient Chinese Minority Costumes.

Across the road is the Parliament Building, an ugly white Communist-era building. The view of the *Stare Mesto*, or Old Town, in the other direction is magnificent, with Baroque palaces and the Gothic St Martin's Cathedral, all nestling below the dramatic Carpathian mountains that sweep down to the river, which is genuinely blue. Below trams trundle along the tree-lined banks of the Danube, and boats bob at their moorings. The great Dane Hans Christian Andersen once called this 'the most beautiful city in Europe' in one of his least eloquent literary moments. When the culture becomes too much you can go shopping. Tesco are here. They make two billion sterling every year and as they say about their annual profits: *Every Little Helps*. I don't begrudge them their profits but I am the only person they ever declined for a Club Card.

Not being one to engage in work when someone else can do it for me, I arrive at the tourist office for the two-hour walking tour of the Old Town. The official literature describes Bratislava as *Beauty on the Danube*. Not unexpectedly our tour guide is another local beauty who should herself be officially classified as a UNESCO world heritage attraction. Katka is a student with perfect English prose and better poise. There are three guys on this tour: myself, an American guy and an Englishman. If I can lose them both in the next two hours then Katka is mine for the day, and mine alone, and all for €13. I always enjoy going on publicly available tours where there are only two or three of us, or even only me. I can get the benefit of their knowledge and when free-loaders try to eavesdrop I can shout at them, 'Get your own guide.'

Katka likes anecdotes. The tower of The Church of the Sisters of St Clare was paid for by a knight who lusted after a novice nun. The mother superior told the knight he could marry the nun if he built the tower. He obliged but the mother superior changed her mind and shipped the nun off to another parish. The forlorn knight went to the Crusades but he never married or loved again. Clearly he should have got a good lawyer and sued the mother superior. Bastova Street is narrow and dark and few pedestrians use this short cut to the Old Town. Katka explains that in the Middle Ages the town executioner lived here and he would hang his bloody axe on a hook outside his home. Legend had it that if you walked by and the axe moved, then you would be up for the chop before the year was out.

In medieval times the city could only be entered through one of four gates, one of which remains. We stop under the Gothic Michalska Gate, where we learn another legend has it that any lady who talks whilst walking underneath will never find a husband. I stalk a couple of trainee supermodels through the gate and yes, their incessant chatter ceases. This must be a great spot to bring the mother-in-law when on holidays. Here too is 'zero point', which shows the distance to many world cities, a spot admired by both tourists and rough local chaps looking for spare Slovak crowns. Beside the gate is the narrowest house in Central Europe with a façade measuring only 160 cm wide, but it's still bigger than any Dublin apartment.

Katka points out the 'beer tower' of the Franciscan Church, so called because the bell was rung for closing time as non-residents left the city before the gates shut for the knights for the night. We pass the Carlton Hotel, where another legend has it that a former owner once checked his accounts and found he was bankrupt so he climbed to the fifth floor to jump to his death, only for others to later check his maths, find that he was wrong and prove that he wasn't bankrupt at all.

We pass a house where a boy called Wolfgang Amadeus Mozart played a concert aged six, and a boy called Franz Liszt did the same aged nine, both presumably as part of a pilot version of the *X-Factor* TV series. Under our feet 178 shiny brass crown logos are embedded in the pavements to signal the route of the former coronation processions. In the main square there is a statue of Knight Roland and legend has it that if you see the statue move you will have great fortune. The statue is stone so it doesn't move much. However on New Year's Eve in 1999 the town authorities hatched a cunning plan, swapping the statue for another version in the dead of the previous night and revolving the statue around on the stroke of midnight of the new millennium, sending the assembled crowds into optimistic delirium.

Katka points to the pink walls of the Primate's Palace. 'There are *Goblins* inside.'

I let her comment pass for a few minutes but I need to know more. 'Sorry, you said *Goblins*?'

'Yes, many *Goblins* inside. Many wonderful *Goblins*.'

I am lost. 'Are you sure? *Goblins*?' She nods. I drop my open hand lower. 'Nasty little *Goblins*?'

Katka is puzzled. 'The *Goblins* are hanging on the walls.'

I don't know what the *Goblins* ever did to deserve this fate? 'On the walls? Animals?'

She shakes her head. 'No. Like what you walk on.' I am still no closer. 'Like rugs on the floor.'

We are now closer. 'Like carpet?' I suggest.

'Better than carpet. They are special ... tapestries.'

'But you said ... *Goblins*?'

'Yes. *Goblins* is same word as tapestries in English.'

'Not exactly. Small animals. Like Gremlins.' I get a few more laughs from Katka as she repeats the word *tapestry* for the next hour. The six tapestries were only found when the Archbishop sold the palace to the city in 1903 so they cannot be that wonderful. I worry there are thousands of American tourists who go home to Kansas and Ohio in the US of A and tell all their friends. 'Jeez, Norm, we had a great time in Bratislava but you wouldn't believe: There's this real neat palace but it's full of goddamn goblins inside.'

The Baroque Old Town (like many of the locals, I am beginning to notice) is perfectly formed and in an excellent state of repair. I struggle to maintain my concentration despite Katka's excellent delivery. At first I think that our tour is taking us through that part of the city where all the model agencies are located, but not so. There are no more beautiful ladies here than in any other European capital but those that are so remain off the very far end of the Richter Scale. Girls like wearing jeans so tight they would have to jump off the top of the wardrobe to get into them. Some say the display of feminine beauty in this part of the world is a throwback to the political resistance of some 40 years' standing. Katka tells us there is a hill memorial to the 6,845 Russians who died 'liberating' the city but she makes sure to mime the quote marks. The Russians did liberate Bratislava. Problem was they took 40 years to go home. So during the Prague Spring, for example, young ladies in short skirts set out to torment the gob-smacked invading Russians. The latter had seen nothing like it but, of course, found every love object achingly unavailable. If I was based in Bratislava in the 1980s I would be on to my commander looking for a rapid posting to Siberia.

If I may digress, and I am not an expert because I have only been to all 27 countries in Europe, but I do not understand how any Slovak man chooses a wife because as soon as he gets hitched to the most beautiful girl in Slovakia, another two or three will come along immediately. I am even more distracted when in the city's leading new shopping mall on a Saturday afternoon. There are security guards here whose legitimate job is to examine everyone here closely. What an amazing job. Even the mannequins in the shop windows are more attractive than your average mannequin in Europe. There is only one unattractive girl who is resident in Bratislava and I can confirm that she does not go out very often.

I make very modest progress (I get a few laughs and prods in the shoulder) and Katka hints that her favourite bars are Medusa and Havana (frequented by fashionable folk otherwise known as the *Brat Pack*), the best coffee can be had at Antik Café and the best sports bar is *The Dubliner* but there is no way I am frequenting an Irish bar when I can do that at home. Katka asks if we have any last questions and I am about to ask her about her plans for the rest of the day, but instead I ask her if she knows the fastest land animal and she correctly answers that's it's the cheetah. We go our separate ways with heavy hearts.

Even banking is beautiful in Bratislava. There are offices here called *Bank+Coffee* and when I peer inside they are more like the interior of a Starbucks than a GnatWest, although they are proper banks. They have comfy leather seats where customers lounge and have a latte with their friendly bank manager who tells them very nicely that they are 10 grand overdrawn, and by the way the latte costs another fiver.

After the tour I sit outdoors at a café on Venturska Street and engage in a local sport. Katka told us that after soccer (at which the Slovaks lose to the Czechs) and ice hockey (at which the Slovaks are former world champions) the most popular sport is

Bratislavan Tennis. This involves ladies walking and rows of males sitting in outdoor cafés watching the ladies walk past, the admirers' eyes moving left to right, like spectators watching a long rally on Centre Court. It's a very exhausting sport and after half an hour I am longing for match point as two ladies appear in SkyEurope uniforms and I scratch my eyes. This style of direct marketing is much appreciated by the crowd. The girls teeter towards us in their ruffles to hand out leaflets advising that SkyEurope is the first airline in the world to offer fares for a minus price, since they are offering to pay us €1 to fly on their airline. So well done to them for innovation (later on their website I see I can indeed fly for minus €1 but it will be €40 to return home a few days later). This is the same airline who will later send me an email at Christmas time advising Santa is giving away free flights to *'all those who were good this year ... and didn't fly with Ruinair'.*

It's a hazard of sitting in any outdoor café in Central Europe that eventually eight English blokes on a stag will pull up the chairs beside you and shout at the waiter for eight beers and then have a 10-minute chat about how fucking cheap the beer is. This time one of the guys, who claims to have climbed the stanchions at Wigan's rugby league ground in a wedding dress, announces there is a fast ferry to Vienna.

'What time does it leave, Lance?'

'Leaves at ten thirty. And comes back at four thirty same day. You get five hours in Vienna.'

'That's not a long time there, Lance.'

'Long enough to get pissed there.'

Later a local youth with most likely a genuine physical disability runs along the street in a visibly awkward manner. One of the stag guys raises a beer glass and shouts after him. 'Run, Forrest, run.'

The Bridge of the Slovak National Uprising traverses the Danube and dominates the city. Pushed out of public life and losing their seats at the university for opposing the Russian invasion, the two Slovak architects who designed the bridge did not even receive invitations to its opening in 1973. The Soviets refused to credit them, lauding instead the cosy workers of the State Planning and Design Institute on the memorial plaque. I walk along the pedestrian route at the lower level, keeping my head down as cars zoom above. At the top of the 85-metre-high single-pylon cable-stayed structure is a restaurant and night club shaped like a UFO. Eighty-five metres is the same height as the significantly more appealing castle on the other side of the river. I take the elevator skywards where in 40 seconds I am invited to *Watch, Taste and Groove.* I do some watching, the restaurant is closed so there's no tasting and I am not grooving at midday cold sober. The view north to the Old Town is glorious, sunshine glinting off the domes, retaining so much splendour and seeming so spacious that it feels like a city built for a much larger population. However the view south from the observation tower is an entirely different matter and initially I am in utter shock.

In 1866 the district of Petrzalka had 594 inhabitants and 103 houses. Now 130,000 people live in this 28-sq-km area: one in four of the entire population of Bratislava. The result is the most densely populated place in Slovakia, and in all of Central Europe. Residents live in *panelaks.* Where one or more *panelaks* are gathered together, and this is usually the case, they are referred to *panelaky.* They are identical pre-fabricated pre-stressed 12-storey apartment blocks knocked up in the socialist period in Czechoslovakia, assembled in much the same way as Dublin property developers jerry-build apartment blocks overlooking the M50 motorway (some of these Dublin apartments are openly advertised as being *'Exclusive'*, so much so that I sometimes wonder if they would ever sell one of the apartments to someone as common as myself). There is an entertainment venue where only Duran Duran perform. Pope John Paul II came in 2003 to say Mass amidst the *panelaky.* The local soccer team, Artmedia Bratislava, crept into the Champions League and thumped Celtic 5-1. But from this distance, Petrzalka appears to be the ultimate concrete jungle, an entire suburb of shocking uniformity and stark ugliness. I count the tower blocks from a safe distance and lose count after 100 piles. Vaclav Havel, a former president of Czechoslovakia, called these *panelaky 'undignified rabbit pens, which are slated for liquidation.'* They are still here, Vaclav.

To reach the *panelaky* is an achievement in itself. They could not be more isolated; perhaps this was the town planners' intention. I watch youths tumble down grassy embankments and others escape across slip roads. I cross eight deadly lanes of speeding motorway traffic via an overpass. Residents pass me in the opposite direction: groups of mums with kiddies in prams, three or four abreast, stubbled men in tracksuits of working age going nowhere fast. At ground level youths play soccer on barren pitches and Alsatians roam voraciously. If this was anywhere else in Europe I would be afraid but I must be safe because one in four Bratislavans cannot be criminals. There are stand-alone shops selling magazines and cigarettes, constructed like bunkered gun emplacements with metal bars over the windows. Tattered flags from some long-forgotten celebration wave from random flagpoles. The streets are pitted and potholed, end walls are graffitied and street signs are bent and twisted. Trees sink into concrete pots and above me grow forests of TV aerials. The ground floor shops seem utterly useless to the residents' needs: banks, solariums and slimming clubs. Up close the apartment blocks are in an advanced state of decay: peeling paint in depressing brown colours, broken windows, rusted shutters, busted railings and crumbling walls. I almost break my neck on the pavement slabs which undulate like hills. The workmanship here is staggeringly bad. I sit on the remains of a bench and I wonder about who lives in a place like this.

From the direction of the car park stacked with old Skodas up on bricks and dusty Ladas decades well past their MOT date, a girl appears. She is in her mid-twenties and is a student, judging by her mid-afternoon return and the academic books underneath her arm. She walks close by and we make eye contact. She smiles voluntarily, then looks slightly embarrassed and momentarily the gloom lifts. She is like so many of the beautiful locals I have seen. She graces the Old Town with her presence in her time off from college. She opens a creaking door to the ground floor and disappears from view. She is home. Here in Bratislava, as in every corner of Europe, beauty lies within.

The Low Fares Airline (2)

THE LOW CARES AIRLINE (1)

A kidney patient said he feared for his life after an airline left a case with his vital medical supplies behind. Colin Price, 43, who is on a transplant list, said he was shocked when he discovered his dialysis fluid had been left at Bristol Airport after he had already boarded a flight to Spain. 'I felt as if I was being left to die,' he said. 'I was told the airline head office had agreed there would be no charge for carrying it but when I got to Bristol they wanted to charge me £137 excess baggage. A supervisor at Bristol Airport read the letter I carried with me from my consultant and the charge was then waived and my bag went through. I got to the Costa Brava but discovered they hadn't even put my bag on the plane. It wasn't as if there were a couple of bandages in the case. I need the fluid to stay alive. I had to go by taxi to the hospital for supplies but I could only have half the daily treatment I needed.' Mr Price said staff at Girona were told because he didn't pay the £137 in Bristol his case hadn't been sent on. 'They let me get on the plane while my bag was left there.' Mr Price faxed a message from his hotel in Lloret to Ruinair in Dublin saying he needed the vital supplies. It eventually arrived two days late. 'I just couldn't wait to get back. I haven't had the amount of treatment I should have and now there's concern and I have to go to the hospital.'

WWW.ICWALES.CO.UK

THE LOW CARES AIRLINE (2)

A disabled woman from Northamptonshire had to be carried on to a plane over her husband's shoulder after the airline's lift failed to turn up. *Jo and Paul Heath from Rectory Lane, Milton Malsor, had booked a flight from Luton Airport to Brest in France through Ruinair. Mrs Heath, who has multiple sclerosis, had pre-warned the airline she would need help boarding. But the usual 'ambulift' device did not arrive, leaving 53-year-old Mr Heath with the option of either taking matters into his own hands or waiting three days for the next flight. Mrs Heath said: 'Ruinair staff said they couldn't help lift me for health and safety reasons. We asked what would happen if nothing was sorted out and they said 'We'd leave without you.' Mr Heath decided the holiday was too important to miss and hoisted his wife over his shoulder in a fireman's lift before struggling up the steps and on to the plane. Mrs Heath said: 'I was scared and very, very embarrassed by it and you could see other passengers were starting to get a bit ratty. I had done everything I needed to for Ruinair to get me on the plane. They failed in their duty of care for a customer.'*

NORTHAMPTON CHRONICLE

THE LOW CARES AIRLINE (3)

It was meant to be a stress-free holiday to Spain but for Lisa Aitken and her father, flying back into Bournemouth Airport ended up being a humiliating and frustrating experience. Lisa and her father Dennis Yorke, 82, who needs a wheelchair after having a back operation and suffering from a stroke, travelled from Romsey to catch a Ruinair flight to Malaga to visit her sister earlier this month. But their return journey turned into a nightmare after a booking Lisa had made for a specific seat on the plane was not upheld and the pair were made to pay extra for priority boarding despite being last to be seated. Lisa, 43, said the final straw came when they landed at Bournemouth Airport, and were told there were no trained staff to operate the ambulift needed to get Dennis off the plane even though it had been pre-booked. She said: 'We were made to sit in our seats for an hour while two of the staff tried to manoeuvre the lift into place. My father had to stay jammed into his seat, in a great deal of discomfort, while passengers for the next flight began boarding all around us. It was so humiliating for him. Eventually they had to carry him off which caused him even more pain. The most upsetting thing was the reaction of the staff who found it all to be a big joke and they were openly laughing about it while he was in tears. I have received an apology from Ruinair about the seats but it's not good enough. It shouldn't have happened in the first place.'

BOURNEMOUTH ECHO

THE LOW FARO AIRLINE

A holiday to Portugal was a welcome break for Mayo couple Michael and Mary Grealish, until it went wrong at the worst possible time— as their flight home was hurtling down the runway during take-off. The couple were sitting in their seats on the Ruinair aircraft, when they got a strong smell in the plane as it was accelerating down the runway. 'Next thing there was awful commotion down the back,' Michael told The Mayo News. 'The people down there were gone mad roaring and shouting "stop, stop, stop" and pressing call buttons because the smell was ten times worse there—it was a type of burning smell.' Earlier that evening, passengers were informed when they arrived at the airport in Faro for their 8.50 p.m. flight to Shannon that there was a problem with the plane, as birds had flown into one of the engines on the incoming leg of the flight. 'We saw the fire engines around the plane when we arrived at the gate to board but didn't pay any heed to this,' said Michael, 'and when we pulled up at the terminal after the aborted take-off we couldn't get off the plane because the wheels were red hot with smoke coming out of them from braking hard at such a speed.' After disembarking, the passengers were given little information, and it was around 11 p.m. before they knew there was no plane to bring them home. 'We were there all night moving from bench to bench trying to get comfortable and didn't get as much as a cup of tea or anything,' Michael recalled. 'There was no Ruinair staff there at all.' The following morning their flight was due to leave at 9.30 a.m. 'It was the same jet but just that they left it on the tarmac overnight.' At 1.20 p.m. on Sunday the passengers departed Faro. 'The pilot came on and said that all the problems had been fixed and that we could have free refreshments, but that amounted to a Mars bar and a can of Coke—which was their way of saying sorry for leaving us in an airport for 20 hours,' said Michael. 'I had to pay for a hotel in Shannon which I was supposed to be in on Saturday night but I wasn't, because I was lying on a bench in Faro Airport.'

THE MAYO NEWS

IL LOW FARES AIRLINE

Two couples ended up making a marathon train journey home from Italy after a flock of birds and a strike caused their flights to be cancelled three times. Howard and Tiree Cawthorne and their friends Scott and Gaynor Bradley ended up stranded in Rome for four days and their holiday cost them £4,000. Their ordeal began when a Ruinair jet made an emergency landing at Rome's Ciampino airport after a flock of birds was sucked into an engine. As a result, the airport was closed and their own Ruinair flight back to Manchester was cancelled, leaving them to go to their hotel and book another Ruinair flight the next day. But, as the airport remained closed, this flight was also cancelled and the friends had to book another flight from Rome's second airport, Fiumicino, with Alitalia. They couldn't believe their luck when this was cancelled as well when the crew went on strike. They ended up getting a night train across Europe and a ferry to Britain at a cost of more than £1,000. Howard, 49, and Tiree, 47, had travelled to Rome with Gaynor, 49, and Scott to Celebrate Scott's 50th birthday. After the return flights were cancelled, they caught a train from Rome to Paris, a second train to Calais and then a ferry to Dover. Their journey home should have taken two hours, but ended up taking 28 hours. The holiday cost them £4,400. Howard said: 'There was very little communication between Ruinair and its customers. It was chaos. We were left to our own devices. It was terrible, but when I was sitting on the train, I found it amusing. I just thought, "that's typical". It would have been easier to fly to New Zealand. It started as a cheap break, but ended up costing a lot of money. We could have gone to Barbados for what we paid.'

MANCHESTER EVENING NEWS

LE LOW FARES AIRLINE

Hundreds of Ruinair passengers were stranded at a French airport on Saturday night, including families who spent the night sleeping on foam mats in a school gymnasium. Around 600 travellers were forced to stay overnight in Grenoble after evening flights to Prestwick, Stansted, Luton and Dublin were cancelled due to high winds. Scottish holidaymakers described the 'chaos' in the airport as queues of hundreds of travellers struggled for information on hotels and alternative flights. Ewan Ogilvie, 41, from Glasgow, was one of 'three coach loads' of travellers forced to sleep on the floor of a school gym due to a lack of accommodation in Grenoble. The sub-contractor and his friends eventually made it back to Glasgow the following afternoon, after spending £1,000 among them on flights. 'It was absolute mayhem in the airport,' he said. 'There was no communication. We were told, "We have no information for you—basically stop asking us, go away." All there was was the airport service desk and the queue for that was so long that we didn't ever make it to the front. We were told that there were no hotel rooms available in Grenoble that night, so we bedded down in the airport, but then at 2 a.m. they announced it was closing for the night. Buses arrived to take us to a gymnasium where we slept on foam mats on the floor. There were blankets but not enough to go around. It was the attitude of Ruinair which shocked me. Any other airline would at least explain what was going on. But the airport was full of people stranded and unable to get information. It was carnage. There was no food, no accommodation and no subsistence. Basically, we were told, "You're on your own."

THE HERALD

EL LOW FARES AIRLINE

A group of 51 pupils and four teachers from the Gaya Institute in San Vicente del Raspeig and a college in Elda, had to spend Saturday night on the seats in Beauvais Airport in France after Ruinair cancelled their flight. One of the teachers, Faustino Barrio, said that Ruinair wanted them to get a train the following afternoon to another airport and pay an extra €245 per person. He says that no hotel was offered and they had to sleep in the airport. At 6 a.m. the police woke them up and took away two teachers who were accused of damaging airport furniture. Finally the matter was solved by their travel agent after representations to the Spanish embassy were also unsuccessful. The group finally made their way home in three coaches changing at Orleans and Barcelona and were due home at 7 a.m. this morning.

WWW.TYPICALLYSPANISH.COM

THE LONG FARES AIRLINE

A woman was stopped from boarding a budget jet because her name was too long. Ulrika Örtegren-Kärjenmäki would not fit on Ruinair's boarding pass. And the dots on the letters invalidated it in security checks at Stansted Airport, Essex. Furious Swede Ulrika, who was with her daughter, had to pay an extra £380 for a flight next day. The same problem happened but an alternative pass was printed and she was allowed to fly home. Ulrika said: 'I did not receive any explanation.'

THE SUN

THE LOW FANS AIRLINE

Ruinair has offered to fly rugby fans to Wales for free after a 'scheduling error' meant a flight on the Heineken Cup final weekend would no longer land in time for kick-off. Hundreds of Munster fans pre-booked the 6.50 a.m. flight from Dublin to Bristol earlier this year in the hope their team would make the final in Cardiff on 24 May, paying less than €50 before taxes. But, in late March, Ruinair told passengers that the departure time was being changed to 3 p.m. With Cardiff 70 km from Bristol and kick-off at 5 p.m., many fans took the refund offered. However, flight FR506 was reinstated earlier this month after Munster qualified at 6.50 a.m. on 24 May, with fares before taxes of €229. The Commission for Aviation Regulation said that the action appeared to be 'a cynical, commercial exercise' and it is being investigated by the National Consumer Agency. Ruinair boss Mick O'Leery told Newstalk fans could fly to Wales for free 'if they write into me before the end of this week'.

IRISH INDEPENDENT

Bulgaria

Flight NE 3204 – Sunday @ 4.55 p.m. – VIE-SOF-VIE

Fare €62 plus taxes, fees and charges €44

I would have preferred to fly to Sofia from Bratislava but SkyEurope only fly there from Vienna, 65 km away. SkyEurope are unique in the low fares airline business in having two bases so close together. The adjacent bases are required since while Slovakians will happily drive west to Vienna, their Austrian counterparts, being snobs, will not cross the Slovak border to drive to Bratislava. Mr Bitter of SkyEurope says, *'Austrians don't see Bratislava as a gateway. There's a mental block. It's close but they think it's far.'*

There is an excellent yet unexciting €6.50 bus service between Bratislava and Vienna but I cannot resist a trip at 60 kmh up the Danube on the *Twin City Liner* high-speed ferry service. Their €21 fare is not cheap but there are no hidden taxes, fees or charges. Like with Ruinair we stand in a queue long before departure, we must present a valid passport or EU identity card because this is exciting international travel, we depart and arrive on time, we travel on a modern jet-propelled steel craft and there is an onboard café selling drinks and snacks at Ruinair prices. Unlike Ruinair the interior is smart with real red leather seats, the first few rows are '*Reserviert*', amongst which I have a reserved assigned seat and there is a pleasant hostess in a smart red uniform to guide any idiots to their numbered seats. The remainder of the reserved seats are taken by a Russian tour group who do not like me being in their midst and give me Cold War stares. Their guide gives a running commentary in Russian but she is likely saying to them, 'Who is this guy sitting in our seats?' There is only one thing pushier than a Russian, and that's a wealthy Russian.

The ferry speeds past a rocky outcrop on the Austro-Slovak border. Americans nearby note as we cruise the EU's longest river, 'This is really a navigable channel.' There are souvenirs onboard to celebrate the closeness of the two cities: T-shirts for Wienislava and Bratiswien. We pass many small wooden riverside holiday homes set high up on stilts, complete with nets on big booms to catch dinner, where particularly tight Austrians can holiday without having to go too far, nor buy an evening meal. After 75 minutes I alight at the transport hub of Schwedenplatz and jump onboard a Vienna Airport Lines bus.

I am too early to check in so I play the waiting game in Vienna Airport's departures area, *'Find the Seat'*, of which I count approximately 15 in the entire building, and all are occupied. Passengers need seats on which to watch the world go by, to admire other passengers trying to check in more luggage than is kept in a Samsonite warehouse and to finish that last bottle of water before Security Control toss it into a bin. I do not venture upstairs to the Food Court which includes 'The Dubliner' *Genuine* Irish Pub. Airside I pass the *Beate Uhse* sex shop which advises us all to *'Sex up your Life'*. The Emirates junior boys' soccer team in matching tracksuits have somehow decided to sit on the floor outside the shop so they can peer into the open door at the various large protruding unmentionable plastic phallic objects. Their middle-aged coach wants them to move on but the boys are not budging for anyone but a Crown Prince, or higher.

The Austrian Airlines adverts advise us, *'You'll be Amazed At How Far A Smile Can Take You'*, but it's not as far as a few hundred tonnes of jet aviation fuel will take you. The other slogan used by Austrian Airlines is *'We Fly for your Smile'*. The slogan used by the flyNiki airline on the road to the airport is, *'The Passengers Come First'*. Who dreams up these advertising slogans? I agree with Mick's view of ad-men and their industry. *'They are all 40-year-old men with ponytails, black suits, black T-shirts and a big buckle on their belt.'*

The SkyEurope flight is as satisfactory as my prior experience. I note Bulgarians prefer to sit in any seat rather than their assigned seat, then wait for someone to ask them to move on, sit somewhere else at random and then wait till they are moved on again like a vagrant, and so on. The safety demonstration is shorter than on prior flights since we are not travelling over water and there is no life vest demonstration. If we are going down, then we are going down on Terra Firma. Full stop. The flight is uneventful save for a guy who brought a guitar on board and proceeds to take it down and play it. Badly. Planes emit enough environmental pollution as it is, without adding some noise pollution too. I want to ask the guy if he knows the tune called 'Somewhere Else', and if so could he play it, but this is not so easily done at 36,000 feet.

I have been to Bulgaria before but it was 20 years ago so I suspect matters have improved. Myself and three other equally broke UCD Commerce students went into a travel agent's (remember those?) on Bachelor's Walk and asked the lady for the cheapest two weeks to anywhere in the sun. She looked at a little Ceefax-style TV screen which was naturally hidden from view and, in the magical mysterious world of the travel agent, produced a trip for £199 to a place called Bourgas, which none of us had ever heard of. We flew to Bourgas on a low fares airline called Vulgaria Air and we ended up in a resort called Sunny Beach, which it wasn't, having neither of the two aforementioned qualities. We coined our own name for the resort as we enjoyed asking the locals on an hourly basis for directions to the resort of 'Son Of A Bitch'. We were frequently approached by locals looking to sell us Bulgarian currency for pounds, which became more entertaining once we discovered that there were 100 *stotinki* to each Bulgarian Lev. Aka 'stinkies'.

Having tired of waiting for the sun, played mini-golf and indoor bowling, eaten greasy chips, drunk cheap beer and terrorised smaller children on the not-so-sunny beach, we were so desperate that we often went shopping in the only Central Department Store in the resort, only because it was so grim. My memory is that this huge store only ever had about four or five items for sale, including rows of bottles of vodka and fridges stacked with foil-wrapped butter and nothing else. I have no idea where people went to buy bread or milk or meat. The fashion floor had rows of identical brown shoes, all made from shiny plastic rather than from leather. One floor of the store selling dire men's clothes was closed and cordoned off with ropes because the sales lady who worked in that area had rung in sick. The only item I bought in the store was a vinyl record (remember those?) to play on my trusty gramophone—Whacko Jackson's *Thriller*. I bought the record because it was a souvenir State pirated copy, it cost 10p and the vinyl was 1 inch thick. I still have the record today since it is bound to be worth something in the future, given that only about 100 million copies were illegally manufactured by the Communist Recording & Artists Production Co. (aka CRAP).

Sofia Airport is a large airport which is only short of a few aircraft. In a throwback to my last visit on my departure I notice the duty-free shops open at the incredibly early hour of 8.30 a.m. and in the wine shop passengers must stand behind counters and point at the bottle they want, for fear they might touch some of the special merchandise without a member of the sales staff being present. There are signs at the Passport Control booths which state that 'No Payments are Accepted,' so it's good to know that notorious bribery and corruption have finally been rooted out of Bulgarian society. The airport magazine contains a quote from John Steinbeck. *'A journey is like marriage. The certain way to be wrong is to think you control it.'* There are plenty of dodgy property adverts inside, one of which from Best of Bulgaria Property Developers has the confidence-inspiring motto of, *'If you did not buy from us, it is not our problem.'* The magazine also contains some Bulgarian phrases which are useful to know when visiting Bulgaria, such as (and I am being serious here), 'Good Morning', 'Good Afternoon', 'Good Evening', 'Write me a ticket, I am not going to give you any cash', 'I love you' and 'I want to marry you and bring you back to the United States.'

The OK *Supertrans* taxi firm is as the name suggests, although Lewis Hamilton could not have travelled the 10 km to the city centre any faster, and all for €4. Sofians drive very fast. Do not dream of hiring a car in Sofia. Ever. Bus lanes here are used by People Who Like To Undertake At Speed and by People Who Don't Think They Will Get Caught. My driver tells me that he has in the past driven the most famous Bulgarian in the world, striker Dimitar

Berbatov. Soon I crash in my hotel. It's been another typically relaxing day of low fares travel, with breakfast in Bratislava, lunch in Vienna and dinner in Sofia. It is reminiscent of the famous British Airways advertisement which once boasted breakfast in London, dinner in New York, to which some local wit scribbled at the foot of the advertisement: *Baggage in Jamaica.*

My first insight into Bulgarians this time comes from the looping in-house video on the hotel TV. Usually these are about the hotel services but here the video profiles the staff who work in the hotel, warts and all. They show a staff member who has been turned down by the local Theatre Acting Academy seven times. They show a manager who walks through the underground car park, past a Bentley, and he turns to the camera and says, 'Please don't film my car.' They show a PR girl who stops the filming with 'Wait. My office is in the other direction,' and a barman who says, 'I forget what I'm to say. Can we start again?' They show a manager meeting a businessman who finishes by offering his business card but then says (as per the English subtitles), 'Hey, but I don't have a business card, ha ha … shit.' This all warrants an Oscar. It's certainly better than the Bulgarian soaps, Turkish belly-dancing and fully-clothed Al-Jazeera weather girls.

Outside the streets are paved with gold. Swathes of bright yellow cobblestones conveniently link all the main sights of Sofia. These paving bricks were a wedding gift in 1917 to a Bulgarian Tsar from the Austro-Hungarian Emperor in Vienna. Imagine wading through your wedding presents from the great and the good, when excitement reaches fever pitch as you come to a gift from a real genuine Emperor only to be obliged to utter some words of thanks along the lines of 'So you got me a few thousand bricks?' The bricks would be an attraction in themselves if they weren't piled up on pavements or missing in other places.

This is the second oldest capital city in Europe, after Athens, and it is also Europe's highest. 1.5 million residents live in this city which has as its motto, '*It grows but it does not age*', which is a tad unlikely. Nedelya Square is at the city centre and it is a large building site. Around the periphery of the hoardings people emerge from underpasses or alight from wheezing buses and wobbly trams. Large ladies rush past with larger bags. Others sell bread rolls, flowers or giant brown bras from upturned Coke crates to the red-rinse brigade. Muscular Bulgarian former world shot-put champions recline nearby, along with their timid husbands. Occasionally a museum-piece red fire tender trundles along the street. Water gushes from open pipes and seeps away into cracked pavements and missing manhole covers. There are some open green spaces with glorious fountains and sculptures. There is a city park where old men sit in the shade and play speed chess on marble-topped chessboards, and try to hustle me to play too, where I would likely lose and have to stump up a few billion Bulgarian Lev. I carefully decline their offer since in Bulgaria, people nod for no, while a shake of the head means yes, although confusingly young people have adopted the usual Western approach to nodding and shaking. Overhead we are watched by the gilded 24-metre statue of St Sofia, after whom the city is named, her figure standing here since as far back as ... 2001.

I gravitate to the most impressive government buildings. Tallest amongst them is the former Communist Party headquarters which sports bullet holes in the walls but no red star. Across the road I am drawn to watch two soldiers in ceremonial nineteenth-century uniform who guard the entrance to the Presidency. They wear smart white and red braided tunics with a tall feather in their hats as they slouch up against the wall, rifle in hand, having a chat with each other, shutting their eyes for a rest and only brightening up when the Montenegran girls' soccer team stand alongside them for a sexy photo opportunity. Like all such guards they do a bit of ritualistic back-and-forth goose-step marching on the hour, every hour. The open-top city tour bus stops beside us and there are six people on board. There are not many tourists here. I hear only a few English voices which I suspect are courtesy of easyJet's London Gatwick to Sofia service. At midday another two soldiers in a jeep spit out their chewing gum, say goodbye to their girlfriends and march out to replace their two army chums who are exhausted after an hour's modelling. The performance is watched by as many as 10 tourists (including myself) plus police officers who stand by two police cars. One car is an Opel Vectra and the other is a

Porsche Carrera 4. Yes, in Sofia the police force has a Porsche. I bet the queue in the force to drive this car is as long as the average queue for Ruinair boarding.

The National Palace of Culture is not a palace and there is not much culture going on. It was built in 1981 by the daughter of a Communist-era leader who had a vision for a cultural centre for all the people, always a dangerous idea behind the Iron Curtain. It is an ugly windowless hive of a building of white slabs and brown metal, fronted by tiers of fountains where the marble is simply not laid straight. Right in front of the Palace I spy another fountain sunk into the ground below street level, which is invisible to passers-by. I peer into the stained brown basement and can only describe it as a subterranean toilet bowl. The Palace lies in a park where locals walk and play amidst untended lawns and broken paving. At the other end of the park stands a 40-metre-high angular monument celebrating 1,300 years of Bulgaria, and based on this monument there is not much to celebrate. There are brutalist Party figures and exposed girders in this monstrous monumental monolith. Again it has concrete slabs falling off and it is so knack-ered that it is surrounded by graffiti-hoarding to prevent more chunks falling down upon people's heads. It's as if the Bulgarians got all the worst architects in the Soviet Bloc and gave them a free rein here for a few decades. The worst eyesore building here is the Trade Union headquarters building, the same as in Dublin city.

I am unsure if the Bulgarians ever achieved much in history, considering that two of their heroes are St Cyril and St Methodius, brothers whose statues stand outside the fine National Library. These were the two wise guys who dreamt up the Cyrillic alphabet. What on earth possessed them to decide, at a time when most folks were happily using the Roman alphabet, to pen a second alphabet and to make the characters so damn difficult to decipher? Cyril lent his name to the alphabet and I guess his brother had a Methodius in his madness. To this day their alphabet remains an obstacle for me as most street signs are only written in Cyrillic and it makes my ambulatory pleasures next to impossible. Just be thankful that I did not try to learn the Cyrillic alphabet and have my publisher present this entire chapter in Cyrillic script.

Sofia is however one step ahead of Dublin in that it boasts a new underground train system. I enter the city centre hub station of Serdika, which contains Roman artefacts from the sixth century, and head towards the north-eastern suburbs. The trains are frequent, clean, air-conditioned, fast and impressive. The main problem is that this is the only journey which I can enjoy on the network. They have only built one line and even then they only built half a line with eight stations, so that from Serdika, commuters can only travel in one direction. It is a fantastic train system if one lives in Obelya but it's not much use yet if you live anywhere else. When travelling on the buses and trains of the Sofia Public Transport Company it is worth noting their advice on the signs at the ticket-selling kiosks: '*Your personal dog can be transpotrated (sic) with a muzzle and with a registered transportation document.*' Also if you get caught travelling without a ticket remember their cordial advice: '*Let us be tolerant in the relations passenger—ticket inspector.*'

Right beside Serdika station I spy another famed Central Department Store. I dash inside hoping for a flashback to my holiday of 20 years ago but I am badly disappointed. There are outlets for Tommy Hilfiger, Fred Perry, Lacoste, Nike, Adidas. There are four marbled floors, more fountains, funky piped music and the poshest public wc in the city. Luscious luxurious sales assistants pout back at the security guards who are not doing much securing. There is a *La Patisserie* and an espresso bar. This place would give Brown Thomas or Selfridges some serious blinging competition, and would appeal to the Mall-teasers who hang around Dundrum Town Centre. Sadly, the Central Department Store has been transformed.

Sofia remains a shoddy shabby chaotic city in need of expenditure. This is already underway on Vitosha Boulevard, the city's main pedestrian street for shopping, wining and dining. The street is named after the landmark mountain which is visible at the far end of the street. The Beautiful People parade up and down in skinny jeans, crop-tops, leather jackets, strappy stilettos, denim shorts, brand names and big sunglasses. I watch the same people walk up one side of the street, cross over and return on the other side, with no shopping bags in hand, only a desire to see and be seen. Everyone is on a mobile telephone and everyone smokes. They dodge the no. 1 tram which rumbles past to queue up at the Bulbank ATMs before money goes out of fashion. They double park their polished black Mercedes SUVs. Those left on foot stop in cafés and bars for beers, salads and cancer sticks. I watch some of them hop in and out of shops in between starters and main courses. Sofia is getting there, but slowly. And not by metro train. Progress will be tortuous. This is a city where I can buy postcards which are *individually* wrapped in plastic.

Sofia's single most memorable building is said to be the St Alexander Nevski Cathedral. It's very easy to locate because firstly, I follow the lovely yellow cobblestones, and secondly it's bloody huge. It was built to thank the Russians for freeing the locals from the Ottomans, a task which took 500 years. I worry that the Ottomans were a vicious bunch of Turks who pillaged through the East and forced their captives to sit on uncomfortable upholstered seats which had neither backs nor arms. From the outside the Cathedral is an impressive multi-domed gold and copper building but inside it's too dark to see the frescoes set high on the walls and ceiling and the only highlight is a few monks doing some sweeping. Outside there is a flea market where entrepreneurs sell antiques, babushka dolls and old LPs (Abba, The Beatles and even another old *Thriller* vinyl album). Mostly they sell historical military kit, holsters, medals, badges, helmets, blades and watches. There is a pack of pornographic Russian Army playing cards which feature topless Russian ladies in various poses and to be honest I would not like to tangle with the Queen of Hearts. I expected to see the relics with images of Stalin and Lenin but those with Nazi, Waffen SS, Iron Cross, swastika and Hitler images are disconcerting. I watch as closet sympathisers discreetly buy and sell this questionable German military history. Here for me the yellow cobblestones have lost some sheen.

Nearby I watch council workmen lay a new surface on the street. They use shovels and pick-axes to rip up the historic golden street paving. Diggers, trucks and machines stand idle until one worker gives up on a crooked kerbstone. In the cultural centre of this city, in a spot most frequented by all, they lay black tarmac. It is disgusting and it is undoubtedly a mistake. In any other city they would ask the Viennese for more yellow bricks (for free) and go paving. But the Sofians are at the end of the yellow brick road.

Readers' Emails

'I feel compelled to write to compliment you on the excellent work of literature you have provided to us (the travelling public). Though unlikely to ever feature on the Leaving Certificate, 'Ruinair' is a work worthy of Dickens and the like, although I have to say that without the rich and fertile material which Mick's crew provide you frequently, the task may be a little more difficult. This is without doubt an accurate and vivid account of one of the aviation world's biggest 'langers', as we say in Cork. Their philosophy is simple—travel as cheaply as possible and to hell with your health (mental or physical). With this in mind I carried your 'bible' with me on my travels. It is a great guide to the Lidl and Aldi of the airways and so many times I found myself on one of Mick's yellow pimp-wagons getting some sneers and looks of disapproval from the staff. On one such occasion an elderly lady leaned over and informed me in no uncertain terms that she found your book 'trite and childlike'—she couldn't understand why anyone might find fault with O'Leery shuttles and that the concept of writing a book to make money on the back of a hard-working industry-changing entrepreneur such as your friend Mick was to her an affront and in her words 'the book should be banned'. I found myself speechless. May God have mercy on your soul. Is Mise le meas. DC, CORK

'I was in the bookstore at Dublin Airport wondering what to buy for the ten hour journey on Aer Lingus back to San Francisco. I guess what made me purchase your book was the price on the cover (similar pricing scheme to a Ruinair ticket). I knew I made the right choice when while boarding our Aer Lingus flight back to San Francisco, a young Aer Lingus employee noticed I was carrying your book and he said it was a great read, he could not put it down.' IE, USA

'On a recent trip to Dublin I purchased your book and as an unfortunate person who has been travelling on Ruinair since 1998, I can really relate to your experiences. I would also add that the cabin crew on my return flight to Berlin did not appreciate me laughing at the book.' NB

'I was a bit bored at Dublin Airport the other day en route to Rome with Ruinair, so whilst the wife read magazines I went for a walk and found a book I had never heard of before. I bought it and pissed myself laughing at boarding as everything happened in front of me as if I was narrating from the book. I was like the cabin crew's best friend when they saw what I was reading. One of the guys took it to show the rest of the crew and came back laughing. Anyway, to sum it up, it was a fecking hilariously accurate book.' RL

'I would like to share a Ruinair story with you. I arrived in the departures lounge in Dublin Airport with 25 other men for a stag weekend in Frankfurt. The group of lads are mainly from the Swords and surrounding areas, so the 6.30 a.m. flight was no problem. All boarded the plane without a problem and we sat fairly close to each other in groups. I myself was sitting with Billy from Glasgow and Bren from Donegal (all three of us live in Swords) when the Ruinair hostess greeted us and checked our seat belts. With that the hostess noticed Billy had a Scottish accent and she asked where about he was from. He replied Glasgow. She said she was from Glasgow too and she asked what was he doing on a Dublin flight. Billy replied that he lived in Swords, to her amazement. She also said she lived in Swords and the small chat then became a conversation. Where in Swords, she asked? River Valley was the reply, and guess what she lived there also. The next question was where did Billy drink? He said The Mill in River Valley. No, she said, I drink in Swords village, but do you ever go there for a drink and where do you go? Billy replied if I am in the village it's normally The Cock Tavern or The Pound. To which her reply and not to be given in front of 25 lads came out. 'Oh, The Cock, I'm very fond of The Cock.' Much laughter, end of conversation. Coming back on the trip three of us sat together. The guy in the middle was fast asleep. So what else could we do but hit the call button over his head *and put the filthiest porn mag in front of him. As the hostess neared, both of us elbowed the man in the middle and both of us fell into an instant sleep. The rest is history.'* IC, DUBLIN

'Well done on 'Ruinair', I thought it was a great read. Although I think the title is a shameless plug. Might I be so bold as to suggest 'Lying-air'. When you write the sequel please don't try to balance it as those mercenary bastards in Ruinair are well capable of making somebody with an important opinion seem foolish. I thought you might appreciate a quote by Ardal O'Hanlon, when talking about Swineair, he said 'The next thing they will do will be to install a large catapult in airports and charge you a fiver to fire you in the general direction that you want to go.' You also may be interested in another little Ruinair story. Myself and my brother were travelling to East Midlands Airport when the announcement came that the flight would be delayed. When we finally did take off my brother started the round of applause that usually should come before the Ruinair on time fanfare. The crew members gave us a very menacing look as everyone joined in and were pissing themselves laughing, they then made an announcement that due to inclement weather conditions there would be no in-flight sales. At this point my brother exclaimed loudly that he was only on board to take part in the Ruinair raffle. The crew member came down and told him if he opened his mouth again there would be a surprise waiting for him when we landed. Needless to say we behaved ourselves and we were rewarded with a very pleasant scowl as we disembarked. Oh the joys of low fares. Take care and good luck to you if O' Leery ever gets his hands on you.' FM

'I have just finished reading your book and thanks for the laughs. Sure that's all you can do with Ruinair. No point in taking them seriously.' PC

'I have read your book 'Ruinair' with great interest as it coincided very well with my own experiences. In fact I have sent a letter of complaint to Ruinair and Mr O'Leery answered me personally, which led to another reply from me, which he answered again. I have also sent him your book as a gift which he thanked me for but he did not comment further.' RS, SWEDEN

'I'd just like to say I'm delighted someone has gone to the bother of putting into print what a huge amount of disgruntled commuters have long known. Ruinair have absolutely no regard for their customers. For each miracle deal Ruinair sell there is a commuter being ripped off, being thrown into tiny constrictive seats, getting hung out to dry with weight restrictions or having to pay extra for wheelchair access (even that surprised me when the news broke). All of this from an airline with an abysmal labour record it was a wonder to me how the staff didn't just mutiny and break the chain of selling shitty lottery tickets, overpriced food and iron maiden seating and take that plane off to the nearest scrap yard. This spectacular dream scenario mightn't be too plausible but Ruinair losing customers from bad publicity is. Best of luck with the book. I hope it gets the message across the globe, Ruinair is a national disgrace.' KD

'I just finished your book, which I thought was brill. At every description of rudeness, shoddy service and general shiteness (if that's a word), I felt myself nodding "that's happened to me", then laughing/cringing, because I've let it happen on a regular basis in the mad dash to get a cheap flight. I'll carry to my grave the memory of being flung a black bin-liner by an ex-Russian bodybuilder (female) on a Ruinair flight from Faro, screaming "rubbish" at me. I am not really sure what she meant.' HW

'My Ruinair flight from Shannon to Stansted was due to depart at 21.25 hrs but was delayed until 02.30 hrs on the next day—that's five hours. Anyway after getting bored and walking round the Duty-Free shop a few times I ended up buying a box of Cadbury's Flakes (a box of 48) and after offering my friends a quick chocolate boost, I offered them to other stranded STN-bound passengers, which quite a few took me up. Once on the plane I mentioned the delay to the stewardess and she said she had finished at 5 p.m. and was on her way home on the bus from Stansted and had a call to return to the airport, which apparently she was obliged to do. She moaned that she hadn't eaten for ages, and was hungry and was missing dinner. I offered her one of my Flakes from the box, and she accepted. I said there are 6 of you on board, at least take 6 of them to get a choccy boost. I got a mention

*from the flight deck in the 'We are this high and will be there soon'
speech with a 'Thank you to the guy who supplied us with the chocolate'.* STEVE, UK

*'I read your book and God but you must have some constitution, or
perhaps just low feelings of self worth. Please read this letter I wrote
to discover the root of my own bitterness—"Dear Mr O'Leery, I know
addressing this letter to you, Mr O'Leery, is tantamount to addressing
a letter to the tooth fairy and expecting a reply, but I presume you,
unlike the tooth fairy, delegate. As you are no doubt a very busy
person (not to imply that you are either inundated with letters of
complaint or required to multitask), I'll keep this letter as succinct as
possible. On Monday last I and my sister were returning from the
environs of Paris, i.e. Beauvais. Luckily I had recently purchased your
handy guide to low fares flying, masquerading as the book 'Ruinair'
by Paul Kilduff. This informative book gave me insights and information so that I knew what to expect from a Ruinair flight. I was not
perturbed when the flight was delayed as I understand these things
happen and delays are definitely not part of your business plan. I was
prepared for the unassigned seating. I was prepared for the cabin staff
hawking wares on the flight as it defrayed the cost of my seat. I was
not more than a bit irritated that one of the cabin staff did not understand or perhaps hear a request, from my articulate English-speaking
sister, for a cup of tea. What I was not prepared for were the taunts of
your cabin staff. I am a woman less in the first flush of youth, more
in the first blush of menopause. While in Paris I purchased a walking
cane as I had a weakness in my ankle and the cane assisted me while
walking on the irregular paths of Paris. While leaving your plane by
the rear door I was not using it but holding the cane in my hand as
the floor underfoot and the apron of the airport are unlikely to be
uneven. As I approached the two staff by the door, one giggled and
said something in the Ruinair native language which included the
words 'Charlie Chaplin'. Because the second staff member, who is
possibly employed on an 'accessibility' scheme for hearing impaired,
did not respond he repeated it again much to both their amusement.
Needless to say I was hurt. But if I am there to amuse and entertain
your staff I feel that I should at least be given appearance money. As*

you Mr O'Leery (or your delegate) are very aware, there is no such thing as a free lunch and, to continue the metaphor, I am not prepared to be the free lunch for your bored, insensitive special needs cabin staff.' GJ

'I recently went for a week to Sardinia and used Ruinair for the trip, for holiday purposes I had brought your book along. On the return trip the flight was scheduled for 7.50 p.m. but did not arrive until 10 p.m. There was no information given and any passengers who asked the staff what the position was were completely ignored. When we took off the in-flight service started. I was quite near the front of the plane so I was in the early rows of service. I asked what hot food was available and was told they only had 1 hot dog. God help the poor people towards the rear of the plane. I got a sandwich which was out of date on Italian time but in-date by 30 minutes in Irish time, it was terrible anyway. We arrived 2 hours 30 minutes late and they still played that ridiculous congratulations song. On the way back the staff were still trying to sell bus tickets, and train tickets to the city centre (I was impressed that the Irish Government had built a rail system from the airport to O'Connell Street in the week while I was away). The low fares airline cost me €935 for return flights to Dublin with a 2 year 3 month old child being heavily levied. Regards.' TJ

'I produce the Guest Services Directory for the Trident Hotel here in Kinsale and when it was printed approx 3 years ago there was a 1580 number available for Ruinair enquiries. A guest reported recently that this number was now a Sex Chat line. I checked the number 33 times to ensure they were correct.' BT

'I am a great fan of Ruinair. I believe that Mick has changed the way we travel. People around my age (23) now travel to the lowest fare location. We are completely open to where we go and could not care less when we are treated with utter contempt by the cabin crew, after all in most cases we only pay 1 cent. What does annoy me is when you are the unlucky one to buy the last seat on the plane costing hundreds of euro and then to be treated like crap. I tend to find that most of the cabin crew have the same face when you walk onto the plane, as if a dog had crapped in their handbag.' MC

'*I just got screwed by Ruinair for being 4 kg over weight—that's baggage, not me. €40. I could write a book about it. My main aim now
is to ensure that no-one in our group today spends anything on board
the flight. Maybe my surname incurs a few extra kilos charge?*' BY
TEXT, FROM MY SISTER, DUBLIN AIRPORT

'*I have just finished reading your book 'Ruinair'. I found it to be very
entertaining and enjoyable. However, I used to work for* FR, *and I and
my then colleagues took great pride in our work and in providing
high customer service levels. The job afforded me great opportunities
to travel and learn new languages and cultures … and meet women!
I still fly with them now, although I do still have my Ruinair rugby
jersey, so I avoid the charges for excess baggage, airport check in etc
and get some perks like the jump seat if I want it, free beers and priority boarding so it's not all bad. Best of luck with the new book on
Central Europe, my wife is Polish and she looks forward to reading it
also, but lay off the staff, they work hard and whatever you think do
take pride in their uniform and work. Best wishes.*' JD

'*I just finished reading your book. I think you are a bit hard on Ruinair.
I guess I must have taken hundreds of flights with them since they first
began operating, I reckon they have saved me a king's ransom in air
fares over the years. I think you are particularly hard on the staff who
are generally pretty cheerful and helpful in my experience and their
English, while often not flawless, is usually up to the job. O'Leary is
indeed an objectionable little bollix, but on one occasion he did check
my boarding card when boarding at Dublin Airport and there was
not a* TV *camera in sight. I couldn't imagine Willie Walsh or Richard
Branson doing the same. The fact that he deliberately tries to rub
people up the wrong way is unnecessary a lot of the time, but on many
things he is right and he exposes cosy relationships and monopolies
which are not in the public interest. I don't make a habit of emailing
authors but I did enjoy the book.*' EM, CAMBRIDGE

'*A few years ago I was standing in a slow-moving queue in an airport
in Portugal and I got talking to an elderly German couple. The usual
stuff, the weather and where are you from yourself, and so on. When*

I told them I lived in Ireland they said they loved Ireland and had a picture in their apartment in Ludenscheidt of the great Irishman. Naturally I asked who this great Irishman was, wondering if it might be Mr de Valera or even Mr Parnell. My jaw dropped when they said it was Mr O'Leery and seeing the shock on my face they quickly added, "Mr O'Leery—Ze man von Ruinair". On a more serious note they said that they had never been wealthy people, but when they retired they discovered the low fares available from this great Irishman and had travelled to every Ruinair destination, usually paying only 1c for the ticket plus the usual taxes, fees and charges.'

GE, ATHLONE

'I thought you might like to hear about a new hair salon which has opened up near to where we live. It's called Ryanhair.'

MD, LUXEMBOURG

Slovakia (Again)

Flight NE153 – Tuesday @ 1.05 p.m. – DUB-KSC-DUB

Fare €40 plus taxes, fees and charges €53

To: Paul Kilduff
From: Ema
Subject: Ruinair

Hey Paul,
   I've spent the last weekend in Dublin partying with Ruinair staff, I bought your book at the airport, I'm halfway through it and loving it :) I work for a low cost airline as well. I feel a bit offended that you didn't give us a go although we fly from DUB too. We're not big enough to be Ruinair's competitor but we're hoping to get there. If you ever visit Slovakia, I'll gladly be your tour guide :)
   Best regards from Slovakia
   Ema

To: Ema
From: Paul Kilduff
Subject: Re: Ruinair

Hi Ema,
   I am glad you had a great weekend in Dublin and that you like the book. Do tell your airline colleagues, especially tell your Ruinair friends, about the book. I assume you work for SkyEurope? If so, SkyEurope is in the next book which I am half way through. I took a flight with SkyEurope to BTS and I am going again on the

'beautiful airline' to KSC *in May. Maybe I can see you there and I*
can sign your book :)
    Regards PWK

To: Paul Kilduff
From: Ema
Subject: Re: Re: Ruinair

Hey Paul,
    Thanks for the reply. So you authors actually write back to your
fans, I'm quite impressed :) *Yes, I do work for the beautiful airline,*
not as cabin crew, I despatch the aircraft, but surely I can arrange
to meet the KSC *flight. I want to get my book signed. I'm really*
curious about your next book. I hope you will write nicely about
us. You better promise, otherwise I'm not gonna buy it :) *Glad you*
enjoyed the BTS *flight, I'll make sure that we repeat the good*
impression on the KSC *flight too, see you there* :)
    Ema

Kosice's tourist office offers the following advice to travellers:
'Arriving by train?—Europe's busiest train routes pass through.
Arriving by air?—there are regularly scheduled flights. Arriving by
bus?—there are regular bus services. Arriving by car?—roads are
good. Arriving by boat?—simply not possible.' I take their advice and
arrive on time in Kosice Airport. Ema is late yet it's not her fault.
Her flight was delayed by a bird strike where our feathered friends
came off second best. It is an inevitable and sad fact of life that
despite much trying, no flock of little birdies is ever going to take
on and successfully defeat a Boeing 737 at 500 mph. I wait in
Arrivals and one hour later Ema emerges with her SkyEurope ID
badge dangling around her neck. She very kindly brings me a
snazzy company gift bag, complete with T-shirt, fridge magnet,
note pad, lanyard, model aircraft and pen. This confirms my view
that SkyEurope is by far the best low fares airline in Europe, and
corporate gifts never influence me. I in turn have brought along
some of my other books. 'I love books,' Ema advises. I use my new
SkyEurope pen to sign the books for Ema.

'Do you like the 'Ruinair' book?' I ask.

'It is funny. A little arrogant too.'

I agree. 'The more I follow the antics of Mick, the more like him I become.'

We take a table at the busy airport café and I go mad and get the soft drinks in. I am amazed that someone who is a mere 27 years old, in jeans and a T-shirt, is in charge of the movements of 15 Boeing 737s on a daily basis. Ema explains all. 'I have a Masters degree, a five-year course in aviation.'

'Do you have perks in your job? Do you get free flights on SkyEurope?' I ask.

'The flights are free but I must pay the taxes, fees and charges.'

'Much like on Ruinair then,' I suggest. 'Have you been anywhere nice?'

'I went from Bratislava to Krakow but I flew via Athens. I can make connections anywhere.'

I recall our prior email correspondence. 'Did you enjoy your visit to Dublin?'

'I did not see a lot of the city. The Ruinair people took me to watch the aircraft landing near the fence at Dublin Airport. And I went to Howth and for a drive to Northern Ireland and to the west of Ireland. And they took me to the bar near the airport where all the Ruinair staff go.' Ema has an idea. 'Next time I am in Dublin I could take you to that bar and introduce you to the Ruinair staff.'

'I fear they would lynch me. But do let me know the next time you are in Dublin.'

I bore Ema rigid for the next hour with my tales of low fares travel. It's very rare that I meet someone who knows more than I do about airlines and aviation. Ema listens intently and flashes her eyes occasionally as she slowly imbibes an orange juice. She is on a flying visit and so is on the return flight to Bratislava. Most of us listen for departures announcements in airports but Ema calls the office on her mobile telephone. I expect if we had more conversation to cover then she'd tell them to hold the flight for 30 minutes. We say farewell and the Beautiful Ema takes the Beautiful Airline to the Beautiful City.

I go to the Sixt Airport car hire desk to collect my Fabia 1.4L (the L is for luxury). Slovak car maker and local star Skoda has manufactured two million of these little beauties in Mladá Boleslav. Sixt conveniently left my car hemmed in by other cars, with luggage trolleys placed strategically all about, plus they left it in first gear with the handbrake off so that I will lurch into another car once I turn the key, and they will bill me big time. I suffer the usual indignity of car hire users since Sixt's website address is displayed on my rear window, which essentially is an invitation for all local drivers to piss all over me from a great height in their far superior motors. The only thing I can see in my rear view mirror on the manic roads near Kosice are registration plates of other cars. There hasn't been this much commotion in the hire car business since Jake Stevens hired a car in Finland on RTÉ TV but later returned to the Hertz desk to complain they had given him a defective car since the steering wheel was on the wrong side of the car.

Outside the city the traffic thins and the drive is not unlike being in Ireland: scenic mountains and valleys, lush pastures and forests, bad roads, appalling driving and roadside billboards for an upcoming visit to the Kosice Steel Concert Arena by Michael Flatley's *Lord of the Dance.* I follow a 'MI' registered truck to Michalovce and then a 'HU' registered truck on to Humenne. The journey northwards for 110 km takes about two hours, since I refuse to overtake anyone in this tiny car. The towns I encounter have eyesore apartments, shuttered shops, pitted streets, beautiful churches and manicured cemeteries (there is real care in the community here). I drive through rural villages so small the name signs are placed back to back. I slow down to avoid hitting men in tracksuits standing with rakes or bottles of beer talking to other men in tracksuits with bicycles or shovels. Nearby their wives hover about on single crutches. These locals are Romany gypsies and are as swarthy as any citizen of New Delhi. They give me long hard stares along the lines of 'See that Skoda Fabia 1.4L. He's not from around these parts.' People are visibly impressed by my mode of transport despite the fact that a Skoda Fabia 1.4L only costs €3,300 here.

Some of the roads are so deserted that I am almost tempted to drift to the left-hand side and so drive on the wrong side of the road. I drive for a few miles parallel to a single-track weed-strewn railway line, wondering where are the trains and why didn't they bother to lay a second track to, or from, my destination. Then the road dips and turns and I find myself at a level crossing, complete with a single red flashing light. I slow down but I do not stop. I don't know the local convention, whether the light is a general warning or whether the light would stay on red if there was any chance of a train coming. I drift forwards and decide to err on the side of caution. I look left and I see a winding empty track with even more weeds. I look right and I see a bloody great train engine with headlights 30 feet away. It's moving slowly but fast enough to do serious damage to a Skoda Fabia 1.4L. I brake hard as the train draws nearer. I look at the width of the train, the location of the track and the manner in which my car protrudes and worry that I will be wiped off the face of Slovakia.

I go for reverse gear, but not having found reverse before in a Skoda Fabia 1.4L, I am unsure if I have found reverse. I could be in second gear. I tickle the accelerator and the car rolls forward. The train is almost upon me. I dare not floor the pedal in case I am thrust forward into Slovak Rail. The train passes by, only feet away from me and from the safe retention of the Collision Damage Waiver clause in my car hire contract. I always worry that if I don't take this optional CDW cover when hiring a car, I will end up in some court trying to explain the country's largest motorway pile-up to a bunch of locals with bicycles or shovels.

Medzilaborce (for Americans, this is pronounced as Med-zil-a-bor-ce) lies in the impoverished Carpathian mountain foothills six miles from Poland and only 30 miles from the Ukraine. Last time I was this far east I was working in Hong Kong. The industries here are farming, forestry and machinery, but also increasingly, and bizarrely, tourism. The population in the town is, much like one of those tombstone boot-hill towns in a spaghetti Western movie, a rather precise 6,741. I follow the signs for the tourist information office to the rear of a grey building but I cannot locate the office. I see an open door and inside there is a hallway with a few city posters on the wall so I step inside. There is no one about so I walk down the hallway past some untidy rooms with furniture and

boxes until I hear voices. I step into the last room to find three surprised people enjoying a meal at a table. It is clear that I am in the
living room of a private house.

There is not much else I can say. 'The tourist office?'

The youngest girl (in her late teens) puts down some food, nods
and gets up reluctantly. She points and I follow her back down the
hallway, out of her home, past a few more doors to a locked office
with a small sign announcing the opening and closing times of the
town's tourist information office. 10 a.m. to 5 p.m. It's 11 a.m. Inside
there are few items of use to a travel writer except for a sparse
collection of leaflets.

'Any English brochures?' I ask.

She shakes her head. 'No English.'

I examine the leaflets. One is trilingual. 'This is in English.'

'Yes. English.'

I purchase the *Turisticky Sprievodca* guide to Medzilaborce ('*the
region is attractive for tourist industry with international importance*')
and leave, allowing her to lock up and return to a late breakfast.
When I emerge I see the gable end of a building decorated with
giant Andy Warhol murals. There are a pair of shoe prints set into
the façade of another building. My €30-a-night two-star *Eurohotel
Laborec* is on Ulica A. Warhola. I could have stayed at the *Penzion
Andy* but I didn't because it's a one-star place. The town square has
a 2-metre-tall metal sculpture of Andy Warhol, with umbrella. If
you take a bus to get here then you can alight at a bus shelter which
is made from two giant halved Campbell's soup cans, one of
Cream of Celery and one of Cream of Tomato, with a sign
announcing, '*Campbell's Soup is M'm! M'm! Good!*' The pop-art
king Andrej Warhola was fond of saying '*I come from nowhere*'.
Well, he didn't. He is from here and here he is everywhere. This is
officially 'Warhol City'. Pop goes Medzilaborce.

The Andy Warhol Museum of Modern Art, also on A. Warhola
Street, is the prime, and possibly only, tourist attraction. The
Museum is devoted to the presentation of his life and works and is
the world's second largest such museum, outside of Pittsburgh,
Pennsylvania. It is a bright, white, boxy new building set in a paved
plaza, and the nicely painted building is in contrast to the

surrounding drab Communist structures plus a few churches, shops and residential dwellings that would be derelict if further west. The only other action in town is the construction of a Tesco store across the road where 10 workers finish the car park and are watched by 20 envious unemployed locals in search of possible gainful employment.

Inside the museum I obligingly comply with the instructions to place red felt covers over my shoes so that I do not bring dust or dirt inside. Once up the wide stairs painted with flower petals I discover that none of the few other visitors have complied and I am the only idiot walking around with bright red feet. The exhibition of 150 images is extensive, with massed walls of one-dimensional icons such as Marilyn Monroe, Grace Jones, Debbie Harry, Joan Collins, Ted Kennedy, Lenin, Mao, Hammers and Sickles, Absolut Vodka, Brillo Pads and Coca Cola. As Andy said, '*If you want to know all about me, just look at the surface of my paintings and there I am. There's nothing behind me.*' Some of the art work is beyond me, such as when I stare at a bright red metal piece on the wall until I realise it's merely a fire extinguisher. There is a letter to Andy from a gallery in New York declining to display his paintings due to 'lack of space', which basically is a polite artistic way of telling him that they didn't think much of his work, I suspect. Music of a bygone flower power era plays softly from wall speakers. '*If you're going to San Francisco …*'

I have to admire someone who can make a living from prints of cans of soup. I learn why Andy painted soup cans. He once asked his interior design teacher in New York what he should paint. She told him to paint something that he loved and to paint something that would be instantly recognisable by other people. Next day he painted dollar bills and cans of soup, one of which endured. The most printed Warhol image is not of a can of soup. It's his self-portrait on a stamp which the US Postal Service printed 61 million times. After tomato, there's a can here of his second favourite soup, personally signed by Andy: Chicken Noodle. Andy said, '*When you think about it, department stores are kind of like museums.*' Andy's personal effects are here, including sunglasses, clothes, Panasonic walkman and camera. There are photographs of Andy with his shock of spiky parted hair and gaunt face, many of them showing him standing away from people and with his arms folded defensively, plus more sepia photographs of him at an earlier age at home in New York. Even as a child he looked a bit odd and so was destined to be an artist.

One of Andy's prints is of a box of Kellogg's Cornflakes, which were sadly not available today at my breakfast in the Eurohotel Laborec, where upon receiving the breakfast menu in Slovak, German and English, my conversation with the linguistically challenged waitress (I use that word loosely) was as follows:

'Muesli,' I pointed confidently.

She waved her hands. 'Nie.'

'Juice?'

'Nie.'

'Yoghurt with fruit?'

'Nie.'

'Rolls?'

'Nie.'

'Toast?'

'Nie.'

'Bread?'

So she took my order. I assume the toaster was broken. With the four slices of bread, she brought me a large plate with a square of butter and a blob of jam. I had bread and water—a prison breakfast. I was pretty close to following her back into the hotel kitchen to see what she kept in there, if anything.

The museum also has rooms of family history and mementos. I learn that Andy's brother Paul had a less successful career as a painter of Heinz tomato ketchup bottles. There are many photographs of Andy's mother, Julia, who kept in contact with her family after she emigrated from Slovakia to New York. Her sister visited her in New York but did not like the city. '*They build tall houses there, all the way to heaven, God will punish them for it.*' She did not like Andy either. '*Andy is strange. He is never quiet. He is always doing something, telephoning, carrying around a box out of which a human voice speaks. Satan's work.*' A cousin of Andy's didn't know much about his life in New York either. '*I knew he was a painter, but I thought he worked as a house decorator.'* Andy sent drawings to relations in Slovakia but they threw them away.

Andy Warhol's parents were not born in Medzilaborce, but in the town of Mikova, 10 miles away. Andy's brother John said, *'Our mother used to often talk to us about Mikova, about her going by wagon to Medzilaborce'*. I have not been to Mikova because it has no Pop Art museum. There is a misleading postcard on sale in the spartan gift shop. It shows Andy pushing his bicycle down the town's main street. With his odd silver-white hair, he is dramatically out of place in the surroundings. Unlike myself, Andy Warhol never visited Medzilaborce, nor Mikova, in his life. He never even visited Slovakia. But his parents' emigration made Andy's life. In New York he was a king. In Mikova he would have been a peasant.

Next morning, and due to Ema's dedication, my return flight from Kosice to Dublin departs one minute ahead of schedule. I am relaxing mid-flight in seat 3C when a member of the crew approaches.

'Mr Kilduff?' asks Jakub.

'Yes,' I reply hesitantly.

He lowers his voice. 'Can you sign a copy of your book for me?'

'You have a copy here?'

'In the rear of the aircraft.'

I make a deduction. 'You know Ema?' He nods. 'Sure, I will sign the book.'

Two stewardesses wait for Jakub and me at the rear of the aircraft. There is a copy of 'Ruinair' on the top of the trolley. One of the girls looks at me hard and points to the photograph of Mick on the front cover.

'Is this a photograph of you? It is like you. We could not tell. We did not know if it was you in 3C.'

'That's Mick,' I confirm. 'He's famous in Ireland. Maybe not so much in Slovakia.' I sign the book.

Jakub takes out a digital camera. 'A photo with me?' I oblige, we chat and then I return to 3C.

Five minutes later Jakub returns to speak with me. 'The photo is not good enough.' Good enough for what? 'Do you mind staying on-board after we land? We will take a photo with all the crew.' I agree.

After we land the four of us stand at the top of a now deserted Boeing aircraft. Most of my fellow passengers are probably through passport control and are sitting in their cars in the long-term car park.

A pilot emerges from the cockpit and speaks to Jakub. 'Ah, 'Ruinair', I see. Did he sign your book?'

Jakub nods. 'Please take a photo of us.' The captain obliges, before going to kick the tyres below.

Andy Warhol famously said that everyone will be famous for 15 minutes. Even little old me.

Ruinair Fan Forum

I am flying again on Ireland's national low fares airline, Aer Lingus. In Dublin Airport I am denied a boarding card at the check-in kiosk because the flight is 'closing'. Undeterred by this technology, a member of staff at a check-in desk advises I am three minutes late, yet he produces a boarding card for which I am exceedingly grateful. Customer service is not about the best punctuality, least lost baggage or cancelled flights. It's about assisting customers, like me, in a flexible manner and that does not happen so much with Mick. *'Our customers are pretty important. When our customers are wrong then we're not shy about telling them they're wrong. If you show up late for the flight, you're not getting on board the flight. We're not going to fall for any of this old management bullshit, or MBA rubbish about clichéd concerns for passengers. Are we going to say sorry for our lack of customer service? Absolutely not. Are we going to apologise when something goes wrong? No, we're fucking not. Please understand. It does not matter how many times you write to us complaining that we wouldn't put you up in a hotel because there was fog in Stansted. You didn't pay us for it. It's unreasonable of passengers to turn up at the airport and expect to be provided with a free cup of tea. Go and buy a cup of tea yourself. Our customer service is the lowest prices guaranteed, on brand-new aircraft, flying safely, on time, with the least risk of a cancellation or a lost bag. Did you get that service? Yes, you did? Fine. Shut up and go away.'*

Onboard I am greeted by smart professional staff, and most are posh blondes, which is fantastic. They play *Orchestral Manoeuvres in the Cabin*, rather than any jingle. I relax in a comfy assigned reclining leather seat. I put my newspaper into the seat pocket. The safety announcement is made in English. And Aer Lingus still remains the *greenest* of all the world's major airlines. Aer Lingus is a fantastic airline. Even Mick thinks so. Sure didn't he spend €400 million of his own money to buy 29 per cent of the company? *'This merger with Ruinair provides Aer Lingus with a secure long-term future as part of one strong Irish airline group, whereas, on its own, we believe it is doomed to a bleak future as a small, regional, high-cost airline which records dismal financial results. If Aer Lingus turns down our offer, they are going to find themselves in five years' time as an eight-million-passenger airline competing with an 80-million-passenger airline next door. Our offer embarrassed the board of Aer Lingus. Five days earlier they were happy to sell the business at €2.20 a share, then they were trying to justify rejecting our offer of €2.80. But it's not a matter for the management or board: it's a matter for shareholders. Aer Lingus has discovered this new strategy of splendid isolation. The last time that was tried was by Éamon de Valera after the war and it led to 40 years of economic stagnation. I'd suggest Aer Lingus is doomed to a similar failure. Helping Aer Lingus to improve its cost base and efficiency to increase profits is better use of our spare cash than putting it on deposit. It is in the national interest for us to help out our national airline.'*

'I am not sure the people ever actually owned Aer Lingus. They never got a dividend and sure as hell did not see any of the money from the sale of Aer Lingus. We can have a philosophical debate as to who owns it. The Government now owns about 25 per cent and the unions about 20 per cent. We own 29 per cent. I have no desire to own Aer Lingus. I would be happy to own 50.1 per cent of it because that would give us the power, tomorrow morning, to eliminate the fuel surcharges and reduce its fares. I am not on a rabid quest to own Aer Lingus in order that civilisation as we know it does not end. The only issue for us as a country and for the Government is whether we want Aer Lingus to be owned and run by a company which operates out of Dublin Airport or whether we want to be talking to Fritz in Frankfurt, Sir Henry—or perhaps Sir Willie at that stage—in London or Jacques in Paris and where all we get is increasing air fares, much higher fuel surcharges and capacity being pulled out of Ireland at a rate of knots. Aer Lingus has an interesting approach to fuel surcharges in that it does not impose them on the short-haul

routes but on the long-haul routes it now adds a surcharge of €100 a ticket. We do not understand the reason for that. Its explanation is that somehow long-haul flying is different from short-haul flying because on short-haul one is flying on Coca-Cola or something whereas on long-haul one is flying on jet kerosene. The reality is Aer Lingus cannot put up fuel surcharges on short-haul flights because we refuse to impose surcharges.'

But Mick makes a second offer to buy Aer Lingus. *'Aer Lingus will be the equivalent of Aer Arann in two years time, some irrelevant, Mickey Mouse, loss-making airline. Another two or three years might be too late. There is no certainty we will make another offer. Did I balls it up the last time by arriving in a hunting, shooting, fishing mood? Yes I did. This offer is guaranteeing the Government connectivity, recognition of the unions, more employment and lower fares for consumers. If anyone else came to the Government guaranteeing more jobs and lower fares they would be welcomed with open arms and be granted honorary doctorates all over the country. I don't need Aer Lingus. We need Aer Lingus like a headache. My board at Ruinair thinks this is some sort of Paddy thing. Most of our sharholders think this is some sort of mental block that we have. Yes, I do play the Irish nationalist card, sometimes you do it because it is the right thing to do. It is our patriotic duty no less to allow the harp and shamrock to come together.'*

I wait at the Meeting Point in Amsterdam's Schiphol Airport for a clandestine rendezvous. Dutch technology is significantly more advanced, in that I can text a greeting to a number and my message will appear on a large red screen above the Meeting Point for all to read. I think about texting 'Don't fly KLM—Fly Ruinair' but I see that they check messages before they appear so they will never display mine. At the agreed time my contacts arrive. In the interests of confidentiality and to prevent reprisals, I will only refer to my contacts by their user names. RuinAdmin is 19 years old and he is the prime mover in the Ruinair fan forum website. RuinairGrad is the technical brains of the operation and he is not just a graduate but a teacher, and Grad is a genuine forename in the Netherlands. They hail from Utrecht, 30 minutes south.

We go upstairs to the Panorama restaurant and I offer to buy them both lunch. I half expect them to go mad and order four or five courses plus a load of beer and wine but being frequent flyers on Ruinair they are both content with a modest sandwich and a soft drink. We sit by the window with an excellent view of the outside balcony where plane-spotters take photographs of the refuelling of KLM *Flying Dutchman* jumbos and elderly men push their wives about in wheelchairs as they enjoy a fun day out at the airport.

'What made you start the Ruinair fan forum website?' I ask once we have exchanged pleasantries.

Admin takes the lead. 'I used to have a web page on Hyves, a Dutch social networking website, about Ruinair. We had about 300 members signed up but it was all in Dutch. We wanted to do something better, and for more people. Grad has the tech skills so he built the website and we put the fan forum on it.'

'Does it cost much to maintain the website?'

Grad shrugs nonchalantly. '€35 a year.' So theirs is truly another low cost website.

'I see your website says Ruinair is the best airline in the world. What do you like about it?' I ask.

Grad is honest. 'The prices. €1 is enough to pay to go anywhere. And I mean including taxes, fees and charges. I don't care where I travel. I go where it is cheap. I went to Gothenburg only because I could. Once I flew with Ruinair eight times in one week. Sure, I have to pay €10 for a bus ride somewhere but that's ok. The great thing is that Ruinair has made Europe smaller.' True enough, and Grad is a geography teacher.

'But don't you feel bad if you only pay €1? Mick O'Leery won't make any profit.'

'There will always be a businessman or two on the same flight who has paid €150.'

'There must be some things you don't like about Ruinair?' I hazard.

'Sure,' replies Grad. 'My first flight on Ruinair, was from Frankfurt-Hahn to Montpelier, and it was cancelled for technical reasons ... my very first flight ever with them, cancelled.'

'Is there anything that you would change about Ruinair?'

Admin nods. 'They could pay their staff better. I know of one person who works for them as cabin crew at a base in Germany. He says that he is paid €1,200 per month after tax. That's not a lot to live on.'

'What about being on board their aircraft?'

Grad shakes his head. 'If you don't like it then don't fly on the airline, I say. It's a hobby for me.'

'What about that Fly Ruinair jingle they play on the aircraft?' I insist.

Admin takes out his mobile telephone and plays his ringtone. It's the Ruinair jingle. I despair. It is very loud. A few nearby diners look over at us as the jingle continues. I am in the midst of true fans of this airline. Admin soon powers down his telephone. 'I don't care if they play the jingle ten times on a flight.'

'What are your favourite posts on the fan forum?' I ask.

'I like the advice on the airports. It's very useful,' says Admin.

It is. The website contains excellent information on Ruinair destination airports, usually written by local experts and often accompanied by photographs which depict a single Ruinair plane on an apron with people walking to and fro, a tin shed terminal building with three check-in desks and two departure gates, a café snack bar with 10 chairs and the bus which will take us the 80 km from a NATO airbase to the nearest large conurbation.

Users also post questions about flying with Ruinair. One Italian flyer wanted to know if several kg of mozzarella can be taken on in cabin baggage. I helpfully replied that yes if it is hard grated mozzarella that's ok but if it is soft buffalo mozzarella in water then it would be a serious breach of the ban on liquids onboard.

A guest user criticises Ruinair on the fan forum and says that they are like McDonald's. A more loyal user immediately posts a reply, advising that he quite likes McDonald's too.

One of the users, the King of Ruinland, living in Basel, Switzerland signs off all his posts with *'Fly Ruinair for the best prices and punctuality. Ruinair = The one and only five star airline worldwide!'* Right.

There are also helpful flying tips, for example on where best to sit. 'If you like to look outside during the flight, perhaps to take pictures, it's important not to take a seat above the wings or just behind, nor in front of the engines (poor view towards below). In short, sit before row 7 or after row 25. Better also not to be on the side of the sun during the flight. And have a tissue handy to clean the window if needed.'

'Do you have a favourite seat onboard?'

Admin nods. 'I like the emergency row seats. I go up and ask the cabin crew girl to move from it. I never pay for the seat but I usually get it. For free.' Me too. Drat. Someone else knows my secret.

Their website addresses a concept previously unknown to me called one-day trips. One user posts about his trip from Charleroi to Stansted to Dublin to Stansted to Charleroi—all in one day. I don't see the point of this. Is it better to travel than to arrive? Others use a day trip to spend two or three hours in a city to decide if they will return for a three- or four-day stay. Others fly to have lunch in the UK. Others try to fly 'triangles'. 'I have tried and succeeded to perform a less spectacular triangle, but a triangle nevertheless: Charleroi-Rome-Dublin-Charleroi. Five and a quarter hours airborne. Quite enjoyable.'

'Why do you think some people make four flights in a day but they never leave an airport?'

'One of our most active users is a retired gentleman. Maybe it's better than staying at home.'

'What advice do you have for passengers on Ruinair?' I ask positively.

'Get a Visa Electron card,' suggests Admin. 'There's no fee if you book with a Visa Electron card. There's no point buying a flight all for only €1 to then be charged a €10 fee to book the flight.'

'Invest some hours and do some research,' says Grad. 'Spend some time at your PC to find the very cheapest flight. One good idea is to fly via Stansted to your final destination. Sometimes a direct flight in Europe is expensive but go through Stansted, there are always cheap flights to and from there. Try Hahn too. If you are not in such a hurry during the day, take two flights, not one, and save some money.'

'Have you ever had any contact from Ruinair about the fan forum?' I ask.

'Not directly. We sent emails to their head of the Benelux area, asking him to make Eindhoven a base or to use a small airport near here at Lelystad. Now and again we get information or maps from their marketing staff which we put up on our website. We do however get some emails from the general public asking us to help with Ruinair flight bookings or to answer their questions. Sometimes they even send us on their credit card details. We pass most of those emails onto Ruinair.'

'Any word from Mick himself? Or his legal people?' They shake their heads.

They have brought along their well-thumbed copies of 'Ruinair', which I obligingly sign. And now the question I have been avoiding since we met. 'So what did you think of the book?' I ask.

'Obviously we don't agree with all of it.'

Some of the users provided a review of the book online. *'I bought the book in DUB, I was going to start reading it on the flight coming home from DUB, but I managed to sit in seat 1C, with 2 STN based Ruinair Maintenance staff sitting next to me and periods through the flight with Cabin Crew hovering by the galley, so I thought better of it.'*

Others opine: *'All along, the author displays a prejudice against Ruinair and endeavours to mock, disparage and criticise it. Of course, the first chapter is about a delayed flight (in a 23 year old 737, meaning it happened a long time ago) and the complete catastrophic horror story as usual. To imply that this happens all the time is rather dishonest, as Ruinair punctuality is amongst the best, and perhaps the very best in the whole commercial aviation sector. The author makes his own contribution by explaining his strategy to keep an entire row of three seats all to himself, so doing his bit not to make a Ruinair experience any more pleasant for others. There are few things more pleasant in life than flying on Ruinair. The author asks about the "FR" prefix: if the "R" stands for Ruinair, someone tell me please, what does the "F" stand for? In my opinion, "F" stands for Fantastic! Or is it Fabulous? The Ruinair fan will read this book with interest, as any book about his favourite airline, but won't learn much new, and won't find it fair towards Ruinair.'*

Finally when I have run out of questions and my return flight beckons, they turn the tables on me.

'We have a question for you,' notes Grad. 'Do you think we are obsessed with Ruinair?' This is after Grad has shown me a log book he has kept for many years showing all the flights he has taken in his life, including each with the flight duration and his seat number, and after Admin has shown me an Excel printout of the flights he has taken with Ruinair, including the price of each flight, which is usually in cents.

'Obsessed? You obsessed with Ruinair? No. Compared to myself ... you are not obsessed.'

The Ruinair fan forum website has truly great potential. This year Ruinair will fly 58,000,000 passengers. To date there are 154 registered fans. There are only 57,999,846 outstanding fans of Ruinair.

Hungary

Flight w6 210 – Friday @ 7.50 p.m. – LTN-BUD-LTN

Fare €14 plus taxes, fees and charges €60

Wizz Air claim to be Central Europe's biggest low fares airline, and they may be right with four million passengers per annum, 500 staff and 100 routes. Their 19 stylish pink and purple 180-seater Airbus 320s can be seen at more than 50 'time-efficient regional airports' across Europe. Wizz's main hub is at Budapest, with other bases in Katowice, Warsaw, Gdansk, Poznan, Bucharest, Cluj and Sofia. And like me you are probably thinking, 'Where the heck is Cluj?' It is in Romania and I too will not be going there. There is a common perception that Wizz has the best, or silliest, name of any airline but there's a Swiss airline called flybaboo. Note that the letter i in Wizz Air is an exclamation mark, as in W!zz. *'Now we can all fly.'*

Despite proudly and rightly boasting of 80 destinations to 40 different countries, Lootin' Airport has not improved since my last visit (and book), with the greasy odour of Burger King still permeating the check-in area. Wizz favour puns and advertise flights to Poland with *'You can do a loty with your zloty.'* There are other Wizz advertisements here which advise, *'Beer £0.49. Thirsty? Book a flight to Poland'*, *'Vodka and Herring £4.99. Hungry? Book a flight to Poland'*, *'Feeling romantic? Book a flight to Poland.'* Right. Here's how Wizz advertise bloody Romania: *'Historical sites to get your teeth into. Book a flight to Transylvania.'*

Check-in is quick and painless but involves more security questions than a job interview at MI5. I sit awhile in one of only 30 seats in the check-in area, which I guess is to ensure we don't loiter here but immediately dash off upstairs to do some BAA shopping. The passage of time is only punctuated by the occasional fire alarm ringing when someone screws up the flame grilling of a *Triple Calorie Killer Whopper.*

Before entering the X-ray machines in security control, passengers again discard half-finished bottles of water into the bins, in case they explode on board. I often wonder what everyone did before the advent of bottled water. When you see black and white newsreel footage from the early 1900s, with those crowds of men with moustaches, flat caps and collarless shirts, plus women in wide-brimmed hats and big bustling dresses, very few of them, if any, can be seen carrying bottles of Volvic, Evian or Ballygowan. The only passengers being carefully frisked today are the 20 or so men in jackets that say *'Shooting Team'.*

On board Wizz, we are in a tired and tatty Airbus that has seen better days. The purple seats are worn yet they are comfortable and they recline. It is the crew who make an impression, or otherwise, on any low fares airline. Diana wears a pink blouse and dark trouser suit with a pink micro belt and natty pink internal lining on her jacket. She delivers the safety demonstration with confidence, a smile and even a laugh, the latter I suspect because she really enjoys her job rather than safety being a laughing matter. The crew are happy and personable and they do not seem to be total strangers. No gift trolley is wheeled past. There are no scratch cards, never-ending announcements or hard sell eastwards. I am disappointed because the in-flight magazine Wizzit features gifts such as a plush aircraft which you can squeeze to hear phrases like 'This is your captain speaking' and 'Fasten your seatbelts.'

I read in the week I travel that Hungary's tourism bosses have promised to ensure Budapest does not get overrun with British stag and hen parties following Ruinair launching five new routes from Bristol, Prestwick, Liverpool, Glasgow and East Midlands. *'You cannot avoid attracting these low-spending clients,'* said Hungarian National Tourist Office director Adam Ligeti. *'But what we are keen to avoid is the mistakes of Dublin and Prague, which have found themselves swamped by people only interested in the nightlife and cheap beer.'* He said they would concentrate future promotional efforts on Budapest's historic past and reputation as a centre for art, music and literature. '*Visitors who are more culturally sensitive tend to be higher spending, and it is these people who we want to attract.*' Culturally sensitive types? *C'est Moi.*

Like other places in Europe I was in Budapest 12 years ago for one week's work. I stayed in the Kempinski, which is too expensive for a low fares traveller. I saw nothing of the city sights for four days until the guilty office locals allowed me to take the Friday afternoon off to see some castles. I flew home on Malev Hungarian Airlines in row 1 of business class. My only memory is of the hot dinner, which was boiled chicken and creamed potatoes in a white wine sauce. As I slowly peeled back the tinfoil and looked at my main meal of the day, my first impression of the amorphous white gunge was that someone had been sick.

Hungary's capital is one of the most beautiful cities in Europe. It is a tale of two cities, divided by the Danube. To the west lies serene Buda with its craggy hills, Hapsburg architecture, cobbled alleys and high river terraces running along the spine of the Old Town. To the east lies jolly lively Pest with its grand buildings, wide boulevards, cosy squares, boutiques, theatres, cafés, bars and restaurants. After 400 years of the Romans, 150 years of the Ottomans and 45 years of the Soviets, now it's my turn to Wizz here.

In its heyday, Budapest, with Vienna, was the elegant joint imperial capital of the Austro-Hungarian Hapsburg empire but the reality is that Hungary enjoyed a far less fortunate twentieth century. Having been on the wrong (and losing) side in ww1 and foregoing two thirds of its territory in war reparations, it was later ruled by the Hungarian Arrow Cross Party, a home grown pro-Nazi party which was supported by foreign-backed fascists. Budapest was bombed by the Allies while aligned with Germany at the outset of wwII, and Hungary remained firmly on the Nazi side in the war until 1944 when the Germans arrived, only then to see them replaced in 1945 by Soviet-installed Communists. All in all, it was not such a wonderful war.

The history of this dual authoritarian period is conveniently and commercially available in one location. The House of Terror on the beautiful tree-lined thoroughfare of Andrassy Street is easy to locate since the giant metal awning at roof level in sunlight projects the large stencilled word of 'Terror' onto the walls, plus on the exterior walls there are poignant cameo photographs of those who gave their lives in the deadly struggle for liberation. The location of this museum is no coincidence, since this building was the party headquarters of the Hungarian Nazis in 1944 (and called the House of Loyalty), and between 1945 and 1956 it was the headquarters of the Communist terror organisation, the State Security Office (the latter being run by a man called Gabor Peter whose only previous job was as a tailor's apprentice). The entrance fee of 1,500 forint is nothing compared to the terrifying price to rent an English-language tour handset.

In the lobby is a full-sized Soviet tank in a pool of black water set against a four-storey wall of arty black and white photographs of mostly male victims. Upstairs are spooky rooms with recessed spotlights, throbbing music and stylish yet sparse exhibits. I find it a little strange there are only three rooms dedicated to the Nazis' tenure, yet countless more dedicated to the Soviets, who indulged mainly in interrogations, hangings and sending the citizens off to prison and labour camps. Informers in factories, offices, universities, churches and theatres passed covert information to this House. My favourite room is one with a 1991 video of the Soviets driving their tanks onto trains and going home. We all must take the world's slowest elevator to the basement and must watch a video in this elevator of a man describing how people were hanged here. Fortunately the video is in Hungarian with English subtitles so I can turn away and it all goes over my head. The basement is full of cells and nasty interrogation rooms but I read they have been renovated. It borders on the kitsch in one small cell which has a never-ending recording of a tap dripping water. Overall the basement feels like a professionally dressed movie set rather than a house of pain. There are more guards on each floor watching the visitors than when this was a place of real confinement.

The Dohany Street Synagogue is Europe's largest, so large that it wasn't used in winter since it was difficult to heat. It survived wwii and now commemorates 724,000 Hungarian Jews murdered in the Holocaust. In only 56 days, 437,000 Hungarian Jews were deported.

A third of the victims at Auschwitz were Hungarian citizens. The difference here is that the deportations were organised by Hungary's own Arrow Cross Party. Before the Germans even arrived in Hungary the Arrow Cross made Jews wear the Yellow Star on their clothes. Random Jews were shot and disposed of in the Danube. As the Hungarian Prime Minister said once at a commemorative speech, *This was a hideous crime committed by the Hungarian people against the Hungarian people.* I wander through the mass of graves at the rear of the building where each memorial plaque marks a life cut short in 1945. Close by in the Raoul Wallenberg Memorial Park is a silvery weeping willow Tree of Life where each leaf bears the name of a persecuted Budapest family. The inscription in Hebrew on the top of the memorial reads *Whose agony is greater than mine?*

I gravitate to the Parliament on the banks of the Danube. Nearby is a statue to former Prime Minister Nagy Imre who led an uprising and whom the Soviets executed. He looks towards the Parliament building, as if he is still keeping an eye on the democracy he fostered. There is a black stone monument to the events of 1956, with an eternal flame burning atop. Close by I stop at a small grave decked with flowers and ribbons in the Hungarian national colours of green, red and white. I read a sign which advises that the grave is symbolic and it remembers the 200 civilians shot by troops in Kossuth Square on 25 October 1956. It also advises that the Hungarian flag flying here is unique in that it has a hole in the centre. When the uprising began citizens ripped the hated Communist symbol from the centre of their flag. It is a still day with little or no wind so I cannot see the hole but as I stand and look up a gust comes from nowhere and the flag opens to reveal the centre hole. The flag flies freely for a few seconds, like a private viewing. The moment is lost as two English tourists stop to read the same inscription. 'Fancy that.'

Budapest's famous landmark is a female freedom figure set high on a Buda hill but the statue of her six-metre-tall liberating Soviet soldier is gone. The soldier had piercing evil eyes, a hammer and sickle flag in hand and a machine pistol hanging from his neck. When proletariat dictatorship statues were no longer deemed to be politically correct, the soldier was moved from his conspicuous location into exile with other Communist-era statuary in Szoborpark (Statue Park), which is a great place to go if you'd like to see 40 pre-1990 statues together in a desolate field 15 km outside a Central European capital city. This is multi-ton socialism at its best, rekindling memories of the cherished Hungarian-Soviet Friendship. The only competition for this park is another in Lithuania called 'Stalin's World'. Statue Park is a sort of Communist Disneyland, but without so much fun or candy floss. It recounts *'the good old days when Hungarians drove Trabants, lived in blocks of flats, stood in banana queues, had two passports, coupon books, no TV on Mondays and no freedom of speech. That was the way it was, Comrade, locked behind the Iron Curtain.'*

There is a stone pair of Stalin's boots, like the ones left on the pedestal when a crowd pulled down his statue in October 1956, but they are 'an authentic replica of the original'. There is a statue of Lenin with one outstretched hand and legend has it that disgruntled Csepel Iron factory workers used to place a slice of bread in his open hand when the security apparatus were not looking. There is a Trabant which despite its being made from pressed plastic units, I can sit inside and watch it visibly rust as I wait to get out of this park. The souvenir shop sells rip-off coffee mugs with a red logo in the style of Starbucks called *'Redstar Coffee'*. And if you are really brave, you can even buy a replica of a Soviet army military medal.

Hungary did more than the other Soviet satellites to tear down the Berlin Wall, by allowing East Germans to sneak over to the West in 1989 via the Sopronpuszta crossing on the Austrian/Hungarian border. The only remaining Communist monument in the city is a gold-topped Soviet War Memorial obelisk which inappropriately lies outside the United States Embassy in Szabadsag Park. One wreath lies on the steps and the obelisk is entirely surrounded by high metal fences so no one can lay any other wreaths here. Edgy gun-toting guards from the embassy of the most paranoid nation on earth watch me scribbling some notes, but they are safe enough today because as a humble writer, I am only armed with the pen.

There is something equally terrifying inside St Stephen's

Basilica, more particularly in the adjoining Chapel of the Holy Right Hand. I should be coming here to pray but like all the other morbid people, I really want to see the Hand. There is an immediate problem and it's not a tour bus of Japanese following an umbrella plus a guide, nor a battalion of aged German ladies marching in unison. Unbelievably, and of all the places for this to happen, there is a church service on inside the cathedral and we have to wait 10 minutes for the priest to finish. Then the zealots open the red ropes to clear the way to the Hand. We stride though the darkened cathedral and enter the side chapel in a deadly hush of expectation. There is a small silver casket set upon a stand, which contains the mummified right hand of St Stephen. This is Hungary's oldest relic. Someone with money to burn inserts a 100-forint coin and the casket lights up for one minute.

I lean closer and I can see the clenched fist although it's small and withered, what with it being 1,000 years old and having spent all of the last millennium in Transylvania, Dalmatia, Vienna and finally Budapest. There is a small photographic display showing an anatomical examination of the Hand in 1999, fingernails and all. It's like something you might see in one of these scary Hammer House of Horror movies. I ask the curator in bad English where the rest of St Stephen lies but he waves his hands in ignorance. So it's not immediately clear where the remaining St Stephen's remains remain.

The Hotel Gellert is an institution built in 1918 and its tiered edifice looks like a sagging wedding cake about to topple over. The hotel is named after Bishop Gellert whom pagans killed by rolling him down the steep hill in a wooden barrel into the Danube. The furniture is 30 years older than I am. The guests are 30 years older than the furniture. The television in the room shows Magyar TV, but it's different to the MTV I watch. At breakfast I watch a waiter carefully and repeatedly smooth out a creased paper napkin on a table, rather than bin it and simply get a new napkin. It might be a subconscious throwback to the old Communist era when nothing was wasted. I read that if you worked in the East German civil service and you wanted a new pencil, then you had to first present the stub of the old pencil. There was probably a form in triplicate. And you'd have to borrow someone else's pencil to complete the required paperwork.

Service is slow in Hungary. By the time you read this chapter, I will still be having breakfast at the Gellert. Check-in is a wonderfully hostile experience since I am able to complain before I got a room key.

'The 47 tram is not operating. I had to walk across the Danube.' The Danube is not a small river.

Big Goran at reception is not in agreement. 'The tram *is* operating.'

'It is not. The bridge is closed for a year for renovations. So the tram does not operate.'

Goran is insistent. 'It does operate. There is a bus by the same number. 47.'

'That's a bus. That's not a tram, Goran.'

I go to my room but it smells like a tobacco factory so I return. 'I wanted a no-smoking room.'

Goran looks at his paperwork. 'You did not *ask* for a no-smoking room.'

'I did ask when I made my reservation online,' I reply.

Goran hands me a piece of paper. 'This is your reservation. Do you see it *anywhere*?' I don't.

The interior of the hotel is aged and shabby but the guests do not come here for the rooms alone. My room has a bath which I will not be using because downstairs is something far more appealing. First I must read a slightly worrying guidance leaflet left in my room. I am advised to change my clothes in my room and enter the residents' elevator in the north wing of the hotel in my bathing suit and bath robe. 'During the elevator trip you will receive a plastic card from the attendant which you will need to get through the entrance gate when you must show the bar code to the sensor screen of the entry machine.'

I exit my room in my Tommy Hilfiger gentlemen's swimming trunks, flip-flops and bathrobe and feel like a bit of a prat as I walk the corridors in the face of other guests who are dressed in hats and coats. The woman in the ancient residents' lift has been going up (and down) in the world for decades. Her name is Regina, she speaks no English but wears an ominous medical doctor's coat although I doubt she is more qualified than to press buttons in a lift. She hands me a plastic card to gain entry. I walk through a lofty foyer and follow the signs to a maze of cubicles where a guy in white shows me the procedure to leave my robe and flip-flops in a locked cubicle and in return I get a numbered tag to go on my wrist. None of the staff can speak English until you ask and they say, 'Go there, turn right, down the stairs, then left.' There is no hard sell here; you have to ask for everything or use your psychic powers; a few of the retail outlets are shut and I suspect the attendants wear the same uniforms given to them by the Communists.

Seventy million litres of 21° C–78° C thermal water spring forth daily in Budapest from 120 natural thermal springs. People have been bathing here since the fourth century B.C. It's all down to the earth's thin crust which gushes hot water wherever you go here. When the Turks ruled Budapest they built enduring baths for their hygiene, health benefits and sociability. Budapest's denizens visit their baths in the same way that Parisians frequent cafés, Finns frequent saunas and the Irish and British frequent pubs. Throughout the veritable ebb and flow of empires, Budapest's citizens have never ceased to bathe.

The Gellert baths, unlike Ruinair, provide refunds if you pay the entrance fee but spend less than two hours inside. The baths are not owned by the hotel but by city authorities—the Communists enacted this proletariat benefit. I enter the fin-de-siècle art nouveau thermal baths, with wonderful sculptures, flora and fauna, mosaic tiles, colonnades of amber porcelain, and tinted glass. A magnificent glass-roofed domed hall with pillars and balconies surrounds the large swimming pool into which lions spew jets of water. The room looks more like a museum hall with a serious flooding problem. I suspect the traditions of style and service, plus the décor, are unchanged here since the time of Emperor Franz Joseph. A Carrara marble statue of Venus lies at the far end and nearby are wooden boards which itemise the treatments.

The menu of cures is more extensive than the hotel restaurant menu. There is a physiotherapeutic department, a physiotherapy unit and an inhalatorium, the latter of which Bill Clinton might have frequented in his student days. There is an outdoor rooftop sunbathing terrace for nudists, but it's not so popular in December. The 13 different pools of thermal water contain sodium, calcium-magnesium hydrocarbonates and sulphates with a fluoride content and are allegedly a fix for degenerative disorders of joints and the spine, chronic arthritis, disorders of the vertebral disks, lumboischialgia (whatever that is but it sounds fairly nasty and it's probably fatal), neuralgic pain and those peripheral circulation disorders, which is no mean feat for mere hot water. You don't have to be sick to come here, but it helps. Based on the claims made for this restorative water I don't know why there is any need to have hospitals in Hungary. In fact in Hungary the National Health Service officially pays for patient visits to the various bath houses.

There is electrotherapy treatment (galvanic treatment, iontophoresis, diadynamic, short wave treatment, stimulus treatment, ultrasonic therapy, interference treatment and magnetotherapy) which I will not partake of since I have no desire to be plugged directly into the mains supply of the Hungarian national power utility, particularly considering that the voltage in Continental Europe differs to the voltage back home, and also because of all that water floating about here, which acts as a natural conductor. There is mechanotherapy (physiotherapy, foot massage, medical massage, underwater massage by water current) for which I learn 'Doctor's Orders' are required, which I haven't got, so I won't be doing that mechano lark either. There is even a dental clinic here and based on the photographic evidence in their glossy brochure, not only would I emerge with gleaming white teeth, but also I would become blonde and very attractive.

There are massages on offer such as Thai, but also lesser-known varieties. There is a massage that is applied in a sitting position to a fully clothed guest during breaks in boring conferences and so it's called the Manager Massage. There's a Hungarian Wine Cream massage, using a cream made of famous Hungarian wines. There's a traditional Dry Brush Massage using stroking techniques applied with a brush of bristles, most likely administered by sadists and only requested by masochists. There's a Tibetan Honey massage, developed from the traditional massage techniques carried out by

Tibetan monks. The honey has a high content of enzyme, vitamins and minerals but it sounds so erotic that I doubt any Tibetan monk ever practised, or condoned, it. So I consider the least terrifying item on the menu, balneotherapy (pool and tub baths, mud therapy, tub bath treatment with carbonated water) and decide to take the plunge.

I descend the steps into the swimming pool but recoil. I expect the water to be warm but it's nippy. There's no going back. I go under, exhale and swim away from the shallow end. Everyone else swims in a clockwise direction so I go with the flow. I am over-taken in the fast lane. About half way down the pool I remember that I am a crap swimmer and I begin to struggle. I look up through the glass window and see a man with a video camera who is filming two young girls in bikinis, making him either the proud-est father or the bravest pervert in Budapest. I have that sinking feeling. My feet search for the tiles but I'm in the 2-metre-deep end zone. A lady lifeguard lazily watches me and I will be mortally embarrassed if she has to plunge in to rescue me and tomorrow morning everyone will point at me with glee at breakfast and I might make the front page of the *Budapest Times*. I resort to an unseen doggy paddle and nonchalantly grab the railing of the steps before clambering out. That's enough freezing cold swimming for one day.

Beside the pool is an inviting crescent-shaped wallowing bath where people bob up and down. I am overjoyed to find it's fantas-tically warm. I could easily pass half a day in here, ruminating, cogitating and digesting, mentally writing the next travel book. There are 30 people lounging on the edges on underwater stone seats. A few ladies built like weight-lifters enter and the water level rises. An Italian couple exchange meaningful kisses in the centre and if it was not for 30 pair of eyes, I sense that they would go fur-ther. Two people wearing plastic shower caps taken from their hotel room just look silly. A few latecomers paddle around the centre of the pool, waiting for a good seat like last diners in a restaurant without a prior reservation. The boys watch the girls and the girls watch the boys and I cannot help thinking this must be a great place to pick up members of the opposite sex because you get to see so much more before that first awkward date. Two American girls in immodest bikinis are visibly excited to be here.

'Let's go to the sauna.'

'Oh, my Gawd.'

Next are two thermal pools where the walls are covered in blue and green majolica tiles adorned with tulips and honeysuckle. The large rectangular baths display signs showing the temperatures: one is at 36°C and one is at 38°C. Being a wuss like most people here I start with the 36° pool which is so fantastic that I could stay forever. Men sit nearby submerged except for their heads and a newspaper held at arm's length. Some octogenarians pass the time of day. Professorial types and businessmen discuss what's new. I sit under a fountain of warm water from a dolphin head and my back takes a pounding, better than any chiropractor visit. There is a gentle hum of conversation. This is in contrast to the 38° pool where I soon sit alongside others and we all look calmly at each other in a sort of couldn't-be-bothered fashion, thinking to ourselves, 'Jeez, the water in this pool is hot.' There is only a difference of 2° but I now know how a lobster feels when first dropped into the cooking pot.

I am extremely fortunate to be still wearing my trunks since signs outside say that these are usually segregated male and female thermal pools with separate entrances. But there are renovations in progress so the ladies have come to the gents'. Otherwise I would be wearing what's called a *koteny*: an apron-like garment made from cotton which only covers the front parts, so to speak.

Next I take some slow steps to the steam room and am relieved to find it's not so hot at all, until I realise I am in the ante-chamber and there is one more door to open. Inside this second room there is a dense misty fog so I can only see a foot or two in front. I take a seat on a bench and assume I am alone. Not so. One by one others rise up out of the mist like gorillas and leave. I endure five minutes until I am gasping for air. I don't know how hot it is, but anywhere else in Europe they would call for the fire brigade. Amazingly enough there are locals pulling up spare chairs to put their feet on as they open a newspaper for a long stay. Like any bad fire I drop my head lower since there should be more air

down below, and there is. I am well done so I exit, receiving a small
burn on the hot door handle. I could have expired in there.

I wasn't ill when I arrived but after two hours I am all aches and
pains from the exercise. Budapest is not the place to come for a
dirty weekend, because you will leave cleaner than you ever were.
The pleasure of taking the waters has little to do with cures and
remedies. I find the relief is mental: it's an escape from the twenty-
first century and the terror of a curvaceous European capital
outside. The citizens using these pools have experienced the poles
of decadence and despair all in one century. So if you find yourself
in hot water in Budapest, do what two million locals do. Relax,
parboil yourself and sweat it out.

The Ruinair Song

http://www.youtube.com

Verse 1
*Ruinair you just messed up my day,
but I'm probably gonna continue buying your cheap flights anyway,
you left me sitting for hours waiting for a plane,
your lack of customer service just drives me insane.
You're meant to be the proud airline of our nation
but you just about get us to our destination,
your constant lottery announcements and your cranky cabin crew,
but I'm a hypocrite 'cause I'll continue flying with you …*

Chorus
*Ruinair, Ruinair, your service is so crap,
the fat guy beside me is practically sitting on my lap,
extra baggage charges and Priority boarding,
if there's any more delays I'm breaking through this hoarding …*

Verse 2
*I can't say I like them but I usually get to my venue,
as cheap as McDonald's and their Super Saver Menu.
Mick O'Leery has a fiery reputation,
takes the piss a bit with airline industry regulations.
Been described in the press as an arrogant twat
but he doesn't really care 'cause he earns a lot
His deliberate targeting and criticism of competitors, governments
  and airport authorities doesn't go unnoticed and he'll have to pay
  for it someday,
oh yeah he'll have to pay for it someday …*

Chorus
Ruinair, Ruinair, your service is so crap,
the fat guy beside me is practically sitting on my lap,
extra baggage charges and Priority boarding,
if there's any more delays I'm breaking through this hoarding ...

COMPOSED BY RONAN TRAINOR, 2008
USED WITH PERMISSION

Slovenia

Flight EZY3245 – Tuesday @ 1.00 p.m. – STN-LJU-STN

Fare €109 plus taxes, fees and charges €34

Ruinair once flew to Slovenia's second city of Maribor but they quietly closed the route and never told me. While they open new routes with a fanfare, they shut routes with a whimper. It's a surprise that the Maribor route closed since it represented the ideal Ruinair destination, being 137 km from the capital. So it's impossible to get to Slovenia on Ruinair unless I fly to Trieste, and that's in Italy. Slovenia's national airline, Adria Airways, fly from Dublin to Slovenia but the fare is way beyond my means, the flights only operate on a Saturday in summertime and they land in Ljubljana after midnight, way past my bed time.

There are 11 scheduled airlines flying to Slovenia and the next best deal is once again with easyJet. So I hop on a Ruinair flight to Stansted and connect to my favourite low fares airline. Mick? *'We want to eliminate the idea that easyJet is somehow a low-cost carrier. It isn't. Its average fares are 70 per cent higher than ours. It's time to sort out who is the low fare airline. It is Ruinair. It is not easyJet. They are a medium-fare airline. The future is not about the competition between Ruinair and easyJet because with the greatest respect that competition is over. Eventually they will lose to Ruinair because we have a lower cost base. They are British Midland Mark 2. EasyJet are not the brightest sandwiches in the picnic basket. Obviously, the Queen, when she knighted Stelios, hit him a bit hard with the sword.'* And what does easyJet management think of Mick? Toby Nicol, easyJet's longest-serving director, said: *'He is widely known within the industry as Michael O'Really.'*

EasyJet's online check-in facility is much better than Ruinair's similar effort. With easyJet I enter my booking reference and surname on their home page and it takes me direct to a boarding card which I print out. Easy. With Ruinair I first go to their check-in page where I must enter my booking reference, my email address and the departure and destination airports. This takes me to another page where I have to tick the boxes to five stupid questions about the size of my carry-on baggage, to confirm that I own a passport, that no one's interfered with my baggage, and so on and on, etc. Next I am taken to another page where I enter my date of birth, my nationality, whether I use a passport or ID card, my passport number and my passport expiry date. Could Ruinair make their online check-in more difficult? Nope. Why do they do it? So that someone (either myself or an 80-year-old dear with impaired vision) makes an error in entering some of this tricky non-essential data, and they can stop us as the departure gate and send us back to pay full fare for a later flight, and all because we selected the wrong nationality drop-down option and said we were Icelandic.

Reaching Stansted's departure gates is easier with easyJet since I can use the transit train. In contrast Ruinair prefer to make me hike over long distances. Why, Mick? *'We're not going to pull out of Stansted, but we're not going to be robbed there either. It's Taj Mahals, gherkins and building projects for wannabe candidates for the House of Lords. BAA should stop buying Noddy train sets which take you halfway round Essex to get you to a satellite building 60 yards away. Our passengers would prefer to walk.'* Who ever asked us? BAA has been bought by Spanish construction company Ferrovial. *'They're a Johnny Foreigner. It doesn't matter whether it is a British highwayman, a Spanish highwayman or an American highwayman. You are still getting robbed and that won't change until you break BAA's monopoly up.'*

EasyJet's Speedy boarding is a superior offering to Ruinair's Priority boarding. Firstly, easyJet board those who paid for Speedy boarding (which is fair), mostly comprising men in linen suits with Panama hats and some who even wear ties. Next they board families with small children who have not had to pay for the privilege, unlike on Ruinair. Because I checked in online, I am in Boarding Group A and I did not have to pay for that privilege, unlike on Ruinair. Lastly Boarding Group B board. Easy.

Across the aisle, an Englishman and a Slovenian teenage girl engage in tentative conversation.

'Why do you visit Slovenia?' she asks politely.

'A friend of ours bought an apartment there and he asked us to come down to see it. To be honest when he told me where he had bought it, I didn't know where the bloody hell it was. What about you?'

'I am from Slovenia.'

'So you are going home to visit your parents?' he asks.

'I am going home to visit my dentist.' Everything is now possible with low fares air travel.

We are about to taxi to take off when a middle-aged Slovenian lady beside me stands up. 'Excuse me, I forgot to turn off my mobile phone. I must turn it off.' Jesus wept. I arise and quickly let her out. The aircraft picks up speed. She stands in the aisle with the phone in her hand, rocking back and forth, and turns to me. 'Do you know how to turn this off? I forget.' Jesus wept again. I try to help but she is the only person with an Ericsson, while we all own Nokias. She finally remembers and sits down. Later in-flight she produces a weighty tome written by Barack Obama and she begins to read his thoughts on the world. I cannot help wondering if George W. Bush has ever produced a book, and if so, was it all coloured in? I buy some water on board and receive lots of coins. This is what Obama calls *'Change .... we can believe in.'*

In-flight it is easy on the eye. The interior of the Airbus A319 cabin is a relaxing white with subtle orange trim and the comfortable seats have head-rests and seat pockets. Unlike Ruinair's Boeings this does not feel like the inside of a cattle truck. The pilot makes clear, informative announcements. The cabin crew exude confidence and authority and are as English and as mature as a good cheddar, and as a result we can understand them when they speak to us. There is an absolute and complete silence in the cabin when they make the safety announcement. When polite Diana asks me if I would like something from the food and drinks trolley, she refers to me as Sir. I don't think anyone on a Ruinair flight has ever referred to me as Sir. Sure, they have called me lots of other names in their time, but not Sir. The easyJet uniforms have recently been upgraded and the all-female cabin crew wear the new uniform with pride. Diana sports a white blouse with a crease as sharp as a wit, along with grey waistcoat and skirt, plus orange neck scarf. Mick follows uniform news closely. *'Last week British Airways said they would introduce new uniforms. It's back to the Fifties, which is where most of these muttonheads' thinking is. If fine wine and food don't get you and Heathrow doesn't persuade you, now you have got shorter skirts to attract you back to* BA.*'*

Unlike his peer at Ruinair, no one knows the Chief Executive of easyJet. Andrew Harrison doesn't dress up in funny costumes, doesn't pull funny faces for the cameras, nor does he use the F-word on every possible occasion. His strategy is simple and clear. *'EasyJet is a fundamentally strong business and it's going to be one of the winners in Europe's short-haul market. We have about six per cent of the market. We aim to roughly double it over the next five years. We have a great brand and we have great people. This means we have a huge competitive advantage. One of the challenges is to keep it simple. Complexity means cost. As soon as you become an aviation anorak you start to lose money. Our philosophy is to do one thing and be the best at it—short-haul European flying. As for our customer proposition, you can summarise it as low cost, care and convenience. Our philosophy is that by making easyJet a happy place to work the crew will smile at the passengers and they'll fly with us again. A happy crew means happy passengers. And in my view it costs no more money to treat people well than it does to treat them badly.'*

Aerodrom Joze Pucnik Ljubljana is a big name for a small airport, and it's an unlikely airport for an EU capital city. The apron is plagued with Adria Airways aircraft, wherever they fly to and from. We are through the tiny terminal in minutes. Outside Arrivals it is tidy, clean and relaxed. The taxi drivers sit on benches in the sun, chatting and eating Magnum ice creams, rather than preying on passengers as in other airports. This all looks and feels a little bit like being in Italy, which is unsurprising because any further west and Slovenia would be in Northern Italy. This small country of two million inhabitants is surrounded by Italy, Austria, Hungary and Croatia and is landlocked with the exception of a precious 46 km of coastline along the Adriatic Sea south of Trieste, where Ruinair would have deposited me. The air is fresh and clean. Hikers and climbers wait with rucksacks and boots. The majestic Julian Alps surround the low-lying airport. Now this looks and feels a little bit like being in Switzerland. An easyJet and Wizz Air bus takes us through winding country roads and pine forests until we join the motorway to the city centre. The traffic is leisurely, what with all the cars having a 'SLO' sticker on their rear bumper. The motorway signs advise our bus driver to *'Keep Safety Distance'*. I overhear some English passengers chatting behind me on the bus.

'This looks lovely,' says one looking at the passing sights. They are not wrong.

'Yes,' replies another. 'I think of it as a clean Prague.'

Another opens a map of the city centre. 'It looks like there is lots to explore.'

'The scale of the map is misleading. It's quite a small city.'

Ljubljana was named by the same spelling fiends who decided that Liechtenstein is a good name for a country. It is Central Europe's smallest capital city, with a population of 280,000. It is small enough to explore on foot and first, and lasting, impressions are impressive. The hub of the city is Presernov Square which has a statue of the Slovenian poet of the same name (he wrote their national anthem), plus on an adjoining street stands the bust of Julija Primic, the girl for whom he nursed an intense, but famously unrequited, love. They can still look at each other, but safely from afar—she was only 16 years old and her folks were not too keen on him calling round. A local businessman in a suit shows three others around his city square, and how proud he appears about what he has to offer! I am slightly perturbed by the small Hare Krishna group who are wailing and distributing snacks, which I accept, but I am unlikely to convert from Roman Catholicism solely based on the merits of their excellent coconut cookies. They soon pack up the cookies and go to wail elsewhere. It's hot and sunny yet it's raining, but only in Presernov Square. There are warning signs with open umbrellas and dark rain clouds about this micro-climate. The clever city fathers have installed a water spray far above the square from which rain of sorts wafts down. Girls in bikini tops cycle around underneath the wonderfully cooling rain. I am beginning to like Ljubljana. Hugely.

I am aware that since I exited my hotel, I have not encountered a motor car. Some hired locals wobble about on giant penny-farthing bicycles and offer free rides. One father accepts the challenge to his children's horror, does very well on the bike and returns to a hero's welcome. There's even a guy dressed as a post-man from 1860 who rides a tricycle and he is a mobile tourist information point. The city centre is pedestrianised and many people fly about by bicycle. There are bicycle lanes everywhere. Hotels offer free bicycles to guests so I return with great trepid-ation to my hotel, where I am given white bike no. 3 from the rack—which is a close escape because bikes 1 and 2 are pink. I haven't been on a bike for years and the last time was in France on a bike that I fondly christened the *Ball-Crusher*.

I cycle off precariously to hilly Tivoli Park, the lungs of this city, then through the leafy diplomatic embassy belt to the old city walls. The only ruins here are Roman, and even they look well. I drift dangerously towards the suburbs to find the recently named Path of Remembrance. It's a 33-km walking, jogging and cycling track that circles the entire city but it wasn't always like this. In World War II the city was surrounded by the Italian army. Never ones for getting into unnecessary combat, and possibly ending up on the losing side, the Italians decided to construct an encircling 33-km barbed-wire fence, behind which they could safely observe and control the lives of the citizens of Ljubljana. I cycle along and see the monuments to where bunkers and checkpoints once stood. For such a small city, this was a big fence.

I risk all on my bike as I travel over smooth cobblestones and rattling wooden decking to cross the Ljubljanica river, which bisects this compact city, using several bridges, each with their own unique history. My favourite bridge is the Triple Bridge, which I cycle over three times. This was once a single bridge but after an earthquake in 1895, the Austrians offered some funds to repair the bridge. There was really nothing wrong with the existing bridge but the cute locals took the money anyway from the Austrians and a famed local architect named Josef Plecnik had the neat idea of building two more bridges alongside. The streets on the modern west side follow an easily navigable Roman street plan whilst the streets in the winding old town and castle on the east side of the river are potentially fatal for someone as useless on a bicycle as I demonstrably am. But around every corner of the old town there are breathtaking scenes. One example is the Stari Trg Street, which curls away from the town hall, past rows of merchants' Baroque town houses and becomes so narrow that there is hardly room for quirky shops, trestle dining tables set up along the centre of the street and me on my clearly defective bicycle. The saddle is loose so that I have to either sit back on the bicycle or allow the saddle to dip forward, leading to more unpleasant gonad trouble.

I brake by the city cathedral which, like many other things here, is small and not wildly interesting but there is more to it than I think. It portrays the entire history of Slovenia, with the Romans, the Huns (i.e. Germans) and the Hapsburgs, right up to Pope John Paul's visit, all shown on one handy bronze door. At the town hall is the landmark Robba fountain, of which the top half is made of Italian marble and the bottom half is not because the bottom half sank in the Adriatic when it was being towed over from Italy. I free-wheel into the market square where locals sell produce in a neo-classical colonnade. I only see one depressing sight on my own *Tour de Ljubljana*—a Russian war monument at the Parliament. There are no beggars, no vagrants, no stray rabid dogs, no jay-walking, no graffiti, no noise, no potholes, no road works and not even one missing cobblestone. This city has left no stone unturned in their desire for the perfect visitor experience. I divide Europe into places where I could happily live and places I could not. I could live here.

Tourism is big in Ljubljana. I have never seen such an array of tourist literature as in the main tourist office near the Triple Bridge. They have every known brochure for every type of person and every possible interest. The only missing brochure is: '*What to do and see in Ljubljana if you are 55–60 years old and like Russian Iconography and Roller Blading.'* They have city walking tours and boat tours along the river, and here the fleet of tourist boats comprises only two flat-bottomed craft, not an annoying armada of the things. There is a tiny toy train service which runs around the old city but I am too old to ride that train. Instead I take the funicular train up to the castle. Usually in Central Europe these trains comprise a small wooden box from the last century which is dragged precariously up the side of a sheer precipice on a thin metal wire. But here the funicular rail is one year old, it is made from steel and glass and has a driver who greets us all. Inside the beautifully preserved castle they show open air movies in the summertime. The current film on show, and this is reflective of how small this city is, is entitled *'No Country For Old Man'* (sic).

Every major attraction seems to be free, even the revival of the wonderful old tradition of punishing dodgy bakers (who bake underweight bread), where they still dip such bakers into the river in a big basket hanging from the end of a log (Cobblers Bridge, Saturdays 10 a.m., cheer loudly). Best of all they do not offer one of those stupid hop-on hop-off open-top bus tours where you pay €20 to sit on the exposed roof of a double-decker bus to see the top 10 sights in two speedy hours from afar, but where no one ever hops on and off because the bus service is too infrequent and we are too lazy, where the recorded commentary comes via a tiny ear piece which is only clearly audible in Italian and Serbo-Croat and where the same tour can be had for a tenth of the price by buying a daily pass on the city's extensive tram, bus and metro network. The tourist office here stays open until an amazing 9 p.m. They even offer free one-hour language classes in Slovenian for beginners. My hotel mailed my postcards for free. These people are keen. They badly want our business. Yet there are few tour parties. As I overheard one American quaintly say inside the gift section of the tourist office, 'These Ljubljanans have really got their shit together.'

One thing that is big in Ljubljana is the Margarita pizzas at Ljubjanski Dvor. I ask for a Small size pizza but they bring me one that's the same size as my bicycle wheel. I spend the next 20 minutes trying to make a dent in the spokes of this wheel with little success. I cut it up into small triangles and try to hide the small pieces under other big pieces. After a while the pizza remnants begin to taste like some of the rubber from my bicycle tyre. When I am beaten the waiter leaves the remains on my table for as long as possible to embarrass me. But it could have been worse. I could have ordered something bigger from the menu. Some children nearby order a Medium Classic size and when it arrives and hangs limp over the side of the table they implore their parents to rescue them from obesity. Some families of eight or more went mad and ordered the Family size, which two waiters must carry over, and they are still there eating.

However be warned that eating horse meat is perfectly acceptable in Slovenia. I came across the *Red Hot N' Horse* fast food outlet, where a burger made from horse meat costs €3.50. I did not partake but it's the sort of restaurant you should visit if you genuinely believe you could eat a horse. The Slovenians seem to have a sense of humour when it comes to food and drink. I accidentally halt my reject bicycle near the *JuiceBox* bar and so can marvel at their extensive menu, which includes the following fruit drinks: a Britney Pears, a Nelly Fruitado, a Bananarama, a Strawberry Fields, a Ginger Spice, a Berry White, a Rick Appley and a Flu Fighter. Eventually I plumped for a refreshing Smoothie Operator. Later I call into a convenience store and purchase a 250-ml bottle of water for a mere €0.29. I almost fall off my bike.

Ljubljana is no rubbish capital city. In fact it is the cleanest city I have ever visited. I hardly see a single piece of trash on a pavement or on a street in four days. They are obsessed with rubbish. In the café and bar area along the river, three city employees dressed like waiters in black trousers, white shirts and bow ties patrol the streets in the vain search for an odd cigarette butt or scrap of paper. Even the city bin lorry on the streets is white and gleaming clean and looks like it has been manufactured yesterday. As it's about to pass my bicycle by I am sure I will receive a disgusting waft such as when I am in my car behind a Dublin bin lorry, but no, not here. The Ljubljana bin lorry is hermetically sealed with no pong at all.

This may also be the safest city in Europe. I only see four police officers during my stay. Two of these pass by on horseback a few times, which I suspect is for effect rather than to chase villains who are also on horseback. The other two police officers, a guy and a girl, walk around the city streets, smile at tourists, distribute tickets to very rare cars and generally look like they enjoy their job. I don't know what a Slovenian police car might look like because I never saw one. Do they have any crime in Ljubljana?

Ljubljana is so different to the many other former Soviet Bloc capitals and most credit Marshal Tito, who led a more benevolent regime in the former Yugoslavia, from which Slovenia gained independence in 1991. This is a big little city, not a little big city, and there is a big difference. It's the best kept secret in Europe, the ideal weekend-sized Lilliputian destination, preserved by the absence of low Ruinair flights and the fantastically high air fares of the national carrier Adria Airways, and long may this continue. Ljubljana remains a city of churches, spires, statues, columns, bells, cafés, bars, restaurants, markets, parks, rivers, bicycles, artists, musicians, Union beer, ice cream cones, shades, awnings, and all combine perfectly.

Everyone in this city soon gravitates to visitor Nirvana along the Ljubljanica river embankment. The area positively hums from lunch time until the early hours. Chilled-out students slouch in expansive wicker furniture with plump red cushions. Elegant ladies dressed in black sit on tall stools and sip chilled glasses of white wine. Table cloths flutter as diners enjoy four salubrious courses. Scruffy people would likely be politely asked to move on so as not to pollute this cosmopolitan vista. I can only deduce that half of the population of the city work as waiters and waitresses so as to serve the other dining half of the population.

So I chuck the bike into the river to dine alfresco at Zlata Ribica on salmon carpaccio with capers and rocket, followed by sea bass, whilst studiously avoiding the foal fillet on the menu, which was a non-runner for me. Through the weeping willows I see the Triple Bridge and the pink façade of the Franciscan Church. The sun is setting as the friendly, attentive waitress brings me a pannacotta with strawberries.

'All good?' she asks.

I am reminded of the Ljubljana tourist office's marketing slogan. *I FEEL sLOVEnia*. 'Very good.'

Advertising Feature

Mick O'Leery, the chief executive of the Irish low fares airline Ruinair, has a mean streak. And for that reason, it's hard not to like him. Consider Ruinair's entry into the Brussels market. At a February press conference, Mr O'Leery called Sabena, the partly privatised carrier that dominated Belgian airspace, a bunch of 'swindlers' engaged in 'daylight robbery' because of their 'outrageously high prices'. That's not exactly how most major airlines announce new routes. Then Ruinair's ads became even more provocative. Beside a picture of the Mannequin Pis, a famous Belgian statue of a urinating urchin, appeared the words: 'Pissed off with Sabena's high fares?' Some papers have translated the ads as 'Fed up with', but Ruinair's spokesman, when he could stop laughing, insisted: 'No, that's a mistranslation. It is suppose to be "pissed off".' Ruinair proudly posts the advert, in English, on its website. The site also allows the public to vote on whether Sabena is a high-fare airline; 99.7 per cent of respondents in this highly unscientific poll voted Yes. 'We're still trying to figure out who the other 0.3 per cent are,' says Mr O'Leery. 'Maybe they are Sabena employees.' Sabena took its case to the Commercial Court of Brussels. Sabena's brief said Ruinair's publicity efforts were 'provoking and denigrating and misleading the consumer in a cunning way.' 'This is marvellous stuff. I can hardly wait to go to court on this one,' Mr O'Leery declares. It doesn't matter 'how weird and wonderful Belgian law is, because it will take a miracle for Sabena to win.' And if that miracle occurs? 'We will make new adverts with the same message.' Certainly Mr O'Leery doesn't lose much sleep over the accusations that he is deepening Sabena's woes: 'Awww,' he says, 'I'm deeply wounded.'

The UK's Advertising Standards Authority has ordered Ruinair not to re-run adverts which contained explicit sexual innuendoes after it promoted its Valentine's Day fares with the slogan: 'Blow me! (These fares are hard to swallow!)' and 'Satisfaction Guaranteed!' with an illustration of two pairs of feet, one on top of the other. Ruinair said the campaign was designed to be humorous in the context of Valentine's Day. The company agreed the adverts were suggestive but denied they were offensive.

BRAND CHANNEL.COM

Ruinair chief executive Mick O'Leery takes a cheeky approach to advertising. However, the airline got a taste of its own medicine from British low fares airline easyJet. In a full-page advertisement in the Financial Times, easyJet congratulated Ruinair on a 'sparkling set of results' for the fiscal year under a headline that blared: 'Congratulations to Europe's No. 2 … from Europe's No. 1 low cost airline.' EasyJet, however, took the opportunity to point out that its revenue had outstripped Ruinair's by over £10 million. 'It's good to see that the airline is in capable hands,' the advert went on, taking another leaf from Ruinair's preferred method of personalising its attacks. 'Who knows, next year they may even regain the number one position.' The advert was a challenge that Ruinair couldn't resist. Thursday's Financial Times featured a full-page personal message to easyJet's Greek-born founder and chairman Stelios Haji-Ioannou from Ruinair's Mick O'Leery, thanking him for the previous day's 'plug' and suggesting that the only reason easyJet's turnover was higher than Ruinair's 'is because you charge higher airfares. Stuff that up your jumper, Stelios,' was O'Leery's parting shot, a reference to Haji-Ioannou's regular habit of showing up in patterned knitwear. O'Leery said easyJet's ad was clearly designed to convince the investment community that easyJet was on a par with Ruinair. 'It will be a cold day in hell before the Greeks get one over the Irish,' he said. 'They're welcome to have a go but they'll get a kickback.'

SUNDAY BUSINESS POST

Ruinair had a complaint against it on grounds of decency upheld by the Advertising Standards Authority of Ireland after a 13-year-old complained their advert was immature, offensive and very unnecessary. The advert read 'Aer Lingus screw YOU with €65 fuel surcharges'. It featured a cartoon of 'Uncle Sam' wearing an Aer Lingus branded hat, sticking up his two fingers. Ruinair said the advert was a parody of an Aer Lingus advert and argued that the fact only one complaint about it was received demonstrated it was neither offensive nor provocative. The ASAI ruled that the advert was gravely offensive.

IRISH INDEPENDENT

A Ruinair advert that ran in Ireland depicts the Pope claiming that the Fourth Secret of Fatima was Ruinair's low fares. Besides the 'usual collection of loonies' calling in on Irish radio to complain, says O'Leery, his own mother told him that this time he had finally gone too far. Indeed, just as Mum suspected, the Fatima advert got to a lot of people. The Vatican fired off a press release around the globe accusing the airline of blaspheming the Pope. Much to O'Leery's glee, the release attracted the attention of newspapers as far away as India, and generated a ton of free publicity. 'I thought I died and went to heaven,' says O'Leery.

BUSINESS WEEK

A discount airline that was accused of sexism in its advertising said regulators are out of touch with the 'Britney Spears generation'. Sweden's Trade Ethical Council against Sexism in Advertising, known by its Swedish initials ERK, accused Ruinair of sexism after the discount airline ran ads featuring a scantily clad schoolgirl promoting a fare sale coinciding with the start of the school year. The ERK said the woman 'is used to catch the eye in a sexual manner that is offensive to women in general'. Ruinair spokesman Stephen McNamara argued that the advertisements simply 'reflect reality'. 'This is the Britney Spears generation,' he said. 'Young women around Europe want to look their best.' Ruinair said in a statement that company officials 'are sure that the anti-funsters at the ERK do not speak for the majority of the famously liberal and easy going Swedes. The advert simply reflects the way a lot of young girls like to dress. We hope the old farts at the ERK loosen up a little,' the statement said. 'Ruinair defends the right of Swedish girls to take their clothes off. This really is a storm in a D cup!'

UPI

French President Nicolas Sarkozy and his new wife Carla Bruni were awarded €60,000 ($88,000) by a Paris court after Ruinair Holdings Plc, Europe's biggest discount airline, published the couple's photo in an advertisement without their consent. Ruinair published one advertisement in French newspaper Le Parisien, using a photo of the couple and with Bruni saying, in French, 'With Ruinair, my entire family can attend my wedding.' The airline apologised and offered to make a €5,000 donation to a charity of Sarkozy's choice. 'Our advertising is always about ads that we think are humorous, topical and witty,' Ruinair Chief Executive Mick O'Leery said. 'I think we did make a mistake with Sarkozy, but only because it wasn't particularly funny. We paid €60,000 to their charity but we got more than €5 million worth of free publicity so we're happy. I'm available to kiss and make up with Mrs Sarkozy any time she wants.'

BLOOMBERG

A complaint by the Royal National Lifeboat Institute (RNLI) against Ruinair has been upheld by the Advertising Standards Authority of Ireland (ASAI). The complaint referred to a newspaper advertisement by the airline which featured a lifeboat at sea with the caption 'DOPES? THEY SHOULD HAVE FLOWN RUINAIR! (WE WON'T

LOSE YOUR BAGGAGE)'. *The RNLI complained that Ruinair had used a photograph of an RNLI lifeboat and a volunteer lifeboat crew while they were involved in a search and rescue and felt that the headline 'DOPES?' implied a description of the actions of the volunteer crews. As a charity dependent on public support, the RNLI was also 'extremely concerned' that an image of one of their lifeboats and volunteer crew was used for a national advertising campaign without permission. Another complainant to the ASAI found the same advertisement misleading and offensive and felt that Ruinair was encouraging drug smugglers to use its services, guaranteeing not to lose bags containing smuggled drugs. Ruinair failed to respond to ASAI queries about the advertisement.*

IRISH TIMES

A Ruinair advertisement depicting Sinn Féin politician Martin McGuinness claiming its flights are so low even the British Army 'flew home' from Northern Ireland has been branded 'crass' and 'deliberately provocative'. Michael Copeland, Ulster Unionist Party East Belfast representative, has blasted the airline for the press campaign. Copeland says: 'The Ruinair marketing department is clearly stupid if they think that an advertisement like this is going to endear their company to a large chunk of the Northern Ireland travelling public.' He adds that the advertisement 'makes a clear political statement on the part of Ruinair'. But a Ruinair spokeswoman has made light of the politician's concerns. 'Michael Copeland should book one of our cheap flights. Maybe he needs a break—he certainly needs a sense of humour.'

MARKETING WEEK

Northern League politicians in Rome are up in arms after low-cost airline Ruinair used a photo of party leader Umberto Bossi making an offensive hand gesture in a publicity campaign. The photo of Bossi was taken when he caused a countrywide furore by raising his middle finger at the Italian national anthem. But the image now appears on the homepage of Ruinair's Italian website in an advert for summer price bargains that also knocks efforts by the Italian government to keep loss-making national carrier Alitalia in the air. 'The government supports Alitalia's high tariffs and its frequent strikes and it doesn't give a damn about Italian passengers,' says the Ruinair banner, before announcing a €10 deal on the Irish airline's flights. Northern League MEP Mario Borghezio said he had asked the European Commission to verify 'if these false statements are not harmful to the image and legitimate interest of a member state' as well as evaluating whether the advert constitutes a violation of competition law. 'As faithful Padanians (the League's name for northern Italians), we are ready to boycott the airline,' he added. The chairman of the Senate's public works committee, Luigi Grillo, pointed out, 'Ruinair also forgets to mention in its advert that it receives a tidy sum from many Italian airports who pay to increase their internal traffic.' Ruinair Chief Executive Mick O'Leery said, 'If there is anything "vulgar and offensive" in Ruinair's advert, it was the vulgar and offensive gesture of Sig Bossi in response to the Italian national anthem.'

WWW.ANSA.IT

Budget airline Ruinair is promoting its flights in the Italian press as a way of escaping piles of trash that are choking the city of Naples. Above a photograph of piles of rubbish sacks—an image which has come to symbolise Naples in recent months where the waste disposal system has ground to a halt—the advert reads: 'Pay the taxes! Not for waste (disposal) but to escape.' Playing on public outrage at the waste emergency and the fact that locals continue to pay a refuse tax even when their streets are shoulder-high in rotting garbage, the airline offered 250,000 free flights where the customer only pays the airport taxes. But the city of Naples is not amused. 'I am disgusted by this exploitation by an airline which has never even flown to Naples,' said Marco di Lello, head of tourism at the regional government of Campania, of which Naples is the capital. 'The only rubbish to be escaped from is Ruinair's advertising.'

REUTERS

Romania

Flight JOR132 – Friday @ 5.10 p.m. – STN-BBU-CRL

Fare €2 plus taxes, fees and charges €104

I am terrified at the prospect of my first visit to Romania. I don't know anything about the country except that their citizens prefer to fly to Ireland to reside in the open air at the M50 motorway roundabout, where they proceed to wash car windscreens at traffic lights and market the *Big Issue*, until they realise the Irish summer is too wet to endure so they appear on RTÉ News and fly home for free, courtesy of the Irish government, which is perhaps the ultimate low fares flying experience, cheaper than my €2 trip.

Blue Air was founded in 2004 and it is Romania's first, and only, low fares airline with seven slightly-used Boeing-737s of varying seat configurations. It flies one million passengers annually. I always worry about an airline with only seven aircraft since if one aircraft goes 'technical' they have no spares. The upside is that I am on their inaugural flight from Stansted to Bucharest so they dare not screw up that flight. The downside is that said Bucharest is widely acknowledged to be Europe's most unappealing capital city. When I told friends in Dublin I was going to Bucharest, their faces lit up as they said, 'Lucky you, that's a wonderful historic city, right on the banks of the Danube,' to which I duly replied, 'No, that's Budapest.'

First impressions of the inaugural flight are good. At the departure gate we receive complimentary champagne or OJ with canapés. An airport photographer asks male passengers in jackets and ties to pose for him, glasses in hand, but he ignores me because

I am too scruffy to participate. Our incoming Boeing 737-300 arrives early and its white hull with Romanian flag is photographed for posterity, but mainly because Blue Air have brought along some glamorous PR ladies from corporate head office who keep the photographer and the ground handling staff fully occupied for 30 minutes of muted adoration. There is much joy and excitement but I would fear for this airline if Ruinair begin to fly from London to Bucharest.

Onboard there are about 40 passengers on a *Mary Celeste* flight. My fellow passengers are old ladies with shocking russet hair and worn fake leather jackets, burly stocky bulls of men in fully co-ordinated faded denim jackets and jeans, plus some young girls with bangle earrings, D&G studded belts, baseball caps, acres of mascara and war paint and more exposed flesh than a German nudist colony. I am likely the only Irish passenger here today and I am certainly the only fully qualified chartered accountant.

We have assigned seating so there is no rugby scrum upon boarding but my seat is my worst ever on a low fares airline. The pitch is severe and there is zero space between me and the seat in front. If I spend the next 2 hours and 45 minutes like this I will emerge from the aircraft like the Hunchback of Notre Dame. Once we take off I move to one of the emergency exit rows where I stretch out. On the return flight I ask for row 12 so I can sit in the emergency exit row again. If you fly Blue Air you can only ever sit in row 12. Their seats make Ruinair's non-reclining blue plastic seats feel like Virgin Upper Class's finest seats.

The smart all-female cabin crew sport sky-blue blouses and natty yellow check waistcoats under navy jackets and trousers. Their service is personable and friendly yet overall the in-flight experience is amateurish. They walk though the cabin with a stack of plastic beakers and free Romanian *Dorna* mineral water in big 2-litre bottles. We are each asked to take a beaker so they can pour us some water. They wheel a food and drinks trolley towards us. I ask for chocolate but they don't have any chocolate. I ask for a menu card but they don't have one of those either. There is no in-flight magazine unless you bring your own from WH Smith. There are TV screens in the roof of the aircraft but like the cabin crew, they are not switched on. The cabin crew repeatedly turn on and off the lighting, either bathing us in a glare or plunging us into darkness. The heat in the plane is so stifling that when the pilot announces that it is -59°C outside, he remains unaware that it is +59° inside the cabin. Towards the end of the flight we receive free sweets and a small rubber toy aircraft as a memento of this inaugural flight.

I hear that Bucharest has a gleaming modern airport called Otopeni but since I am on Blue Air we land at Baneasa, which is favoured by other low fares airlines including Germanwings, SkyEurope and Wizz Air. As a natural-born writer, words seldom fail me, but Baneasa is something else. Apparently it has recently been renovated, some say at the specific request of easyJet, but it's hard to know what was improved. The entire airport is the size of an average departure gate at any larger airport. There are hundreds of people standing in the tiny circular hall which serves as both Arrivals and Departures. But the only alternatives to getting here are by train (in which case one arrives at the Gare de Nord) or by bus (but quite frankly if you arrive in Bucharest by bus then something, somewhere, has gone very wrong in your life, and no amount of vaguely humorous travel advice and anecdotes is going to be of help to you).

Shortly after landing I hear music. It's not emanating from someone's iPod or mobile telephone but from outside the aircraft. It is so deafening that it sounds like a rock concert is underway beside the airport runway. When the aircraft doors are opened, I step outside and realise a rock concert *is* underway beside the airport runway. The legendary Romanian heavy rock group Iris are in full flight in a thirtieth-anniversary celebration 100 feet from the terminal building. It is like stepping off a flight in Dublin to find Bono, The Hedge, Harry and Adumb playing *Vertigo* beside the D Gates. There is also a spectacular light show, so much so that I wonder how the pilot found the runway and avoided the 15,000 frenetic concert-goers. I am impressed by this innovative location and wonder if perhaps Bucharest is going to be a fun destination.

When stepping into a taxi anywhere in Bucharest, and particularly so at this airport, as a foreign national or a local it is best to immediately resign yourself to being ripped off. I fully expect to have to pay a fare which is five times the legal rate yet I remain optimistic because the exorbitant fare for 10 km will still represent excellent value for money for anyone who daily suffers the cost of living in Dublin. The phrases you need to know when in a Romanian taxi are as follows: 'Can I have the bill please?'—'*Pot sa am nota, va rog?*' 'How much is it?'—'*Cat costa?*' 'Do you speak English?'—'*Vorbiti engleza?*' 'Please write it down.'—'*Va rog scrieti.*' 'There must be some mistake.'—'*Trebuie sa fie o greseala.*'

But I have researched the taxis. There are several reputable taxi firms which ply the airport but the first yellow taxi at the rank does not belong to one of those firms. In fact the taxi does not have a company name on the side. Danger. I watch locals amble up to the taxi, ignore it and walk past. I am increasingly convinced that even if this was the last taxi in Bucharest, no one would clamber inside. I stand nearby as the driver spits on the ground, eyes me up with avarice, scratches his balls and eventually comes up to me to ask if I need a taxi, which I surely do, but not his. I pretend to be waiting for someone and use my mobile to make a call to no one. Twenty minutes elapse. I have visions of over-nighting it at the airport taxi rank.

An empty taxi pulls up beside me. It is from a company called Perrozzi. They are on the approved taxi list. They even use meters. I jump inside. Pandemonium reigns at the rank. The first driver and his best mates try to drag me out of the back seat but I pretend not to understand them. They tell me the taxi is 'on command' which I eventually deduce means it has been ordered by telephone. The Perrozzi driver wants to drive me and I want him to be my best friend in a foreign land. He says he will telephone for a taxi for me. I get out and stand under the glare of the livid gangsters at the rank. Mr Perrozzi shouts to me that I can now get back in. He seems to have called himself and strangely enough he is free and he is even already at the airport. We speed off but halt a few yards down the road when he turns to me.

'It's ok … you share … with others?'

There is zero chance of me getting out of this taxi until I reach my hotel. 'Share with who?' I ask.

He points outside. 'Those two men.' I now have visions of losing all my cash and credit cards within the first 20 minutes of being in Bucharest. 'That man is my brother. The other man is his friend.'

Two guys with stubble and wearing tracksuits under polyester coats hop in alongside. The alleged brother looks nothing like Mr Perrozzi. He speaks a little English. His friend has no English. 'Iris,' he says.

I'm not sure how he knows my nationality. 'Yes, I'm Irish. From Dublin. Roy Keane. Guinness.'

The brother points outside to the crowds and starts to nod his head back and forth. 'Iris.'

Now I know what he means. 'Yes, Iris. Great rock band,' I lie.

'You know them?'

'They are big in Ireland.'

'Yes?'

'Huge.'

His taxi driving brother reacts positively and plays his favourite CD. Iris's greatest hits (both of them) pound away inside the Skoda. Soon all three are bouncing back and forth in the car and screaming the lyrics. I have no choice but to join them. We look like that *Bohemian Rhapsody* scene from the start of the *Wayne's World* movie. The fare is metered and comes to the amazing low price of 20 Ron, or €7. Romanian taxi drivers are the best in the world, provided that you find the right driver. His name is Nick. He offers me a city tour and to return me to the airport and he doesn't even offer me any 'nice girls mister'.

Next morning I set out to explore the city whilst noting the words of warning on my hotel key card. *'Do not show your key card, money or credit cards to anybody. Police does not ask for them. Do not count the money on the street. Be aware of the fake policemen. Our Loss Prevention Department is here to assist you.'* With an even tighter grip than usual on my wallet I am irresistibly drawn to what is not only the largest building in Bucharest, but also in all of Europe. It's hard to miss Casa Poporului on the hill but finding the correct side of the building to enter is impossible since the signage is pathetically confusing. The building is two miles in circumference and I walk all four sides of it eventually. Casa

Poporului was never that popular when it was built but now it is increasingly popular as the biggest attraction in town.

It is not permitted to simply turn up here, look around the place, open a few random doors, check out a few rooms and leave. Visitors must take an official organised tour. An entrance ticket costs 15 Ron but you have to stupidly pay extra if you wish to use your camera inside. I loiter with about 50 other tourists until a twenty-something girl with the face of a kindly angel, the diminutive body of a waif but the lungs of a regimental sergeant major shouts at us. 'The English tour starts now. You must pass through that security X-ray machine. You must place all telephones, cameras, wallets and bags in the tray for the machine.' We all line up and show our tickets to this little madam. She allows us pass a barrier one by one but she makes us wait to pass through the X-ray machine. This is worse than any airport. I don't know what she thinks we will bring inside the building but at least it keeps the 10 security guards gainfully employed.

A timid Dutch couple make the mistake of walking forwards to the machine before she gives them explicit permission. 'Wait until I tell you. I said this is the English tour. Don't you understand English at all?' A very brave Italian guy who went through first has taken the liberty of climbing up the first marble steps. She shouts up at him. 'Stop. Come back now. Do what I tell you.' The tours start on the hour so our tour commences at 11.13 a.m. Before we begin she stands in front of us. 'My name is Oana. You can come closer to me. I won't bite.' Most of us are not fully convinced about this and think she probably does. I am looking forward to this tour immensely. We have the rudest tour guide on the planet. If Oana fails in her current choice of career, she could effortlessly secure a position as a cabin crew supervisor with Ruinair.

Oana takes us along an impressive corridor and into an auditorium. It is large but it's smaller than the Albert Hall. She tells us that the bigger rooms are named after famous Romanian politicians. But there are none named after the man who built this building, one Nicolae Ceauşescu. Oana asks us if we are impressed. We are not really but we are so terrified of her that we meekly utter a collective yes. 'Do not be impressed. This is nothing. There are

1,000 rooms here.' She pauses for an evil grin. 'We will not visit them all today.' Oana asks if we have any questions. I want to ask her if she enjoys her job but I dare not.

Oana provides a detailed and informative tour, which is fortunate because we dare not complain to her. This whitest of elephants is of gargantuan proportions: 3.7 million square feet and second only to the US Pentagon in size. It is 12 storeys high and dominates the skyline plus it has four underground levels including an enormous nuclear proof bunker and rumours of its own metro station. We see a chandelier in one room with 7,000 bulbs, which, when it was switched on by Nicolae, surely darkened the remainder of the nation's living rooms. There are furlongs of Transylvanian marble plus carpets so big they had to be woven on site. Someone in our party asks for more information about what is underground. 'I do not know. Today you will see two per cent of the building. I myself have only seen ten per cent of the building. Who knows what lies below?'

We stop at an impressive set of marble steps in the main lobby area. Oana asks if we can guess how many times the steps were built. We guess once or twice. 'Nicolae was a small man and even Elena, his wife, was taller then he was. He wanted the steps to be shallow for his personal use. He made the workers rebuild the steps five times until they were the perfect height for him to walk up. Five times.'

We pause at a series of tall biblical paintings on the walls of one corridor. They are appealing yet peeling. 'You might think these are great paintings? They are not. There was a movie made here in 2003 because this interior looks very like the Vatican Palace. They made these paintings. Please touch them.'

We enter the Human Rights Room, which is a square space with a large circular table and 60 chairs, with another crystal chandelier overhead and a round carpet in the centre of the floor. 'People can be married here. Nadia Comaneci was married in this room. There was meant to be 61 chairs in here—60 for the deputies and one gold chair for Nicolae. But he never got to sit here so they never installed his chair.'

It is October yet it's sunny and 21°C and inside it is hot and claustrophobic. I risk all and ask if this opulent meaningless building has air-conditioning? 'No air-conditioning because Nicolae feared that he might be poisoned by gas. So he ordered that only natural ventilation be used in the building. Of course he did not realise that he could be poisoned by gas equally effectively through a natural ventilation system. Any questions, comments, complaints?' I am slowly beginning to warm to Oana. I think she despises Nicolae. She has grit and I am sure she could take Nicolae apart with the best of them, if so requested.

Oana stops at one stage by a set of his and her doors. 'You may take a toilet break. Please note that the toilets are normal toilets. There is no chandeliers nor gold nor marble inside them.' She is correct. But there is something very satisfying about urinating long and hard in this increasingly depressing place.

For the climax of the tour we walk into the biggest room in the building, which is the height of two houses. 'This room was to be used as a concert hall. The first, and last, concert here was performed by Yehudi Menuhin. It was then discovered then that the acoustics were too bad for music. Now it is used for conventions.' On the walls are the national emblem of an eagle which on mature reflection looks like something the Nazis might have designed. We step through some tall French doors onto a balcony which offers a panoramic vista over the city below. Everything within view appears to be symmetrical. I walk to a balustrade and imagine how Nicolae would have felt standing here. It's a balcony Hitler would have liked.

'The first person to speak from this balcony was the singer Michael Jackson, who screamed out, "I Love Budapest". Please examine this view carefully. What is it that you do not see?' We are stumped. 'Churches. When this building was constructed Nicolae ordered that three churches should not be visible from this balcony. So two large apartment blocks were built in front of two of the churches. The other church was placed on rails and it was moved 285 metres to the west in 1985 so that it could not be seen.'

In 1984 Nicolae sadly razed one quarter of old Bucharest, the Uranus district, which included 10 churches, three synagogues and a maze of old streets, villas and small houses, to create this monumental folly fit for a megalomaniac. Systematisation was his greater plan to raze half of Romania's villages and rehouse the inhabitants in new agro-industrial centres, on the basis that their villages were decrepit and that these new centres would free up valuable land for agriculture and thus raise the standard of living.

So this is the house that Nicolae almost built, having copied Kim Il Sung's place in North Korea. In fact Romanian architects rarely seem to have original ideas. The Gare de Nord here is a copy of a more famous train station in Paris and the 85-foot tall Arc de Triumf is an exact copy of another similar-sounding Parisian landmark. Nicolae's building was designed by a 29-year-old architect, which explains a lot, and it was built when his national austerity measures were at their harshest. From 1984, workers toiled in three shifts, 24 hours a day, yet today the building remains one quarter unfinished. Nicolae never did enjoy all the 1,000 rooms to be used by countless bureaucrats, who could sit around all day in suits in pointless party committee meetings in grand rooms and basically do feck-all. The building remains an obscenity when the time, effort and scarce resources could have been used on health, social welfare, education or housing.

Nicolae went one better in the 1980s when he constructed a civic centre. Eight square kilometres of the old historical centre of the city were levelled, including more monasteries, churches and hospitals. Some 40,000 people were evicted with only a single day's notice to make room for the construction of some Stalinist apartment buildings topped with neoclassical follies. It is said that Nicolae drove through this district in a motor cavalcade, pointing out the homes that he wished to be destroyed. People were moved to high-rises in the suburbs and some of them later committed suicide in their not-so-nice new homes.

I leave the ironically named Casa Poporului and walk down Boulevard Unirii. It is lined with apartments built for the Party faithful and the Securitate, and is proudly longer than the Champs-Elysées by 6 metres. It is a street of empty offices, ugly graffiti, broken windows, wandering locals, lost souls and government departments such as the exciting Institute of National Statistics. It is more shocking to recall that 30 years ago this longest and widest street in the city simply did not exist. The walk takes me forever and I cannot help thinking that Nicolae wanted to keep his big building as far away as possible from the general population. He could have located a metro station nearer to his building but that was probably planned too. Bucharest remains one of the least walkable cities I have encountered on my euro travels.

Piata Unirii at the far end is vast. Anywhere else it would be grand, but here it is barren. There are fountains spraying jets in all directions, through which roads wind and traffic snakes. The pavements are cracked and the roads are potholed. For a city council that laid so much concrete and tarmac in the last century, you have to wonder as to why they never learned how to lay it down flat. The parched grassy areas are brown and dry. There are few seats and those that I sit on are old and broken. The view is grim and Casa Poporuli, surrounded by railings up on the hill, still dominates. We can look but we cannot touch.

I take the underground metro from Piata Unirii. It is surprisingly efficient and reliable. But even this project was not safe from Nicolae. In 1978 there was the 'hole that was not a hole' incident. A new underground station was being constructed and a vast hole of 12,000 cubic metres was excavated as an entrance to the station. However, one morning the civil engineer in charge of the project turned up for work to find that his big hole had disappeared. It had been there the night before, but now in its place were trees and benches on park land. The engineer first doubted his sanity and then asked one of Nicolae's aides what had happened. He learned Nicolae wanted to make a welcoming speech to students at the polytechnic and he wished to use the park. So he ordered the hole to be removed until after his speech. All night hundreds of labourers and machines had worked to fill in the hole. Trees were uprooted from other parts of the city and grass was taken from the rest of the park to cover the hole. The job was finished by 6 a.m., 30 minutes before the engineer had arrived for work. So the hole incident was fully explained.

Sitting in the train carriage provides me with the first microcosm of Bucharest's citizens and it's not a pretty sight. I am the only blue-eyed and brown-haired passenger in a train of deep inky black eyes and jet-black hair. I cannot help thinking that the

passengers look subdued, broken, hunted, even guilty about something. Middle-aged men should really not wear baseball caps
with sports jackets, grey flannels, white socks and trainers. Others
wear tracksuits, a particular favourite being the Adidas Romanian
national soccer team colours. Because of the weirdly un-
coordinated clothing, I assume the nation's citizens must share
wardrobes. Every train seems to have an onboard security guard.
The metro stations are decayed and their walls have posters to
'Emigrate to Canada' and posters to find missing 'Disparut' boys
and girls. The Pet Shop Boys are still big in Bucharest and they
have an upcoming concert per the voluminous bill posters. The
battered escalators are decades old and the steps and hand rails
shudder at different speeds such that half way up to the exit you
almost break your neck as your body is unexpectedly elongated.
Outside the metro stations little old ladies in headscarves who
grow smaller and more bent by the hour count small change with
wizened bony fingers as they sit upon newspapers on concrete
ledges.

Life here under Nicolae was hard. Petrol was rationed and
electricity consumption was curtailed as citizens could only use
one 40-watt bulb in a room. People used to secretly fantasise about
having their very own 60-watt bulb and what they might do with
it. Only one in every three streetlamps was switched on. Power cuts
disrupted industry and hospitals as operating theatres would be
plunged into darkness and life support machines would fail. Fuel
shortages led to ambulances not attending emergencies if the
patient was over 70 years of age. Heating was minimal and the gas
pressure so low that cooking was virtually impossible. Citizens
with empty milk bottles waited outside shops from 4 a.m. to
7 a.m., when the milk supply would arrive. By 1981 bread rationing
had been introduced and there were severe shortages resulting in
hours of standing in queues. Nicolae dismissed the problems with
some comments that Romanians eat too much and in 1985 he
announced a 'scientific diet' for all Romanians, thus controlling
their nutrition.

His Securitate police tapped private telephones and opened mail
and required all typewriters to be registered. When Nicolae received

an anonymous death threat he madly ordered the Securitate to obtain handwriting samples from *all* of the population. The state-controlled media reported in great detail on Nicolae, glorifying him and heaping praise on his wife, Elena, continuously reporting on the great advances the country was making in all fields of industry, agriculture, science and international relations. Television was restricted to a two-hour programme, the bulk of which showed Nicolae on his various visits receiving praise from crowds of people lining the roads or attending his speeches. Imagine the horror of it, only two hours of TV per night and not even the remotest chance of seeing any decent Champions League football.

Under Nicolae all Bucharest town planning was of the central variety, which is worse than no planning at all. Piata Universitatii is another fine example of the way to make 2.1 million citizens feel small and lost, by building five-lane boulevards in either direction intersecting at a roundabout and if the citizens wish to cross the road they can scurry like rats into the dark underground warrens, with the stench of stale urine and where a solo teenage girl approaches me to urgently ask for money or something worse. The alternative is to cross the 10 lanes on foot and to dice with death and the notorious local driving practices.

What impresses least here is the tiny chipped stone memorial on a traffic island to 12 citizens who died in the revolution of 1989. Sadly this square was the scene of further brutality after the revolution when some loyal hard-hat miners arrived here to quell a student demonstration and 100 students died. Again there are pathetic wooden crosses to the students who died. It is time to build something lasting. Nearby Piata Victoriei is equally grim and it eternally symbolises the victory of traffic over mankind.

It could have been so different, as I see when I stumble across the heart of the old city, now on life support. The Lipscani quarter could have been like the Left Bank in Paris with its narrow cobbled streets and secession architecture. Instead the neglected area looks as if it had been bombed yesterday, with crater-like excavations, derelict buildings with trees growing inside, scaffolding and more hoardings. It's no secret that Nicolae hated this district because he wished to pretend that nothing existed in Bucharest before his arrival. Nearby I am involuntarily drawn into a small church with blackened ceilings and wooden icons where a priest in glittering robes chants a solemn Sunday Mass to worshippers, yet when I leave I see the repulsive apartment blocks only feet away from the church. Under Nicolae, religion was never an orthodox matter.

Lipscani is rising from the ruins. There are some gems of buildings, which even Nicolae could not pilfer, now undergoing renovation. Some trendy shops have opened, selling what else but shoes? There are alfresco book vendors selling yards of books upon wooden planks. The Market 8 café has '*design, style, food, music, books and news*'. Timberlake and Timbaland pump from another street café where locals imbibe coffee on timber decking. There is interesting historical information in English on posters and one shows a glorious sepia photograph from 1929, when these fashionable streets were crammed with shops, people and cars. This rundown area is very much a work in progress but it will be magnificent—in 10 years' time. Buy now.

Tourism is not established in Bucharest. Aside from the Casa Poporului there are neither chugging tourist buses nor hordes of tiny Japanese explorers arriving before the rest of their nation. No one stands in the streets to take photographs of any glorious sights. This is the only European capital city without a convenient hop-on hop-off open-top bus tour. I ask the concierge in my five-star hotel for the address of the official city tourist office in Bucharest, but he confirms that no such office exists. In fact, it's official. Bucharest is the only capital city in the EU not to have a Tourist Information Office. I try to buy postcards in the shop in the hotel but they do not stock postcards there because I guess no one needs to buy them. Finally I see postcards in the gift shop in the Museum of the Romanian Peasant (the shop is hidden behind two sets of closed doors and it is only locatable if you ask) and even then all the postcards are of peasants, sheep, haycocks and tractors. Don't even think about trying to purchase a postage stamp.

This is not one of Europe's great consumerist cities. I always worry about a country that utilises a banknote of 1 Ron, equivalent to 30 cent. Even getting cash from an ATM becomes a struggle since many don't work and I resort to using a machine at the Bank of

Transylvania, surely the ultimate in blood money. It is always worth taking care using an ATM here since it is known that Romanians' favourite leisure-time activity in the UK is skimming ATM cash cards for gain. In a city of contrasts I see a man driving a tractor and trailer along a street and the next minute he is over-taken by a flash bastard in a silver Lambo. Later a genuine fuming Trabant wheezes by and a lost taxi driver reverses around a round-about. Others drive 20-year-old Dacia cars (made in Romania in partnership with Renault) which look like a Renault 11 of the 1970s, while men double park outside Bucuresti Mall in gleaming Lexus SUVs to chat on mobiles, mainly because in this capital city there are as yet no pedestrianised shopping streets to spend your Ron.

There is a slow and reluctant acceptance of the free market economy. If you wish to buy chocolate here you must first try to find a window stacked with cigarette boxes, then locate a small aperture in the window of a few square inches upon which you knock. When the window opens you pass through 2 Ron and say, 'Mars'. A little lady inside takes the cash and goes off to a box in some rear room, passes you the bar and shuts the window. Self-service it is not. Browsing is not encouraged. The rawness and hardship of daily life are visible at the open-air street market at Piata Obor where locals buy fruit and meat, ugly-shaped root veg-etables, pots and pans, water tanks and mirrors, crockery and brushes, toys and spices, where queues snake from nearby shops perhaps out of habit (queuing for anything in Bucharest makes boarding a Ruinair flight look like a Sunday picnic in comparison) and abrasive-looking bog rolls cost only 0.25 Ron.

Walking back to take my last increasingly depressing metro ride, I pass an elderly man who stands on the cracked pavement in front of an old dusty set of weighing scales. People stop to step onto his scales, hum and hah at their amazing weight and pass him some coins. He has invested in some basic mobile machinery and he provides a low-cost service to consumers. Around these parts he is known as a self-employed business entrepreneur. This is the lasting legacy of Nicolae. I have been in poorer parts of Central and Eastern Europe but I have not sensed this level of helplessness, aimlessness and apathy. As chef Gordon Ramsay is prone to say when stumbling upon another awful Kitchen Nightmare, 'Fuck me.'

Bucharest has gone to the dogs. They are everywhere: rabid, flea-bitten, stray hostile mongrels. Estimates say there are 40,000. In 2006 Hajime Hori, a 68-year-old Japanese head of a local unit of a ball-bearing manufacturer, was fatally attacked by a dog outside his apartment on the exclusive retail artery of Calea Victoriei, near my hotel. He came here to savage the competition but ended up on the receiving end. Residents feed the dogs with scraps. Nicolae is to blame for the dogs too. When he evicted residents from their apartments of the old town into high-rise estates, the dogs of this social war were thrown onto the streets. Their surviving descendants roam freely despite the efforts of the Mayor who had 200,000 dogs slaughtered between 2000 and 2004, earning him the nickname of King Herod. Now the Mayor is the Romanian President, one of the few politicians elected on a canine manifesto. His only opposition came when Brigitte Bardot became interested as ever in the poor plight of the dear little doggies. Ask Hajime.

Among the gifts Nicolae received over the years was a black Labrador puppy from British Liberal Party leader David Steel. Nicolae named the dog *Corbu* and he became so enamoured with the thing that Romanian citizens were soon calling it 'Comrade Corbu'. Unfortunately, *Corbu* became a part of Nicolae's and Elena's fantasy world and soon the dog was to be seen being driven through Bucharest in a limousine, with its own motorcade. *Corbu* slept with Nicolae at night and during the day it slept in its own villa, complete with bed, furnishings, television and telephone. The Romanian ambassador in London was under orders to go to Sainsbury's to buy British dog biscuits which were then sent home in the diplomatic bag.

In his final years iron-fisted Nicolae grew increasingly madder and badder. He became so paranoid that foreigners would poison his clothes, or that he would catch a fatal disease from shaking hands, that he started wearing only clothes that had been under surveillance in a specially constructed warehouse and he even once washed his hands with alcohol after shaking Queen Elizabeth II's hand. He took his own bed sheets when he went to stay at

Buckingham Palace. Perhaps most embarrassing was his honorary knighthood bestowed on him by the Queen of England, and revoked only hours before his death. The *'Geniul din Carpati'*, or Genius of the Carpathians, was once congratulated by telegram by Salvador Dalí on his excesses, which included his use of a kingly sceptre. Despite an official salary of around $3,000, Nicolae found the cash for 15 palaces, a superb car collection, yachts, fine art and bespoke suits.

I recognise Piata Revolutiei from the TV news. I stand a few feet away from the low balcony of the Central Committee building where on 21 December 1989 Nicolae made his most widely seen, and last ever, speech to 80,000 people (like all televisual history the clip is available for all eternity on YouTube). This was meant to be a rousing rally to show support for their leader after riots broke out in Timisoara following the arrest of an outspoken priest. Nicolae wears his best grey hat, coat and scarf and he begins confidently, pausing intermittently after soundbites to allow the camera to pan to the front row of the crowd where a stage-managed rent-a-mob with banners and flags encourage him. Eight minutes into his lines the crowd begins to chant, 'Timisoara, Timisoara' and his face con-torts with confusion. I don't know what he is saying because I don't speak fluent Romanian but he is dying up there. The camera switches to a shot of the crowd and building as party handlers assess the unprecedented situation. Two minutes later he resumes but the cheers are long gone and the jeers resume. It is the begin-ning of the end. 'Jos.' 'Down.'

Just before the TV censors pull the plug, the camera pans to a view of 20 party animals alongside on the balcony. The expression on their fat, well-fed faces is clear. 'We've had a good innings but the game is up, lads. We're fucked.' On the next day, like in Saigon, Nicolae and the wife flew away in a helicopter. Later unarmed civilians hid behind tanks as special forces fired into crowds and buildings in this square. Defiant locals walked onto our TV screens waving the blue, red and yellow flag with the hated Communist symbol ripped from the centre. Only one month earlier at the fourteenth Congress of the Romanian Communist Party, Nicolae had been re-elected as their leader and not one of the 3,308 party members voted against his re-election. Nicolae and Elena's trial on Christmas Day took 55 minutes and the sentence of death was carried out by firing squad in an army barracks, with the evidential end result shown on TV.

An old marble monument points to the balcony while a revolution monument pays tribute to 1,104 people who died. The latter signifies freedom breaking through barbed wire but some say it looks like an olive on a cocktail stick. I think it looks like the giant lemon which U2 took around the world in the Zooropa tour. Below it are plaques with the names of those who were martyred. Nearby one burnt-out building has been purposefully left in ruins whilst an office block was built within the shell. Today the square is devoid of tourists (no surprises here). There are visible bullet holes on the façade of the Humanitas bookshop but they are several metres above me, proving the special forces were either bad shots or aimed to miss.

Throughout all the hardships Nicolae resided in a home in the northern part of Bucharest, which is inhabited by the A-list. I exit the metro at Aviatorilor and find myself immediately in the diplomatic zone, with embassies, consulates and ambassador residences, the sorts of places where locals subsist only on *Ferrero Rocher*. This district is not that salubrious but it is as salubrious as Bucharest gets. I stroll down Boulevard Primaverii, where the UN consulate has four proud peacocks in their compound. There are abandoned black Mercs with smoked windows and CD registration plates. At the junction with Mircea Eliade I'm sure that I see Nicolae's former residence. It is a grand tiered classical building with large grounds yet like much of his construction work, it is derelict, boarded up, dirty and vacant. I stand and loiter but I am immediately eyed up by a few edgy policemen standing in security cabins in this sensitive zone. I peer into Nicolae's garden and see a 'For Sale' sign advertising the 1,290-square-metre building. A policeman inside the garden approaches me and I have little option but to engage him in conversation.

'Is this the former home of Nicolae Ceauşescu?'

He shrugs his shoulders.

'Can you tell me if this is his house?'

Another shrug.

'Are you allowed to answer?'

Another shrug. Maybe he does not speak English.

'Can you speak English?' I ask.

He visibly relaxes. 'I do not speak English.'

With its tree lined boulevards, glorious Belle Époque buildings and a reputation for the high life, Bucharest was known as Little Paris in the 1920s, which would still be true today if Paris was a derelict wasteland. Bucharest is a city of great potential and will always remain so. As they say here, 'What is dark and always knocking at the door?' Answer: 'The future.' Bucharest is dirty, dusty, dated, dilapidated, decayed, dreary and decrepit but if you like that sort of thing on a grand scale then this is the place to visit.

And never forget that we owe it all to the cobbler, dictator and non-believer Nicolae Ceaușescu (1918–1989) who lies in restful repose with his wife Elena and eldest son in Bucharest's Ghencea cemetery under a modest white Orthodox cross embedded with a small red Communist star, for old time's sake.

Mick's Local

I leave Dublin and drive in a general westerly direction. The M50 motorway is barrier-free but sadly it's not yet toll-free nor pain-free. All the traffic cones in the developed world have been gathered together along the remnants of the N4. One hour later, travelling at a maximum speed of 120 km and an altitude of zero feet above ground level, I approach the Mullingar area but this time I am not visiting Mick's house. I see the road sign and exit the M4 a few miles after the urban metropolis of Greater Downtown Kinnegad. I negotiate a sharp U-bend and kill the engine in a deserted car park in the townland of Coralstown. I am only here because a reader sent me an email to tell me that I might find something of interest about Mick.

From the exterior Mary Lynch's looks any other well-established country public house. It is an early-1900s building, complete with old pub signs, kegs, tubs of flowers and ample outside seating. It occupies an enviable location on the banks of the Royal Canal, which provides *Coarse Fishing*, a sport one would think Mick would greatly enjoy. The Dublin to Sligo (and back) railway line runs perilously close by on the other side of the road. Out back there is a modern Bed & Breakfast annex, an upturned bath on the tarmac and a beer garden which would be ideal if it was hot and sunny but this is Ireland and it is August. On the front window there is a sticker for Westmeath Football Supporters Club, Mick's favourite GAA team. There is no sign of life inside but a sign adver-tises *Lunch from 12.30* and sure enough, on time a front door is opened.

Inside I am the first and only customer. I order soup and a sandwich but I am distracted almost immediately. On the wall by

the bar are six colour photographs with a typed sign saying
'Cheltenham Gold Cup—St Patrick's Day.' Mick is in all of the
photographs but for a change he is not pulling funny gormless
faces. He sports a navy blazer like the one he wears to very posh
events plus a blue open-necked shirt. The photographs are lami-
nated and held up with Blu-Tack. This is a shrine to a local hero.

I sit at the bar beside the photographs and politely ask the bar-
maid for more information.

'Mick came in here on the day that he won the Gold Cup.' I tell
her that I was told to come here by a reader. I have a copy of
'Ruinair' with me. She looks at me as if I might be dangerous. 'I'll
get the owner.'

John is from Kerry, so he is happy to chat. 'We didn't know Mick
was coming in. We had regulars here that St Patrick's Day who had
been here all day but they simply couldn't drink any more. They
had to go home. Then Mick arrived in about 9 p.m. They missed
him. They asked me why didn't I tell them he was here. I said to
them, "You have to be here. I'm not sending texts to everyone to
tell them Mick is in my pub."'

I ask about the people in the photographs. 'That's me and my
wife with Mick. That's Mick and his wife. That's his brother Eddie
and his wife, and his other brother and his wife. The brothers came
in first and they had a look around. I knew something was up
because they had a Martell Cognac trophy box with them.'

*If my brother Eddie wasn't involved, I wouldn't be involved. You
want to be up early in the morning to be ahead of the guys in the Irish
bloodstock industry. Eddie is the judge. He decides what we buy or
don't buy. It's important to have someone like that. Someone you can
trust. It's like any walk of life. Eddie's advice is vital. I fell off a horse
at the age of four and I realised it was a stupid activity. My brothers
and sisters didn't realise how stupid it was and kept going.*

One photograph is of Mick saying a few words with a micro-
phone. 'He gave a small speech. He spoke about getting the Gold
Cup off Camilla. She invited him and his wife back to the Royal
Box. He declined and said he was going direct to the first pub in
Westmeath for a drink. Camilla told him that she has never been
in an Irish pub in her life. Sure enough Mick came in here a few

hours later. We are the first pub on the road from Dublin. If he went into Kinnegad there would be too many pubs to chose from.'

'The Cheltenham Festival is a great Irish institution—for me, the Olympics of racing, although still an occasion to be routinely beaten up by the English. There is an annual exodus of drunken Paddies coming for four days of gambling and other recreation. I came to Cheltenham on Ruinair with 188 other Irish passengers. The plane was full.'

In another photograph Mick holds a pint. He is the only man in Ireland still drinking Smithwick's. All the photographs feature people holding the Gold Cup, and it's tiny. I don't know what all the fuss is about.

John surprises me further. 'I know Mick. I used to be his boss. He worked in a bar in a hotel in the town for me. He was a very good worker. He always knew what was going on in the bar, not only with his own job. Like, he'd see dirty glasses or something else and clear them away. Even then you could see he had something extra. He's modest enough. When he won the Cup they wanted him to sit in an open-top car with the Cup for the St Patricks's parade next day but he told them he'd prefer the girls in the local school to carry the Cup. He's a shrewd man too. At the time he was trying to buy some land near here and he was up against some local farmers. Sure, none of them could afford to outbid him. He got the land in the end. But when he was in here he made sure to talk to the farmers and to buy them all drinks and that mends a lot of fences. His mother and father still live near here, as does his brother. His mother runs the show.'

Our conversation is interrupted by a woman who enters the pub, looks around and goes directly to the toilet. John shakes his head. 'Another one who's missed the turn off for Galway a few miles back. They come in all the time. Never buy anything. Just use the toilet. No thanks, either.' Five minutes later the lady exits the toilet and makes for the front door. John is rarely lost for words. 'Thanks for leaving me something anyway, dear.' She disappears, very quickly. John is a comedian and should be on a stage.

I try to settle my bill. John says lunch is on the house. I refuse and hand over some of my royalties. John promises to send me some photographs by email. I sign the copy of the book and leave it on the bar.

John smiles at the books cover. 'It's priced at 1 cent. Very good. I've been on the airline to Rome Ciampino and it was ok. I got on early and I got a good seat and I kept to myself for the flight. It was fine.'

'So this is Mick's local?' I ask finally, wondering if I can return covertly to buy Mick a Smithwick's.

John shakes his head. 'He hasn't been in since.'

Cheltenham Mug

Cyprus (and Turkey)

Flight LS405 – Sunday @ 4.30 p.m. – DUB-LBA-PFO-ECN-SAW-STN-DUB

Fare €A Large Amount plus taxes, fees and charges of €Another Large Amount

There are no direct scheduled flights from Dublin to the island of Cyprus, since XL Airways went bust, so I must travel via the UK. I spend all of €0.00 on my Ruinair flight from Dublin to the glamorous destination of Leeds Bradford. These days, anyone who pays more than €0.00 for any Ruinair flight from Ireland to the UK is either mad, sad or both. I obtained the very lowest fare on one of the seat sales where they advise: 'Book Until Midnight Tonight.' It's the same advert they have up on their website every day.

I know nothing about Leeds Bradford except that Leeds United are a rubbish soccer team and Bradford is where MI5 pick up Al-Qaeda sympathisers who have an inherent propensity to explore the properties of combustible liquids. Leeds Bradford International Airport is tiny with a single runway and it is the only airport I have visited where you can sail in an adjacent boating lake if your flight is delayed. Whilst waiting in the airport for a departure in more than one hour's time, the screens tell us to 'Relax and Shop'.

Jet2 are the low fares airline for northern England, a sort of *'Flies and Prejudice'* airline. They fly to southern European destinations, to Egypt and to New Jersey's Newark Airport. They have 30 aircraft and fly four million passengers annually. They are so proud of their northern roots that some aircraft have *'Jet 2*

Yorkshire' and *'Jet 2 Manchester'* daubed on their fuselages. Jet2 began life as Channel Express, flying us nice flowers from the Channel Islands. It is not immediately clear to me whatever happened to Jet1.

Mick O'Leery and the Jet2 CEO Philip Meeson are not best friends since Mick described Jet2 as *'a crappy competitor who will go bust'* because of high oil prices. Mr Meeson retorted: *'It won't be Jet2. I'm sorry, Mr O'Leery, but unlike you, Jet2 has bought all its fuel for this summer, this coming winter and next summer at attractive rates. And because people enjoy flying with Jet2.com, we are having a great year yet again. Our passengers can rely upon us for many years to come.'* However Mr Meeson, a former RAF pilot, took a leaf out of Mick's book of sound bites when during a French air traffic control strike he said, *'It seems to me that either the air traffic controllers or the students run France at the moment'* and he called for *'the lazy frogs to get back to work.'* He added: *'Pouvez-vous nous expliquer pourquoi exactement êtes-vous en grève?* [Could you explain to us exactly why you are on strike?] *It's not a diplomatic incident, it's the roast beefs and the frogs having our natural little bit of sparring. Our passengers are being inconvenienced and we are entitled to have a go.'* Jet2.com posted a cartoon on its website of a French frog blocking a runway, holding a placard reading *'I am lazy.'* Mick won't like it either that Jet2 was voted the best short-haul airline in the UK by readers of the *Guardian* and *Observer*. Ruinair came in fifteenth.

Check-in for Jet2 is in a low-ceilinged warehouse that could otherwise be used to sell gardening equipment, paints, tools and nails on a Bank Holiday weekend. There are signs inviting us to pay to use their priority check-in and 'avoid the queues', but there are no queues here. Jet2 offers *Jet2Plus*, which includes priority check-in, security fast track, VIP lounges, seats in the front of the aircraft and food and drink. This sounds suspiciously like the old business class which we used to see often on flights. *'We should outlaw business class traffic. We should pack them into economy class rather than have the fat and overpaid flying around on flat beds farting and burping after they've all eaten and drunk their fine wines.'*

Onboard the English crew have sensible names such as Emma and Jane or Andy or Tony. They wear black and white uniforms with a red trim. The *No Smoking* and *Fasten Seat Belts* signs in the B757-200 cabin are written in English and in Chinese so this is an old second-hand aircraft that they picked up somewhere east. It is jaded inside. Jet2 offers a hot *Flying Feast* meal for £8, which includes roast beef, vegetables, gravy and of course a Yorkshire pudding. The mineral water is Pennine Spring from Yorkshire. Jet2 rent us a hand-held TV/game console for £4 plus it's another £4 if we want to see a movie. *Airplane?* They offer us an Adult Snack Box or a Kids' Snack Box; presumably the former has a few xxx magazines.

Two of the passengers proudly wear Leeds Rhino rugby league jerseys, sponsored by the 'big yellow skip hire company'. Some of the passengers appear to come from Hull. Wayne Rooney is on our flight, or at least that's the name on the back of his T-shirt. I would have to ask why a fully grown adult male would set off on his annual holidays wearing the full replica soccer kit? We are surely in footballing territory since there are a few glamorous WAG types with big sunglasses on board. Everyone in the cabin speaks with a strong northern accent and they greet each other with words such as 'Hey … up.' It's like being on the set of *Coronation Street* or with shop keeper Ronnie Barker in *Open All Hours*. Others near me repeat a catch phrase in the same northern accent. 'Sophisticated? I'll 'ave you know … I've been to Leeds.'

Mick would love Paphos Airport since the recognised airport abbreviation is PFO, as in Please Foxtrot Oscar. He would also like the fact that the airport is basic, efficient, small, modern and prob-ably cheap. I fully expect to be ripped off by taxi drivers at 11 p.m. at an airport without a bus service and I am not disappointed. A wizened sun-ripened driver rushes up to me, bundles me into an ancient stretch black Mercedes, switches off the meter, takes me on a 10-minute diversion through an industrial estate and charges me €35 for a 20-minute ride, proof that not only was I taken to Paphos, but also to the cleaners.

Paphos is *Little Engerland*. The Rose and The Red Lion pubs. Nemo's traditional English Fish N' Chips, *eat in or takeaway*. Full English Breakfast only €2.60. Cottage Pie. Tea For Two. Pizza Express and KFC. Starbucks and McD's. Dining at *El Sombrero* Mexican restaurant. The Six Bells, 'a traditional Greek tavern'.

Drinks in Flanigans (sic) Irish Pub and Café or in O'Solomons Irish bar (the world's only Irish/Jewish bar, which results from a communication breakdown between a bar owner and Paphos's newest sign writer). The garish kitsch nightclub strip of Bar Street does exactly what it says on the tin, as does *Club Topless*, or so I hear. The *Daily Mail* and the *Daily Express*, today's editions. Tiger Boat's extreme roller-coaster boat ride in a flashy craft named *Sweet Chariot*. Two boat trips on offer ('€5, a mad price')—the Glass Bottom Boat Cruise and the *Real* Glass Bottom Boat Cruise—where the salesmen ignore only myself.

Great sea bass at the Poseidonas Fish Tavern, washed down with a draught Keo beer (*Brewed on the Island of Cyprus*). Gem shopping at Homer's Diamonds. Mediterranean sea sponges from the island of Kalymnos. Men in their Umbro away kits displaying bare-chested lobster paunches. Ladies with bad legs and varicose veins. People asking for ketchup at breakfast, but only after they have placed their towels on the sun-loungers. (Do you know that in Germany you can buy a beach towel by mail order with one word on it: '*Reserved*'?) The long-term English visitors struggle with the major crises of life, such as 'We can't get Sky Sports One.' It's as good as being back home, what with the plugs being the same size and locals driving on the same side. There are good old British ER post boxes but they are painted in ochre yellow, not pillar box red. The no. 11 bus to Old Paphos town up on the hill might as well be operated by London Transport. Everyone here, including the natives, speaks right proper English. The best selling T-shirt in the souvenir shops proclaims: '*I am not fifty—I am 18 with 32 years' experience.*' I am the youngest person on the Promenade. I will return to Paphos, but it will be in 30 years' time, when I can blend in effortlessly.

In the local tourist office I overhear a Dutch couple speaking with the nice girl behind the desk.

'Is it dangerous?' they ask.

'No, it is not,' she replies.

'Is it forbidden?' they persevere.

'No, it is not,' she answers with some evident weariness at their pointed line of questioning.

I know where they are going to because I am going there too. Next morning I pack and check out. There are no trains in Cyprus. I could hire a car but I am not going there (see Kosice, Slovakia). The bus service is one option but here they use a bus calendar rather than a bus timetable. There is only one bus service daily, which leaves at the ungodly hour of 7.30 a.m., another typical Ruinair departure hour. So I book the island minibus service, and I share the eight-seater bus with our driver, a Mr Grumpy, two local ladies going to the hospital, two construction workers who do not possess a motor car and two nice tourists from Sheffield who *Thomas Cooked* it here and ask me if I am from *Southern* Ireland, when no such place exists. We speed along the A6 past jagged escarpments and deep ravines, past parched tinderbox vegetation and olive and vine groves, past ominous convoys of Cypriot army trucks and Massey Ferguson tractors in the inside lane, and past the half-finished shells of holiday villas and the advertising hoardings of Leptos Estates extolling the many virtues of buying the afore-mentioned homes. The fine for littering on the motorway is a whopping €834 but you can speed past the traffic cops for free. I change minibus in the ugly sprawl of Limassol and head north. Two hours and 150 km later I enter Nicosia, Europe's last divided city.

To understand the present, one must understand the past. The Museum of National Struggle is a struggle in itself to find, since it is located in the eastern fringes of the city amidst a warren of one-way or dead-end streets more suitable for a Hampton Court maze, it is only open in the morning and it is located in a discreet building. I am the only visitor. Inside I find documents, weapons and memorabilia of the 1955–1959 national liberation struggle when the Cypriots sought independence from Britain. I learn Archbishop Makarios was exiled to the sunnier climes of the Seychelles—he could have done a lot worse. There is a Wanted poster offering a £10,000 reward for the Cypriot leader General Grivas, where he is described as having 'a small Hitler-style moustache'. I learn that the British decreed that anyone found with a gun would be arrested so the Cypriots tied a gun to a donkey and let the donkey amble about the streets, thus making an ass of the law. There are disturbing photographs of dead bloodied Cypriots, all of whom are described as heroes, plus mug shots of their 'English interrogators/torturers'. It is clear that the Cypriots fought long and hard and sacrificed much to gain eventual independence. I see the wooden gallows on which Cypriots were executed (the actual rope is here and sadly it is frayed). One local hero was schoolboy Evagoras Pallikarides who went to the gallows aged 18. I am beginning to see why English tourists do not frequent this museum. It is amazingly generous that the impressive exhibits are described in both Cypriot *and* English. There is a staff car which was used by General Grivas. I cannot help wondering if General Grivas ever dreamed that his ancestors would gladly welcome the English in Paphos with a full English breakfast.

Debenham's store on Ledra Street is the next stop, not for shopping, but because it houses the Ledra Museum Observatory. Eleven storeys up, past cosmetics, lingerie, haberdashery and the restaurant, there is an unrivalled view of all four points of the city. A short presentation outlines the development of Nicosia from a walled city built by the Venetians to one with a line of green dots between the north and south. The Cypriot nationalist group EOKA, backed by hard-line Greeks, ousted President-Archbishop of Cyprus Makarios III in a coup in 1974. In response, at dawn on 20 July 1974, Turkish armed forces invaded Cyprus. Four weeks later, on 16 August, a ceasefire was called. The point to which Turkish troops had advanced by 9.30 a.m. on that day was to divide Cyprus for the rest of the century. The Turkish population fled to the north, Greeks fled to the south. A 180-km line was drawn across the island, starting in Nicosia and working outwards, leaving a little less than half of the capital city in the new south.

Today 270,000 people live in the south of Nicosia and 85,000 live in the north of Nicosia. The Greek Cypriot tourist office maps show 37 per cent of the island's land mass as being 'Under Turkish Occupation since 1974'. The Turkish Cypriots proclaim the part of the island as the Turkish Republic of Northern Cyprus (TRNC). I stand and look north and see the gigantic Turkish and Turkish Cypriot flags displayed on the mountains and visible to all daily. The stones on the hillsides were clandestinely painted over a number of weeks, then were all flipped over one night to provide extra some shock value to the Greek Cypriots. I don't know why these Turkish Cypriots would wish to wave their flag in the faces of their fellow residents.

The brochure in the Observatory provides the contrary view. 'From the Observatory, you can enjoy the view of a developed city to the South, East and West, compared to the misfortune of occupation in the North. Ours is a city which was built to be united, not divided. You can see Nicosia without dividing lines.' Major buildings are referred to by their name plus *'Occupied'*. At the exit they sell six postcards of views of the city but everyone buys the card with the picture of the eyesore flag on the mountain in the distance.

Outside I take a seat on a bench to down a badly needed ice cream. I get chatting to a tourist from Israel but I make the basic mistake of telling him that shortly I will approach, and then cross, the border.

He shakes his head. 'You must not call it a border. That implies it is a permanent arrangement.'

I am admonished. 'What do I call it then?'

'Call it a separated area. That's what it is called in our Hebrew book.'

I am slightly taken aback. 'This is mentioned in the Bible?'

'No, not that Hebrew book. A Cyprus guide book that I have … that is written in Hebrew.'

I walk the rest of Ledra Street until I can go no further without causing an international incident. A Cypriot army sentry post is to my left where fatigued khaki-uniformed youths carry scuffed and well-used rifles. The soldiers look back at me and I am not sure which of us is the more anxious. On another street two dusty white 4x4 vehicles with 'UN' on the doors cruise by and then disappear out of view. A few feet away to my right the street ends in a barrier of concrete-filled oil drums, barbed wire and sandbags. There are two spy holes and I look into no-man's land. It is overgrown and it smells and I know why. No one has passed this way in three decades, certainly not the city refuse trucks. Cats prowl about. For the first time in my visit to this island, flies swarm around me. It's not clear if they are Greek Cypriot flies or Turkish Cypriot flies.

Depending on who you are, this ceasefire line that divides the city is called the buffer zone (because of the UN presence), the Attila line (because it marks the limit of the Turkish advance), the green line (after an English officer's crayon mark on a map), or, if you are a Turkish Cypriot, it is the peace line. Once there was Jerusalem. Beirut. Berlin. Belfast. Now there is only the city of Nicosia left to resolve. There is nothing like a United Nations buffer zone to add a bit of an edge to your average sun holiday.

Inside a side room with jet black walls and metal bars on the exterior, there is an exhibition of large black and white photographs. *1,600 Greek Cypriots are missing. Where are they? Cyprus is still bleeding.* The photographs show civilians with their hands held up in the air or clasped behind their heads. There is a large print extract from the EU Court of Human Rights in the matter of Cyprus v. Turkey. *Greek Cypriots were held by Turkish forces and their treatment could properly be characterised as inhuman within the meaning of Article 3.* In other photographs old ladies hold up pictures of loved and lost ones. There is a printed extract from the United Nations General Assembly in 1976 where Turkey refused to provide any information to the UN. I am not an expert on international affairs but I tend to side with the EU and UN.

A Cypriot flag and an EU flag fly freely. A Greek flag flies over the adjacent Ledras Police Station. A single tree stands against the blue sky. A sign says, *'This is the last divided capital.'* Nearby are empty shells of long-deserted homes and shops, vacant for 30 years, with bullet holes in the walls. Visitors stand silent and sad and take photographs. The crossing to the separated area is via a roped-off route. A sign points to an unspecific 'Entrance'. People arriving from the other side are met with either disinterest (tourists showing their UK passports) or with disdain (either Greek Cypriots who crossed to shop or perhaps Turkish Cypriots who can cross). Idiots walk up to the relaxed Cypriot policeman, point away and ask if that is the Turkish side. The policeman is in denial and he rightly doesn't bother to reply. An English lady stops at the ropes, looks towards the far side and asks her hubbie, 'So what's down there then?'

I am terrified at the prospect of getting past the Turkish Cypriot 'border' guards. They will ask me why I am visiting and I will say I am on holiday. They will ask my job and I will say that I am a writer. Their eyes will widen and they will ask me if I am a journalist and if so am I writing something about their island. They will examine my baggage and find the incriminating trappings of my trade—city maps printed from the web with buildings and streets circled in pen, scribbled comments and arrows all over plus bus timetables and airport details and all the usual stuff that spies are found with before being shot. I could be staying in the TRNC for much longer than I planned, maybe 10 to 15 years, mandatory. I mean, have you seen that movie *Midnight Express*? But I have a copy of 'Ruinair' which I will produce and they will look at the cover and laugh and say to each other 'Ah ... Mick O'Leery. Very funny Irishman. When will he fly to the TRNC?'

I bide my time and choose the optimal moment when two CD-registered cars park up and smart suited diplomats alight. They walk down towards the crossing and I consider it safe to follow them. I show my open passport to the Greek Cypriot policeman but he is uninterested. I suppose if you see someone departing your country for the enemy side then his is the right attitude. The suits stop in front of me and go no further. Greek Cypriots walk towards me from the other side, carrying shopping bags from a shop called 'Free Choice'. I walk down the slope into no-man's land. I feel guilty, ashamed, like a rat or a traitor, to be leaving Cyprus and the EU. While others are evidently crossing for an hour or so, I am the only person crossing with luggage. I might as well have a big red Turkish flag emblazoned on my suitcase.

At the mid-point I look left and right to see big gates with *No Entry* and *No Photography* signs. These are the gates through which only the UN patrol back and forth. I walk on. A woman ahead of me has a child in a push chair plus some bulging Debenham's shopping bags. I see that she crosses this 'border' solely to purchase Kellogg's Cornflakes. There are tubs of flowers and new awnings, all part of the EU's Master Plan for Nicosia. So there is hope. It is at times like this I remember that this crossing only opened as recently as April 2008. Before that date, if I wanted to reach the rest of Ledra Street, I would have had to drive 80 km south to Larnaca Airport and take a plane to Athens; from Athens, I would take a plane to Istanbul; from Istanbul, I would take a plane to an airport north of Nicosia: which all in all would be a day-long, 2,500 km journey just to arrive less than 20 metres away from where I started.

I pass under the two large flags, one of Turkey and one of the TRNC. The Turkish immigration apparatus hoves into view. Theirs is a minor industry with six gleaming white booths staffed by uniforms. They love this 'border'. I fill out a visa form with my name, my passport number and my nationality, much like Ruinair check-in. Osman the nice 'border' guard takes my passport. 'Have you been before?' he asks.

'No.' I am saying as little as possible and I am volunteering nothing.

Osman visibly lights up. 'First time.' He examines my well-travelled passport. 'Ireland.'

'Yes.'

Next to me an old lady is being turned back by another 'border' guard. He hands her back her identity card and he points away. 'This is in Greek. I cannot read Greek. You must go back.'

Osman stamps my visa form but fortunately he does not stamp my passport. Who wants a stamp in their passport of a 'country' that is a considered to be an international pariah? I already have stamps from San Marino and Liechtenstein and they are embarrassing enough. Osman smiles at me in a smug, arrogant and obsequious manner. I don't know what he is so smug about since his chosen career is as a 'border' guard at a 'border' that is not a 'border'. He hands me back my paperwork. I am in. I replace my passport in my luggage. If I lose my passport in this non-country, then I am completely screwed.

The customs guy in the next booth does not give me a second glance. The last booth is manned by a genial man from the Northern Cyprus Tourist Office who has stacks of glossy brochures which he needs to get rid of. 'English?' he asks me with open arms, absolutely delighted to be welcoming me to his place of work and ready to answer all my questions except the question about why he is here at all. I nod and I receive a large wedge of literature plus a bad dose of paper cut on my bloodied hands. His brochure says, 'The island has been occupied by a succession of peoples from

Europe and Asia.' You said it, mate. His city map ends at the
'border' and it shows neither streets nor street names in the south.
On this side of the divide there are no sad memorials to the
invasion of 1974, nor any mention of the EU or UN.

First impressions are that this part of city is stuck in a time
warp, probably since 1974. While the southern part of Nicosia is
high-rise and modern, the Turkish Cypriot part is low-rise and
almost feudal. I walk down the first street from the crossing point
to find hucksters' shops selling counterfeit goods at low prices.
Dolce & Gabbana for €10 is amazingly good value. Hostile shop-
keepers loiter outside shops, but they will take euro as well as
Turkish Lira. Their windows are full of half-naked mannequins, as
if they couldn't be bothered to fully clothe them. This part of the
city seems cheap in every sense. While the southern end of Ledra
Street is buzzing with people and life, this dead end is dark, dirty
and depressing.

I sit at an outdoor café overlooked by a police barracks in
Ataturk Square to digest the northern part of Nicosia. There are
Turkish and TRNC flags everywhere—I can count 10 from my
chair—and there are even two perched on top of the Selimiye
Mosque, once St Sofia Cathedral but handily converted by the
Ottomans. The centre piece of the square is the Venetian Column,
which is a chipped obelisk set in a waterless pool now infested with
pigeons. It was once crowned with a lion of St Mark but that was
nicked and it was replaced by a rather boring globe. More flies
hover about and this time I am certain that they are Turkish
Cypriot flies. The traffic comprises 30-year-old Renaults and regular Mercedes Benz army trucks whose drivers rev their engines
whenever they see a good-looking woman, which is not often
around these parts. There are 40,000 Turkish troops stationed on
this side of the 'border', making the TRNC one of the safest places
on earth. Taxi drivers sit around at ranks playing backgammon.
Youths loll on kerbs and chew gum. Everyone smokes like a
Turkish army trooper. There is a branch of ING Bank so it seems
that this international banking giant condones the TRNC. The
major industry here seems to be scruffy waiters who take dark cof-
fees and cold water on trays to nearby shop-keepers on the hour.

There are few people about. Tourism is not so well catered for. The lady in the tourist office at Kyrenia Gate tells me that the brochures are in Turkish. 'We don't have it in English.' A few other tourists (we're the ones wearing shorts) sit and stare, thinking that this place is awful and it's time to return to the south. But I am staying one night.

I search for an evening meal in vain because it appears that most of the establishments would not pass a food hygiene visit by any environmental inspector. Eventually I cross back to the Greek Cypriot side, merely for a bite to eat. It is noticeable that when I leave the Turkish Cypriot side the 'border' guards are much less friendly. They don't make eye contact. They love to welcome us but they hate to see us leave for the opposition. The last straw for me is when I pull the curtains in my grim three-star hotel room on the wrong side of the tracks. I see flashing lights up on the mountain, near where the dreadful flags are located. A star lights up, a crescent lights up and finally an entire TRNC flag lights up. This illuminating process repeats itself all night. The Turks do like to rub the Greek Cypriots' noses right in it, 24/7.

Perhaps aware of the Museum of National Struggle on the Greek Cypriot side, the Turkish Cypriots have the emotively titled Museum of Barbarism, which would only likely be outdone if the other side opened a Museum of Unspeakable Acts Committed by those Nasty Turks. I take a bus to the suburb of Kumsal. On 24 December 1963, Greek Cypriot irregulars forcibly entered the house of Dr Ilhan, who was a major in the Turkish army but who was away that night. The doctor's wife, three children and a neighbour were killed by machine gun fire. The house remains almost as it was found that Christmas Eve. The inside of the bathroom where the killings took place is left intact, with captions explaining that the fading red spots upon the walls are the actual blood of the victims. It's an outrage and I am sure there were many such other outrages, committed by both sides, but I am unconvinced that it all warrants an invasion.

Next morning I gladly checkout and take a taxi to the airport. I should be flying from the rather convenient Nicosia International Airport but that's stuck in the middle of the UN buffer zone and it hasn't seen a plane for 30 years. So I travel to the new Ercan Airport on the Turkish side. We speed through a wasteland of squat apartment blocks, car showrooms, factories and warehouses. If there is one thing that the Turks are good at, then it's driving taxis. Passport control at Ercan is ridiculously slow as we queue to get out of this place as quickly as possible. In the TRNC you must bring your mother and father plus extended family who can all have a chat with the 'border' guard in the smart uniform in the passport booth. An Englishman is baffled at the delays. 'I think he's asking that guy about his school report in 1984.' There are a WC, a nursery and small mosque in Departures, one of which I use. Duty Free sells mostly cigarettes plus some Jack Daniels chocolate. They also sell boxes of Turkish Delight—something you will never find on the southern part of this island. Everyone smokes freely everywhere in this stinking airport. This place is five years behind the rest of Europe and it should be called the Turkish Republic of Northern Cigarettes.

Pegasus Airlines are a Turkish low fares airline who offer flights from the TRNC to Stansted for £33. They fly Boeing 737-800s with nice reclining padded seats. For the in-flight service the two girls wear canary yellow aprons emblazoned with *'Flying Café'* while the two guys have to wear the same aprons, but in a nice shade of sky blue. We leave on time and the flight experience is professional and reassuring.

My fellow passengers are English folk with property in the TRNC. This is impressive until I see the property adverts in the *Cyprus Star* where apartments start from a mere £35,000. I guess property can be this cheap when the builders got the land for nothing—they simply took it from the Greek Cypriots. A tiny Turkish man in a tiny suit but with a big moustache sits alongside and it might be his first trip on a plane. He is amazed when I can recline my seat (clearly we are not flying on Ruinair) and he tries to do the same without success until he holds the button in and heaves with all his weight backwards. We both hear an English voice behind. 'Thank you so very much for doing that. We're trying to have a nice cup of tea here.'

We are one hour into the flight and I'm comfy and settled when the pilot comes on and announces to my amazement that we will be landing shortly. Where? Jet2 took four hours to get here so there's no way that Pegasus is going to make this return trip in only one hour. Out of the cabin window I see a vast city straddling an isthmus between east and west and deduce that we are approaching Istanbul. A passenger confirms this fact and that we will make a stopover here. We land at Istanbul's Sabiha Gokcen Airport.

The Turkish Republic of Northern Cyprus is not recognised by any country in the world other than by Turkey. Funny that. I am not even sure how a country is recognised. Can it be walking along a street in Nicosia one day and another country will pass it by on the opposite side and give it a subtle nod of acknowledgment and it has been recognised? Thus Ercan Airport is not recognised by the governing international aviation body IATA. Istanbul Airport is the essential means by which a planeload of passengers emanating from a non-country is transformed into a planeload of passengers emanating from an EU member-applicant state. Otherwise no airport in the world would accept our desperate flight.

I could write a chapter about Istanbul and Turkey but I only spent 50 minutes there. We couldn't leave the plane and I spent some of that time in the WC and they wouldn't let us stand up and walk about inside the plane. So I don't know that much about Turkey. And I don't wish to take sides.

The Low Fares Airline (3)

THE LOW FIRES AIRLINE (1)

Ruinair has sent one of its rostered pilots a P45 backdated by six weeks. It means the aviator had completed dozens of flights for Ruinair while technically unemployed. Ulrik Holm, a Danish pilot based at East Midlands Airport near Derby in England, had been in dispute with Ruinair over his contract, but said he was 'gobsmacked' to return home from a flight to find mail that informed him he had been 'fired' six weeks previously. Between 10 August, the day Ruinair terminated his contract, and 17 September, the day he received his P45, Holm flew 48 Ruinair flights mainly from England and Ireland. The then 60-year-old had been asked to sign up with Brookfield Aviation, a subcontracting company that provides pilots to Ruinair. The airline explained to him that it was against company policy to employ pilots over the age of 60. An internal e-mail shows a Ruinair manager described the contract granted to Holm as a 'mistake' because he was 'the only person in Ruinair who is over 60 and is working for us on a Ruinair contract. It is not permitted'.

THE TIMES

THE LOW FIRES AIRLINE (2)

A former Ruinair pilot has claimed that CEO Mick O'Leery told pilots, 'You're some crowd of fucking idiots' during a major dispute over their right to union representation. Joe Peard, who is taking a constructive dismissal case against the no-frills airline, said Mr O'Leery also warned them: 'If you want a fucking war, put your hard hats on, get your banners and go on to the roundabout.' Mr Peard, from

Terenure in Dublin, admitted he sat on his hands so people would not notice how much he was trembling during his first experience of a meeting with Mr O'Leery. At a hearing at the Employment Appeals Tribunal, he claimed the budget carrier boss used tactics he had not 'experienced since school' when pushing through a training package for pilots. Mr Peard, who now works for Emirates airline, is claiming that Ruinair subjected him to a 'systematic and ongoing campaign of harassment', forcing him to resign. Mr Peard worked for Ruinair for four years before handing in his notice. He said Mr O'Leery had told pilots he was sick of hearing they were working for 'Siberian salt mines' and told them to find a job elsewhere if they did not like it. Mr Peard said he was earning between €32,000 and €36,000 when Ruinair put out a press release that said pilots earned about €120,000 a year. During a meeting with Mr O'Leary, he said he approached him directly to tell him he was struggling financially. Mr Peard said the CEO did not know who he was but said, 'You'll have your command within a year', which meant he would get a €30,000 pay rise if promoted to captain.

IRISH INDEPENDENT

THE NOT FAIR AIRLINE

Claims that Ruinair's gift vouchers are almost impossible to redeem - — and may end up costing consumers more than they're worth—are under investigation by the National Consumers Agency (NCA). The NCA received several complaints from frustrated consumers claiming that they were unable to get through to telephone reservation agents to book flights using the vouchers. They can only be redeemed by ringing a dedicated reservation line, which charges callers 13 cent a minute, according to company policy. The consumer watchdog said it would re-open its investigation yesterday after several furious gift-voucher holders rang the Liveline programme on RTÉ Radio claiming it was next to impossible to redeem the vouchers by telephone as required. One caller, a pensioner named Martha, said she had been trying to make reservations for the past six months and gave up the other day after being put on hold for 45 minutes before being cut off. 'I feel like just crying,' Martha said. The €300 voucher expires tomorrow under the budget airline's policy which restricts validity to just six months from the date of purchase, she added. Martha said she had rung every Ruinair phone number listed, and even spent €5.90 to send a registered letter to headquarters, hoping to resolve her booking nightmare, but had not heard back. Fellow pensioner Noel Long said it cost him almost the entire value of his €50 gift voucher in calls to the reservation line, which was finally answered after three attempts, in order to book a flight to London three days before it expired. 'To use my son's €50 gift voucher, I had to pay €49.30 for the phone call,' he said. 'The €50 voucher cost about €100.'

IRISH INDEPENDENT

THE LOW USABILTY AIRLINE

Ruinair has come bottom of an online Irish shopping survey. Ruinair's website, Ruinair.com, finished in last place in the survey of consumer practices at 25 online firms by Irish internet consultancy firm AMAS. 'Ruinair fell down on several points of good practice,' said Fiachra O'Marcaigh, director of AMAS. 'It's very difficult to avoid paying for extras as consumers have to opt out repeatedly. It takes a very determined effort for a web-savvy user to book a flight without any additional charges.'

WWW.ELECTRICNEWS.NET

THE LOW FANS AIRLINE (1)

Ruinair has been voted the worst airline by British travellers for the second year running. A third of people in the UK polled by online travel community TripAdvisor voted the Irish no-frills airline their least favourite. The main reasons given were delays and cancellations, unfriendly staff, uncomfortable seats and poor legroom, according to more than 2,500 respondents to the travel survey.

WWW.TRIPADVISOR.COM

THE LOW FANS AIRLINE (2)

Low cost carrier Ruinair have hit out at the consumer magazine Which after they published a survey indicating more passengers pre-ferred to travel with rival airline easyJet. The survey was conducted with 30,000 Which members and examined many airlines and the service they provide to their customers. The Which survey published on their website concluded that whilst easyJet did not excel in several key areas they were superior to Ruinair in 'helpfulness and efficiency of cabin staff, cleanliness of aircraft and handling delays' with Ruinair apparently scoring poorly in all these areas. Ruinair had the following to say about the results of the Which survey: 'If you want low fares and great passenger service then follow our 60m passengers and fly Ruinair. If you want to buy a useless magazine with no insight whatsoever into air travel, then we strongly recommend Which whose annual loony member survey is about as useful as a baggage tag in Terminal 5.'

WWW.WHICH.CO.UK

Malta

Flight FR7242 – Thursday @ 7.05 a.m. – DUB-MLA-DUB

Fare €0.02 plus taxes, fees and charges €50

I have taken so many flights on Ruinair that I know all of my fellow passengers, intimately:

'*Sporting Athletes*'—gangs of Dublin lads dressed in sporting apparel. I assume that despite missing selection for the Irish Olympic Team, they secured lucrative sponsorship deals from Nike, Adidas, Lacoste or Le Coq Sportif, so much so they do not even need to have day jobs. Some dress for Eircom's national soccer team or for Carling's favourite Scottish soccer team. They are fit—fit for not much more than hanging around overseas airport bars looking for a smoking zone. They all visit the same barber in Dublin who supplies them with copious amounts of hair gel. When seen in sunny Spain, they glow bright red.

'*Ugg Girls*'—three or four girls in Ugg boots and grey Abercrombie & Fitch hoodies, plus leggings, usually going to Mummy and Daddy's place near Nice, Malaga or Faro. They are better tanned from a bottle than they will be after two weeks in the sun. They begin conversations with sentences like 'I only have €900 in my bank account,' to which another says, 'We'll have to sleep in the streets,' to which the first replies 'Well, I'm not sleeping in the streets.' They are sometimes able to answer their own questions such as 'Where did you get that new white top, Zara?' They have been to known to stand outside an aircraft wc for a few minutes and watch the green light before asking a friend, 'Does vacant mean the same as empty?' Ironic.

'Virgins'—two or three girls who do not know what to do, maybe because they arose at 3 a.m. in the countryside to drive two hours to Dublin Airport long-term car park to catch a 6 a.m. Ruinair flight. They are greatly confused about numbers, such as check-in desks, departure gates, rows and seats. So much so that they asked me to move from my seat in row 12, which I obviously refuse to do, even when they show me their boarding cards with a big number 12 on them. 'That's our departure gate,' I reply. They produce €50 notes to pay for €5 drinks, which the crew refuse to accept, so they offer a credit card. It may be their first flight. We have all been virgins on Ruinair at least on one occasion but eventually we all get screwed.

'Hen Parties'—most commonly seen on the 7.30 p.m. Stansted to Dublin flight on Friday evening and thus a flight to be avoided at all costs. On some occasions the combined number of Hens en route to Temple Bar outnumbers all other passengers on the flight. They travel in groups of four to eight and wear matching T-shirts, one with Bride, one with Sister, one with Mum and the others with Friend. Often they wear pink wigs.

'Connected Youth'—they travel with minimal baggage, usually with only an Apple lap-top computer. They do not care if we are late or probably even about where they are flying to as long as they can lie on the Departures lounge floor and can plug their lap-top into a hole in the wall for free juice. Simultaneously they have an iPod plugged into both ears and one free hand on a shiny new Nokia mobile for blind texting.

'Sad Suits'—solo businessmen who are well turned out in dark suits and bright ties and who all look smarter than the average Ruinair male crew member, even better turned out that Mick himself. They loiter uncomfortably at departure gates and display doubts about whether this airline will get them there. They sit onboard with hunched shoulders and their hands on their knees, to avoid contamination by touching the seats. They pray silently that post-recession their large corporate multinational will relax the travel cut backs and permit them once again to travel on a real airline, such as on Aer Lingus or British Airways.

'Decklander Families'—those who accumulate the maximum amount of material possessions in life, such as BMW SUVs, 50-inch flat plasma screens and homes in suburbs with a barbeque and outside decking. He is dressed by Tommy and Dockers. She wears more jewellery and bling than Posh Spice. They crave the very best in life, such that I have seen Him sit in the emergency row for extra leg room, while he puts Her and the two children in the row behind (children not being permitted to sit in the emergency row). They freely engage in conversations with other passengers, mostly about places they have visited. 'We were there last year for a week. We stayed in a five-star place. Good shopping there.' They take more holidays than I do, which is no mean feat.

Safety Experts—people who sit in or near the emergency rows and broadcast their alarming knowledge to others. 'We're the ones who will have to open the emergency exit door. That's it there. You can't push it outside right away due to the air pressure out there. You have to pull the door inside first and then twist it and push it outside.' Also been heard to say, 'You can't leave bags on the floor here. It's in case the aircraft suddenly swerves in mid-air,' or 'That's a picture of the brace position. You have to lean forward like this. Chances are we won't be asked to do this. Getting into the brace position is rare enough.'

'Italian Nuns'—they are usually seen in a queue to board a flight to Ciampino (near Rome) or to Bergamo (near Milan). The stand patiently, shrouded in all black. Their vow of poverty means that they must choose the lowest fares airline. Their vow of silence means that they cannot complain about the delay in boarding. Their vow of humility means that they must be last in the queue. If they ever paid good money for Priority boarding they would likely be excommunicated from the Catholic Church by the Pope. For them, with their desire for suffering, contrition, penance and possible self-flagellation, Ruinair represents the ideal airline.

Mick knows his passengers better than I ever will. '*People may pretend they don't fly Ruinair but everyone does it. Tony Blair, half the Royal Family. If I showed you our passenger list, we'd have half the House of Lords, lots of* MPs. *The chatterati hate mass tourism but they travel with us to their Italian villas. They all love a bargain. If they use it, why should they exclude others? It's just snobbery. I hate this censorious attitude to what people do. If you think they're setting a bad example I would point you to lunatics like Robert Mugabe. He didn't go on a stag night, he starved his entire people. Willie Walsh is the one with the high fares and the fuel surcharges.* BA *is neither on time nor efficient. They used to claim to be the world's favourite airline, now they're not even Britain's favourite airline, Ruinair is. We have twice as many passengers. Eventually there'll be one last British Airways flight with a bunch of old toffee-nosed snobs on it but all the kids of the toffee-nosed snobs will be flying on Ruinair. The budget airlines are visionaries who are creating a more equal society. Low fares have transformed Europe politically. There's much more movement of young people across the Continent. We've done more for European integration than any old fart politician in Brussels.*'

There is a reason I can fly from Dublin to Malta for 1 cent and the Prime Minister of Malta spelt it out in his budget speech. '*We introduced schemes to attract a low-cost airline. It is pertinent to point out that these schemes will cost the government more than Lm 1 million. I am saying this to explain to everyone that the price of a low-cost airline ticket is cheap because we are all paying part of it.*' But there is a second reason. I am on the inaugural Ruinair flight from Dublin, which will likely be met by dignitaries and the press pack at Malta's Luqa Airport. Ruinair certainly do not wish to arrive with a half-empty aircraft.

The Maltesers are jittery. 10 per cent of the 400,000 inhabitants derive a direct living from tourism, which accounts for 24 per cent of GNP and 25 per cent of exports, but their industry is in crisis. Whilst European destinations report ever-increasing numbers of tourists, Malta's number of visitors fell by 50,000 in the last year. The occupancy rate in Malta's hotels in the winter months is a miserly 41 per cent. Last year 18 hotels closed while only four new hotels opened. The entire board of the Malta Tourist Authority resigned en masse due to a lack of strategic direction and policy implementation. A Maltese travel agent sued the Authority because they introduced a website where visitors can *pay online* for their holidays. Shock, horror. There are rumours that a major British tour operator will remove Malta from their brochure. Some blame the decline on Air Malta, a bloated government-owned airline, where a flight from Dublin would cost me hundreds of euro, and that's assuming I could get their online booking engine to function. Personally I attribute the decline to those low fares airlines who lure holidaymakers to middle-of-nowhere places, rather than to an historic cultured hotspot such as Malta. The Maltese government agree with me and they have stumped up to Ruinair.

Onboard my newspaper coincidentally reveals that Ruinair's vast fleet of aircraft will belch out more carbon dioxide emissions this year than an entire country plus its population: Malta. From the air the other polluter is the largest of an archipelago of seven islands in the midst of the Med, a creamy oval rock without mountains, forest or rivers; an island of low stony hills, terraced fields and a coastline indented with bays plus one of the finest harbours in the world. It's an epic flight of three and a half hours' duration, my longest ever journey on Ruinair, and the 30-inch pitched seats mean that I will exit the aircraft like a cripple. There is a man of undersized proportions, a dwarf, on the flight and he is the only comfortable passenger. The flight is so long that a cabin crew member finishes a *Harry Potter* novel at the rear of the aircraft.

There is never much news on an island 17 by 9 miles in size so the press met the inaugural flights from London Lootin' and Pizza (Florence). Mick arrived in an open-neck shirt and jeans with a Maltese flag and made contorted faces for the photographers. *'I was told to go to Malta because there is all-year-round sunshine and the moment I step off the plane it starts raining. That's it, I'm pulling my airline out of Malta.'*

We left 30 minutes late but in a feat of military precision we land exactly on time to the second to be greeted by airport officials and media. We are 149 passengers, which is a satisfactory load factor. Inside the terminal a band plays local music and pretty ladies in traditional garb offer us free wine, chocolates and flowers. I know my first 'Ruinair' book was moderately successful but this sort of special welcome is clearly excessive. A Dublin guy grabs his leggy girlfriend and points over at the party scene. 'See, impressive or what? I went to all this trouble for you. It cost me a bleedin' fortune but it's worth it for someone like you.'

Later that evening the arrival of our aircraft is the second story on the Channel 7 news. Next day we are the lead in the *Times of Malta* (with a *'story continues on page three'*). I learn that the Malta Hotels & Restaurants Association love Ruinair but Air Malta hate their guts. *The Independent* runs the story on its back page with a photograph of us deplaning. I recognise some of the faces from the flight but I am not in the photograph, which is just as well since I don't do media work unless my publicist is first consulted. The excitement here at the arrival of Ruinair would only be surpassed by the second coming of Jesus Christ.

Outside I wait for a bus. A local lady speaks to me in a foreign tongue and then in English.

'Where are you from?' she inquires.

'Ireland.'

There is immediate recognition. Her eyes light up. 'Ah ... Ruinair.'

There is 7,000 years of history on Malta—megalithic temples and fortified cities—but nothing is as old as the buses which traverse this island nation. There are 508 buses, of which 300 are more than 35 years old with proud names such as the *Plaxton Supreme* and the *Bedford Dominator*. They are much like the 1950s Leyland buses which stop in neat rural villages in *Miss Marple* episodes on BBC TV. The buses sport a white roof, a striking orange band and a deep yellow body and you can buy postcards of Malta bus models and liveries over the years. Exactly half of the buses operate each day. All are privately owned and most are driven by the owners themselves so don't put your dirty feet up on the seats. The owners share their income each fortnight. Buses are the main form of public transport; there are no trains because Malta is small enough that even when you become lost, you will always arrive at your intended destination.

The number 8 airport bus is geriatric but at 50 cent for a 30-minute trip to Valletta, I cannot complain, being an embarrassingly small 1/18th of the price of the Dublin Aircoach service from the airport to my home. Our driver appears surly at first but later he toots the horn at locals and other drivers, stops the bus between the stops to chat to good looking-women and whistles at playing children, as he takes the bus down impossibly narrow one-way streets, wing mirrors only inches from ancient mortar and plaster. The roads here are worse than in Ireland and that's saying something.

Up close for the first time Malta is old, run down and dilapidated but is so in a fantastically appealing manner. There is no air-conditioning so in a breach of health and safety regulations, the bus wheezes along streets with the door open. Drivers like to play music from local radio stations mainly featuring Bonnie Tyler, Jennifer Rush and suicidal Johnny Cash tracks. Malta uses all the buses that the rest of the world no longer requires and instead of a decent burial upon a scrap-heap the buses work out their last days in semi-retirement ferrying people to outlying towns. The buses are an embarrassment to the locals but tourists love to stand at the Triton fountain in the centre of the bus terminus to snap the single most decrepit knackered bus for their digital photograph album. The drivers are sufficiently uninterested in public opinion that several have slogans written on their windows such as 'I Don't Care What People Say', 'The Road to Nowhere' and 'That Don't Impress Me Much'.

The Phoenicians, Carthaginians, Romans, Arabs, Normans, French and British came here, the latter leaving red post boxes and telephone kiosks, left-hand side driving, a judicial system and the English language. But of all the invaders, the Knights of the Order of St John made the greatest impact, against all prognoses, by saving the city in the Great Siege of 1565 when the religious order dressed men, women and children in uniforms and propped them up atop castle walls, fooling the Turks into thinking they were out-numbered. French Grandmaster Jean La Vallette had a city named after him and Valletta became the first planned city in Europe, with streets in a grid like Manhattan, the pattern designed to encourage natural ventilation through the streets in the searing summer highs. This World Heritage Site and fortress city is renowned as being a city *'built by gentlemen for gentlemen'* so I blend right in. The Knights ran Malta for more than two centuries until Napoleon arrived in 1798 and asked for safe harbour to supply his ships, but he turned his guns against his hosts once safely inside the Grand Harbour, which is a particularly sneaky trick to pull.

Republic Street is the spine of the city and was originally called Kingsway by the British before being renamed when Malta became a republic in 1974. It begins at City Gate (once only a hole in the walls but now a monumental entrance between two giant cavalier fortifi-cations) and it rises and falls towards Fort St Elmo on the tip of the peninsula of Valletta. Close to the top at Freedom Square is the only eyesore in Valletta: the WWII ruin of the Opera House, yet to be rebuilt. Republic Street is for posing, shopping, café society, meeting friends and the last tourists left standing. On both sides are narrow streets of stacked limestone homes in honey and lemon tones. Sometimes wicker baskets are mysteriously lowered by residents from fourth-floor balconies only for skinny cats to leap out for their daily exercise once grounded. Dotted around the city are *auberges*, one inn for each nationality, where knights could crash for the night. On street corners I see religious decorations and statues, demanded by the knights to maintain standards. It is said that Republic Street has gentle steps because knights in armour found steps easier to navigate than hills. I walk up and down the weathered steps moulded by centuries of wandering city pedestrians and imagine myself as a knight off to slay the infidels in my full metal jacket.

The wealthy Knights were originally hospitallers who built hospitals mostly for themselves it seems, served the sick using dishes made of hygienic solid silver (although condemned crimi-nals and galley rowers had to make do with pewter) and turned their hand to building churches, palaces and residences. Beneath the *Sacra Infermeria*, I discover the chivalrous world of the

Hospitaller Knights and experience the anguish and glory of 700 years from the Crusades to the Great Siege, the glorious hospital and the Plague. I learn that they had the fairly hopeless task of extracting a large number of nasty pointy arrows from fallen knights and hoping a bandage would mend all. Following medical progress the knights used red-hot irons instead of ligatures to control haemorrhaging during amputation and any gunshot wounds were cauterised with boiling oil of elders, which obviously made a huge difference. I step into the main ward, which at 161 metres long was the longest building in the world at the time. In the basement exhibition I see models of the interiors of hospital wards in the Middle Ages which appear fairly similar to present day NHS facilities. The Knights' mantra was 'Live in truth; have faith; repent of sin; give proof of humility, love justice, be merciful, be sincere and whole-hearted; and endure persecution', which all in all was a demanding lifestyle.

The Knights built St John's Cathedral. Once past its austere façade I discover an opulent Baroque interior filled with floor-to-ceiling frescoes, marble statues of Grand Masters, an altar of precious stones plus a Japanese camera crew offering me a chance of stardom on Japanese TV. I loiter in the background just to make things difficult for these space invaders. Beneath our feet are 400 inlaid marble tombstones dedicated to famous interred knights so the staff ask the Japanese presenter to remove her six-inch heels and she's even more diminutive. Slippers can be purchased for 25 cent and bare ladies can borrow a shawl or wrap. At the end of my visit I walk into a small side oratory and come face to face with a dramatic Caravaggio masterpiece showing something fatal happening to St John the Baptist and his head. This is Caravaggio's largest painting, with a canvas so expansive that I feel like I am standing at a UCI multiplex cinema screen, and it's the only work he ever signed as he scrawled his name in the blood draining from St John's slit throat. *Michelangelo.* Outside in Great Siege Square the alfresco *Café Matteo* offers an excellent closed Maltese bread roll with ham, basil, Gozo cheeselets, olive oil and tomato but do sit under a canopy since the over-active pigeons have a tendency to dive bomb your lunch.

I am here on the *Feast of St Paul's Shipwreck,* which is a unique excuse for a public holiday and commemorates his shipwreck in 60 AD, believed to have taken place at the aptly named St Paul's Bay. One imagines Paul out for a night on the town with other saintly types, having a few meads too many, taking his boat out on the high seas and trashing it on the rocks whilst under the influence. But St Paul was an accidental tourist who later became the patron saint of Malta, staying for three months and converting the Maltesers from chocolate to Christianity, before returning home to Rome where he too was beheaded.

At first the locals were not impressed with ragged beardy Paul but that all changed when a snake bit him on the wrist and the venom had no effect, and thus legend has it that Maltese snakes ceased to be venomous. The main celebration takes place in Valletta with street decorations, countless statues, marching bands, confetti-throwing and a firework display (there's no better way to burn money), culminating in a monumental figure of St Paul being carried through the streets. His shipwreck is mentioned in the Acts of the Apostles 28:1-2: *'And falling into a place where two seas met, they ran the ship aground. And when they were escaped, then they knew that the island was called Meli'ta.'* Some sceptics don't think St Paul ever landed in Malta but it says so in the Bible so it must be Gospel.

I find the locals are reassuringly welcoming to tourists. The inhabitants of the smallest and southernmost EU member state and Europe's most densely populated country have a reputation for talking like Arabs (and being equally indecipherable), gesturing like Italians but really wanting to be British. They are all devoutly Catholic with 400 churches in all and some of the churches have two clocks telling different times, which is meant to confuse the devil about the time of Mass. I find the locals swarthy and earthy, almost organic in nature and outlook and as naturally sun-ripened as any on-the-vine tomato.

Malta is holidaying a la carte. It offers a kaleidoscope of a little bit of Southern Europe, a little bit of North Africa and a little bit of the Middle East but in reality it is none of the above and remains uniquely Maltese. It is one big open-air museum, with a history built layer upon layer of cultures, races and religions. There's the lush sister island of Gozo. Another sister island, Comino, has no cars. There's a Hard Rock Café, a TGIF's and the usual burger joints. Catch of the day is on the menus. There's a daily morning flea market on Merchant Street where they sell rosary beads and model Maltese buses. There's a casino where Napoleon stayed and Lord Horatio Nelson moored his ship outside. There's sunbathing too. Sicily is only three hours by boat away. There's nightlife in St Julian's, Paceville and Sliema, even *Saturday Knight Fever*.

But Malta still attracts an older British clientele who are more hip-op than hip-hop. I see them in the hotel at breakfast where I am given a table near the door, whereas the older guests have tables near the ample buffet so that they don't have far to walk. The elderly gentlemen wear faded polo T-shirts with white Fred Perry tennis shorts, and open-toed sandals with beige knee-length socks. I don't begrudge them their attire. In fact I admire them tremendously. Based on overheard conversations I learn the last time they were in Malta was 60 years ago manning a gun battery defending the island against the then Axis of Evil. Malta is peaceful except for the rejuvenated Saluting Battery, which sounds off from its unique vantage point in the Upper Barrakka gardens, an arcaded bastion terrace overlooking the Grand Harbour. The Maltese still refer to 'sharp noon' as *'nofs inhar bumm'*, the last word being a reference to the sound of the gun. The official Malta Heritage Trust brochure advises that 'the noon-day gun is fired daily at … midday.'

Other frequent tourists are some A-list celebrities, here to work not play, making Malta the Hollywood of the Med. Brad Pitt came to film *Troy*. Matthew McConaughey came to play submarines in *U-571* in the water tanks of Mediterranean Film Studios. Guy Ritchie shot his ex-wife Madge here in *Love, Drugs, Sex and Money*. Oliver Stone made the disastrous *Alexander* as Valletta became Alexandria. Russell Crowe acted his scenes for *Gladiator*, not to be confused with the more hardcore *Glad He Ate Her*. There is an official movie map and guided tours are available for movie buffs. But perhaps the most famous, and saddest, cinematic location in Malta is the corner snug in *The Pub* at 136 Archbishop Street, Valletta where Oliver Reed breathed his last. A small shrine now exists to the actor with old photographs and a framed press clipping entitled '*Ollie's Last Order*', which I read consisted of 'eight lagers with the wife, 12 double rums with a group of sailors from HMS Cumberland and a quick half bottle of whiskey'. Oliver Reed left £10,000 out of his estate to be spent at his local pub, but only for 'those who are crying'.

The *Wartime Experience* in the Embassy shopping centre recounts experiences during the Siege of Malta. The siege lasted from 1940 to 1943 but the movie show only takes 45 minutes. Italy declared war on Britain on 10 June and the first bombs fell on Malta next day at 6.55 a.m., another unsociable time much favoured by Ruinair for their first departure of the day to ensure maximum utilisation of their aircraft. Malta suffered 3,000 bombing raids in three years and in the first six months of 1942, there was only one day without an air raid. 16,000 tons of bombs were dropped. There were so few aircraft on Malta that three obsolete Gloster Gladiator biplanes were first used to defend the island, and were immortalised as *Faith, Hope and Charity*. The British believed that Malta was indefensible and so stationed only 4,000 soldiers on the island with five weeks' worth of food. During the greatest times of starvation food was rationed to three boiled sweets, half a sardine and a spoonful of jam a day, which do not combine so well. Some days the communal Victory Kitchens fed 170,000 citizens and soldiers.

The National War Museum at Fort St Elmo houses memories of the Siege. The defence endured. Hermann Goering described the island 'an unsinkable aircraft carrier'. He wasn't wrong since the stone city flanked on both sides by water remains an immensely solid protrusion into the sometimes equally hostile Med. At the end of the museum drill hall is their prize possession. The refurbished *Faith* is here and in good nick but she won't be flying again. It is a little-known fact that there was a fourth plane which was never assembled and was used instead for parts, and in any case if they had decided to use it, they would have had trouble finding a nice name for it. The resistance of the population earned Malta a George Cross. A replica of the cross is on the Maltese flag and I see the real thing in a glass case in the museum along with the original covering letter on fancy Buckingham Palace note paper and signed by George VI. '*To honour her brave people, I award the George Cross to the Island Fortress of Malta to bear witness to a heroism and devotion that will long be famous in history.*'

It remains a staggering feat of military under-achievement that the Italians failed to capture an island only 93 km south of Sicily. The closest they came was on 26 June 1941 when a small Italian assault force tried to land in the Grand Harbour at 4.44 a.m. They were spotted early on radar and were repelled by 4.50 a.m., that is within six minutes. The assault is known as the Battle of Valletta but based on its duration it would appear to me to be more of a minor altercation or a misunderstanding. The Italians who first flew to Malta in 1940 proceeded to bomb the island from a safe height of 5,000 metres; they dropped down to 3,000 metres to improve their accuracy; went back up to bombing from 6,000 metres after encountering flak from the Gladiators and anti-aircraft batteries and eventually preferred to drop their bombs into the sea 30 km off Malta and return to base safely. I learn one bomb pierced the cupola of the *Mosta Dome* church in the midst of a Mass for 300 parishioners, bounded off the interior wall twice and skidded across the whole length of the church but it failed to explode, an event immediately attributed to the divine intervention of the Virgin Mary. A replica of the 200-kg bomb remains on display in the church, albeit defused.

The War Museum curator is a chatty fellow and he asks me if I have any questions. I tell him I am writing a book about Ruinair and he seems to agree that there are more tourists from the UK and Italy of late. I ask him if Ruinair will be a success. 'How can they sell seats for so little money? The market will decide. We will see the statistics. Then we will know.' I am about to leave when he returns to my side and leans closer in a secretive manner, as if about to reveal the Fourth Secret of Fatima. 'One more thing you should know. Do not take a ride with the men in the horse carriages outside. Big rip-off. Plenty money.'

Since my pilgrimage, Ruinair opened eight additional routes to and from Malta. EasyJet, Vueling, Clickair and a biblical swathe of low fares airlines followed them a year later. Now Italians can fly direct to Malta without the risk of being shot down, from Pizza (Florence), Bari and Venice (Treviso). The British can fly here from Lootin'. Ruinair remains a latter-day saint for those who profess a strong faith in the low fares business model and for those who pray for more tourists who appreciate the charity of 1-cent fares. Ruinair has become the saviour of Maltese tourism: their very own next knight in shining armour.

Financial Ruination

It must be the Chartered Accountant in me, usually a terminal condition, but I still have a burning desire to summarise the cost of travelling to every country in New Europe. Honestly, I wish I had an Excel file.

Country	Airline	Route	Fare	Taxes Fees & Charge	Total
Lithuania	Ruinair	DUB-KUN-DUB	€0.02	€46	€46
Latvia	Ruinair	DUB-RIX-DUB	€15	€54	€69
Estonia	airBaltic	RIX-TLL-RIX	€45	€23	€68
Czech Republic	Ruinair	DUB-PRG-DUB	€3	€41	€44
Poland	CentralWings	DUB-GDN-DUB	€10	€68	€78
Slovakia	SkyEurope	DUB-BTS-DUB	€28	€20	€48
Bulgaria	SkyEurope	VIE-SOF-VIE	€62	€44	€106
Hungary	WizzAir	LTN-BUD-LTN	€14	€60	€74
Slovenia	easyJet	STN-LJU-STN	€109	€34	€143
Romania	Blue Air	STN-BBU-CRL	€2	€104	€106
Malta	Ruinair	DUB-MLA-DUB	€0.02	€50	€50
Cyprus	Jet2, Pegasus	[let's not even go there]	[a lot]		
Total			€288	€544	€832

Lesson learned? I saw 11 countries within my budget but can Ruinair please fly to Cyprus? Soon.

Mick's Plane Speaking (2)

On Ireland: *'We all know the world is in a mess at the minute, we all know we're going to have to cut back. What needs to be done is to cut back public spending massively, sell off all the useless semi-states and get rid of all these useless quangos. We have had an explosion of quangos, putting the Celia Larkins of this world on the board of the National Consumer Agency and paying her a fee to do what? Get rid of her. And the other guy, that fella in Cork, the 'Show me the Money' guy, what's his name? Eddie Hobbs. Sack him. What are we paying any of those guys for?'*

On the Irish Civil Service: *'Sack civil servants. We have far too many bloody civil servants. Decentralisation was a great idea, but two days later to come out and say, 'Sorry, nobody's going to lose their jobs.' If you're a company and you're going to relocate to Mullingar and your employees don't want to go there, it's amazingly simple, either you go to Mullingar or you don't have a job. But what we did in the Bertie Ahern era was, we would have decentralisation but nobody need lose their job. Well hang on, in the real world if you don't want to move, go find another job. We give all these numb nuts a guarantee that it's alright if you don't want to move. You can stay here and do what? Nothing.'*

On a proposed new airline. *'As for our transatlantic plans, we will never fly transatlantic. We are working on a plan that I hope will emerge out of a major downturn, to set up a transatlantic low fares airline. The only time to set up an airline is when they are parking planes in the desert. We are not very far from that at the moment. It would provide a premium service in business class. We are contemplating opening up transatlantic services from day one from major airports in Rome, Barcelona, Frankfurt, Brussels, Paris and perhaps somewhere in Ireland. It probably is at least two years away. Its focus would not be to operate an Irish-American transatlantic route for the blue rinse grannies.'*

On Irish politicians: *'People just want some leadership. I think if they take the tough decisions, but lead people in the right direction, tell them: 'Look, there's a reason we're doing this, it'll be short-term, but there's a tax cut', you'll get away with almost anything. By all means increase tax for rich people like me. We can afford to pay more tax. I think that in Brian Cowen you have a very good Taoiseach. In Brian Lenihan you have potentially a very good Minister for Finance. I don't know Mary Coughlan. I have no dealings with her, and one way or another, she's not that important. The Tánaiste is about as useful as the role of vice-president, not worth a bucket of warm spit as Lyndon Johnson used to say. We elect politicians to run the country and to run the economy. The last thing they need is either the opinions of rich business people, many of whom either don't live here or pay taxes here, or the trade unions.'*

On UK politicians: *'Politicians call for eco-taxes but that's just spin— it's just taking more money off us. David Cameron may be holidaying in Cornwall but he flew halfway round the world just to see some huskies. David Cameron can hug trees because he won't have to do much to get into power but it is not a way to run a country. Gordon Brown is only staying in Britain because he is too frightened that if he leaves someone will nick his job. England's a wonderful country but it isn't right for every family or every holiday. Sometimes you need to get away. It's just government by poll and spin-doctor. Thatcher and Blair didn't dither, they just made their decisions. Where do all these carbon offsets go? Corrupt African dictatorships and staff in New York. The money doesn't actually go to planting trees. The green lobby are like those old guys in the medieval marketplace, shouting about the end of the world. Climate change is not the biggest threat to mankind. If it is, why is the summer so crappy?'*

Epilogue

I have always been fascinated by maps and there is no map more fascinating than the constantly evolving multi-pronged Pan-European destination map of Ruinair. Even after three years of travelling to all 27 countries in the European Union, there is so much more to discover. Each time I view the map I marvel at the places I have never heard of, let alone been to. I'm convinced that half of these places are made up. I am curious.

I am like every other Ruinair passenger at this stage. We have done the hotspots of Rome and Barcelona, the fleshpots of Amsterdam and Berlin, the cultural spots of Prague and Krakow. I do not intend to retrace my steps but what about the other places? I mean, I know so little about Zweibrucken in western Germany, except that it must possess two bridges, but there's 38,000 people there ... with an airport.

'We've never done market research on any of our new routes. We don't go in for demographic analysis. We simply look for airports with efficient facilities and a low cost base. There are a lot of people, particularly in London, who are always looking for somewhere different. If you can fly to somewhere in Europe for under £10 then you are going to fill 200 seats a day to almost anywhere. People have laughed at some of our more unusual destinations, but we've never stopped flying to any of them due to lack of interest. We have very few complaints. Almost none are about out of the way airports or the kind of apocryphal tales you're always reading. There's all kinds of places in Scandinavia and down through Germany where NATO had bases during the Cold War. Even in the UK there's dozens of airports. When you look at an ordinary map you think there's no more airports; in actual fact the place is absolutely awash with airports. We look for the

signs which show there's an airport somewhere and go and talk with them. It's not as if JFK was in Central Park or Heathrow was in Pall Mall. I don't give a toss where people want to go. I'm in the business of creating a market for people to go where they never have heard of.'

Billund in Denmark is the world headquarters of Lego so is the town built from large multi-coloured inter-locking plastic bricks? Would Salzburg exist if it were not for the *Sound Of Music*? What would I do in Karlsruhe and would I follow the Germans and fly off to somewhere else ... anywhere else? Would I blend in effortlessly with the cool surfer dudes in the Atlantic resort of Biarritz? How close is that tower in Pisa to toppling over, and taking its entire tourist industry with it? Is Basel pronounced as in the American herb or as in the mad owner of *Fawlty Towers*? Are some places from Aarhus to Zadar more likely to represent a cartographer's rare spelling mistake? Is Aarhus homely? Is Brest rude? Is Baden-Baden bad? Is Nice nice? So many places, so little time.

I log on, check a few new websites, book flights, get my backpack and set my alarm clock for 5 a.m.

I'll call the book *The Ruinair Guide to Other Places*.

Waiting for the back door of a Ruinair plane to open (people all standing at their seats with bags in hands), a man turns around and says to an Asian man in the seat behind him (whom he obviously knew):
'Hey Mahmood, I was just thinking sometimes it's great to be a Pakistani.'
'Why's that?' asks Mahmood.
'Cos ye nearly always get a whole row of seats to yer self.'

Shortly after landing on a Ruinair flight at Dublin, the intercom goes through all the usual stuff and says at the end: '90 per cent of all Ruinair flights have landed . . .'
My sister looks at me: 'What happens to the other 10 per cent?'

On a Ruinair flight from Lübeck to Dublin. I'm sitting at the window. Coming in to land there's turbulence, fog, you name it. Very bumpy.
After rough landing genuinely relieved pilot announces over intercom, 'Clear of the active runway sir, thank fuck, I hadn't a clue where I was going.'
15 seconds later...
'My apologies there ladies and gentleman, I, errrrr....' (pause)
15 seconds later... (other pilot)
'Ladies and gentlemen, welcome to Dublin.'

I was on a Ruinair flight from London to Dublin. The plane landed on the runway at Dublin quite rushed and roughly. I was walking through to baggage reclaim and I saw the captain and co-pilot walking through to the same area. I saw these two skangers who were on the same flight (seated near me) walking up to baggage reclaim also. They spotted the captain and the co-pilot also. One of the skangers walks alongside the captain and says, 'Captain Kirk, what fuckin' way did you land that plane back there? You fuckin' bounced down that runway. Me auld one could have landed that better.'

On a Ruinair flight to Rome, the plane was getting ready to take off, but the cabin crew were having trouble getting some Italian folk to sit in their seats—they were standing around chatting.
Intercom clicks on.
bing bong
'Eh, it's the captain here, could you Italians sit down so I can fly this yoke?'
Intercom clicks off.

When finally boarding the Ruinair plane in Dublin Airport after a four-hour delay:
'Ladies and gentlemen, please take your seats as soon as possible so we can leave on time.'

On a Ruinair flight to Edinburgh the air hostess kept pausing during the safety demonstration.
'In the event of a drop in cabin pressure, oxygen masks will drop down. Pull the mask down and place it over your face.'
She pauses.
Young lad down the back shouts, 'And insert €2 for oxygen.'

I was boarding a Ruinair flight from Dublin to Glasgow when the passenger in front said to the air hostess, 'Where do I sit?' and she replied, 'On your bum'.

'Privately and personally, I don't think I'm quite as obnoxious as I come across.'

The author welcomes feedback from readers,
particularly those with Ruinair anecdotes.

paulkilduff@eircom.net

or visit

http://www.paulkilduff.com

Or become a Fan of Ruinair on
www.facebook.com

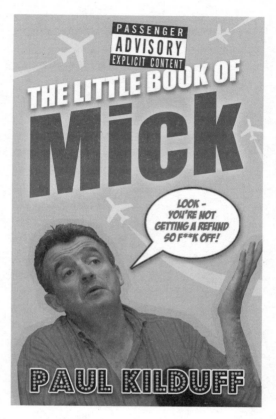

Michael O'Leary, the retiring Chief Executive of Europe's largest low fares airline Ryanair, speaks his mind.

The European Commission are 'communists', airport operators are 'overcharging rapists', British Airways are 'expensive bastards', environmentalists are 'eco-nut bags' and travel agents are 'f***ers'. 'Do we carry rich people on our flights? Yes, I flew on one this morning and I'm very rich.'

Paul Kilduff, author of the bestselling *Ruinair*, has gathered O'Leary's choicest utterances. Prepare to be informed, possibly offended — but most certainly amused.

THE BESTSELLING *LITTLE BOOK OF MICK* IS AVAILABLE IN BOOKSHOPS NATIONWIDE

Stung by a ten-hour delay and a €300 fare to Spain on his native 'low fares' airline, Dubliner Paul Kilduff plots revenge – to fly to every country in Europe for the same total outlay, suffering every low fares airline indignity. Armed with no more than 10kg of carry-on baggage, he endures 6.00am departures, Six Nations-style boarding scrums, lengthy bus excursions, terminal anxiety and cabin crew who deliver famed customer service.

On his pan-European exploration he reveals the secrets of the new travel phenomenon favoured by one hundred million passengers annually. And his advice to fellow travellers in what is perhaps the ultimate airport holiday read? 'Don't get mad, get even – get a one cent airline ticket!'

NUMBER 1 BESTSELLER *RUINAIR* IS AVAILABLE IN BOOKSHOPS NATIONWIDE FOR ONLY €0.01*

*price excludes fees and charges of €12.98